PARENT'S GUIDES ®

As a parent, you're swamped with conflicting advice and parenting techniques that tell you what is best for your child. THE EVERYTHING® PARENT'S GUIDES get right to the point about specific issues. They give you the most recent, up-to-date information on parenting trends, behavior issues, and health concerns—providing you with a detailed resource to help you ease your parenting anxieties.

THE EVERYTHING® PARENT'S GUIDES are an extension of the bestselling Everything® series in the parenting category. These family-friendly books are designed to be a one-stop guide for parents. If you want authoritative information on specific topics not fully covered in other books, THE EVERYTHING® PARENT'S GUIDES are the perfect resource to ensure that you raise a healthy, confident child.

Visit the entire Everything® series at *www.everything.com*

THE EVERYTHING
PARENT'S GUIDE TO

Children with
Depression

Dear Reader,

As a psychologist, I have seen my share of depressed patients. When they first come in, they each have a unique life story to tell, and their symptoms are affecting them in many ways. What they all have in common is that they are suffering, they are unhappy, and they feel hopeless. You can see it in their eyes, hear it in their words, and observe it in their behaviors.

When a parent has a child who is depressed, she is desperate to get help and will do just about anything to make her precious baby okay again. My goal in writing this book is to demystify the illness called depression. Knowledge is power, and this book is meant to give you, the parent, that power to help your child.

My favorite part of my job is when I see life coming back into a patient who has been in the dark tunnel of depression. On the days when I wonder why I do this job, these are the moments that remind me.

May this book bring you understanding and comfort as you strive to take care of your beloved child. There is hope, and there is a way out.

Sincerely,

Rebecca Rutledge, Ph.D.

THE

EVERYTHING®

PARENT'S GUIDE TO

CHILDREN WITH
DEPRESSION

An authoritative handbook on identifying
symptoms, choosing treatments, and
raising a happy and healthy child

Rebecca Rutledge, Ph.D.
Technical Review by Thomas Bannister, M.D.

Adams Media
Avon, Massachusetts

For Jim, my biggest fan, and for June, with gratitude and appreciation.

• • •

Publisher: Gary M. Krebs
Executive Editor, Series Books: Brielle K. Matson
Managing Editor: Laura M. Daly
Associate Copy Chief: Sheila Zwiebel
Acquisitions Editor: Kerry Smith
Development Editor: Brett Palana-Shanahan
Associate Production Editor: Casey Ebert

Director of Manufacturing: Susan Beale
Production Project Manager:
Michelle Roy Kelly
Prepress: Erick DaCosta, Matt LeBlanc
Interior Layout: Heather Barrett,
Brewster Brownville, Colleen Cunningham,
Jennifer Oliveira

• • •

An Everything® Series Book.
Everything® and everything.com® are registered trademarks of F+W Publications, Inc.

Published by Adams Media, an F+W Publications Company
57 Littlefield Street, Avon, MA 02322 U.S.A.
www.adamsmedia.com

ISBN 10: 1-59869-246-X
ISBN 13: 978-1-59869-246-8

Printed in Canada.

J I H G F E D C B A

Library of Congress Cataloging-in-Publication Data
Rutledge, Rebecca.
The everything parent's guide to children with depression /
Rebecca Rutledge, Ph.D., with Thomas Bannister.
p. cm. – (An everything series book)
Includes index.
ISBN-13: 978-1-59869-264-8 (pbk.)
ISBN-10: 1-59869-264-X (pbk.)
1. Depression in children–Popular works. I. Bannister, Thomas. II. Title.
RJ506.D4R88 2007
618.92'8527–dc22
2007010851

*This book is available at quantity discounts for bulk purchases.
For information, please call 1-800-289-0963.*

*All the examples and dialogues used in this book are fictional, and have
been created by the author to illustrate medical situations.*

▶**childhood depression**
(child-hood di-presh-en) n. An illness that affects a child in four categories:

1. Behavioral—acting out and impulsivity.
2. Emotional—moodiness or feelings of sadness, dissatisfaction, anger.
3. Physical—weight changes, sleep disturbance, low energy.
4. Cognitive—lack of concentration and indecisiveness.

Acknowledgments

I wish to thank the following people who helped make The Everything® Parent's Guide to Children with Depression *possible:*

To my patients who have shared their stories with me and given me tremendous insight into the world of depression. You have each been a gift.

To Thomas Bannister, M.D., my friend, colleague, and technical reviewer for this book.

To June Clark, my agent, who has listened to me obsess over the writing of this book and has never stopped cheering me on. To my husband, Jim, who is the greatest husband in the whole world and is without a doubt my biggest supporter.

Contents

Introduction

Most people have felt sad, blue, and generally unmotivated at some point in their life. When asked what was wrong, inevitably they'd say, "I'm depressed," or "My life is so depressing," or "I've had the most depressing week." The way in which they dealt with those emotions varied depending on the circumstances. Some lay in bed watching movies, waiting for the "depression" to go away. Others ate or drank their way through it. Still others got busy, thinking if they could just get their mind off of their "depression," they'd be fine. Eventually, the "depression" would lift and things would go back to normal.

That wasn't depression; that was the blues, a few days of feeling yucky and a few days spent medicating one's self in the best way you knew possible. For those who have suffered the real thing, they would tell you that you have no clue how it really feels. The word "depression" has been bantered about so much that it has lost its meaning in most contexts. It is now used to describe anything that feels unpleasant.

Real depression is devastating. It feels as if it is going to last forever, and it rarely just goes away. Those who have been through it will tell you that it's a long, slow road to recovery. Only through the identification of it as an illness and its subsequent treatment can most people overcome it.

According to the World Health Organization, by the time your children reach adulthood in 2020, depression will rank second as the cause of a loss of healthy years in one's life (number one is heart disease). While most parents do not want to think it's true, the prevalence of depression among children is growing at an alarming rate. Unfortunately, most research is focused on the treatment rather than the prevention of depression.

How can the amount of people suffering from depression be reduced? It seems obvious that you would start with your children. While much depression is hereditary and related to problems with brain chemistry, a child who has had a parent with depression is not necessarily destined to become depressed. Depression *can* be prevented in many cases.

There are myriad things you can do to help prevent your children from becoming depressed or to treat those who are already suffering. It is a teaching process, and it involves much hands-on parenting. No one expects parents to know how to do this, but it can be learned and therefore passed on to our children.

Since depression prevention programs are still few and far between, you, as the parent, must become the first major team player in the prevention and treatment of your child's depression. Part of your work requires that you become as educated as possible about the causes, risk factors, and chemical factors that can cause depression. You'll also need to acquire healthy parenting skills that will prepare your child to become resilient, self-reliant, and emotionally flexible. These are the skills that your child will need to not only beat depression but also to have a successful, happy life.

The most effective way to combat depression is through a multifaceted approach. This book will outline what to look for, how to spot it, and how to begin getting your child the help he needs. It will also push and encourage you to become the very best parent you can be to make your child healthy and happy. Are you ready?

CHAPTER 1

Getting a Handle on Childhood Depression

T o think that your child is depressed is a scary prospect. Sometimes it seems that the more you read and research about depression, the more daunting and overwhelming it becomes. Yet knowledge is power, and when it comes to mental illness, it is better to know too much than not enough. By getting a thorough understanding about childhood depression, you will be prepared to make the best decisions designed to meet your child's individual needs.

Do Kids Really Get Depressed?

Even though people prefer to think of childhood as a happy time, free from worry and stress, it is not always the case. As life has become increasingly more complex, children are faced with more challenges than ever before. If adults are having trouble navigating their worlds and all of the problems that naturally occur, imagine what it must be like for children! Popular thought used to be that children didn't suffer from such complex disorders and thus labeling a child with depression merely provided an excuse for the behavior being exhibited.

Adolescence

As for adolescence, it is a period filled with hormones, rebellion, and moodiness. How easy it is to dismiss an adolescent's latest phase as "just being a teenager!" One mother used to call it the "uglies" whenever her daughter flew into a crying rage. She readily admitted that she secretly believed the child was behaving like that in order to get attention. It wasn't until a teacher mentioned the possibility of depression that she looked a little more closely at her daughter. While teenagers can make you feel utterly helpless and hopeless, some of the behaviors they exhibit might actually be the result of depression. You wouldn't be the first to miss the signals, and you most certainly won't be the last.

Just as you are forced to keep up with the latest trends in music, dating, resources, and schools, you have to keep up with what is seemingly "normal" for your child. It becomes easy to compare children, but let's face it, there are no two alike. That is why communication becomes key in order to stay hip and to recognize if anything's out of character with your child.

Essential

In order to recognize and address depression quickly, it's crucial to have an open dialogue with your child. Resist the urge to do all the talking. A child will talk more freely in a relaxed atmosphere. Listening and being observant during this time will teach you more than you realize!

Staying hip does not mean you must act like an adolescent yourself. What matters is that you realize what is important in your teen's particular world and how these trends and situations are affecting him.

Is It Depression?

Kids *do* get depressed. Some are mildly depressed, which, if that is the case, will probably go away on its own. Others get seriously depressed so quickly that it incapacitates them before anyone realizes there's a problem. Maintaining a balance between worrying too little and too much is hard to do. However, just because children get depressed does not mean they always know how to tell you. In fact, they are superb at pretending everything is fine. But deep down, they look to you for guidance and help. They need you to understand that something is not quite right and that how they feel needs to be taken seriously.

Alert!

When your child says to get off his back and quit worrying so much, follow your gut. If you feel there is something wrong, check it out. Resist the urge to be liked by your child. Don't be afraid to ask questions and to bug him. He will get over it!

The good news is that depression is not only preventable but also treatable if it occurs. Parents have a lot of trouble admitting there might be something wrong with their child, but neglecting the problem is not the answer.

Prevalence in Children and Teens

Quoting the exact percentages of children and teens that are depressed is like nailing jelly to a tree! The numbers change every day. Research studies often focus on certain aspects of depression, or use a group of children from a certain region of the country. Many things affect these studies and their outcomes. Unfortunately, what is known for sure is that the prevalence for depressive disorders is on the rise.

The Numbers

Among preschoolers, depression is thought to affect between .3 percent to 1 percent of the population. Anywhere from 1 percent to 9 percent of school-age children and approximately 8 percent of adolescents will have a major depressive episode. For teenagers, that's one out of every eight. According to a 2004 study by the National Survey on Drug Use and Health, 10 percent of kids ages twelve to seventeen had had at least one major depressive episode. The number of boys and girls who suffer from depression is about equal until adolescence. Girls have twice as much of a chance of experiencing depression from adolescence into adulthood.

Question?

Why does depression among females rise so drastically at puberty? No one is sure, but a common belief is that the hormonal changes that girls undergo at puberty and into adulthood have a more significant effect on both their bodies and emotions than what boys experience.

You might prefer to look at the numbers and figure out the odds are in your favor that your child won't be one of the unfortunate to have depression. No matter how you try to wish it away, however, no one knows why some will become depressed and others never suffer from it.

Does Depression Come Back?

Most of the time, the depressive episode will last a year or less. It is believed that 70 percent of children who have depression will suffer a recurrence at some point in their lives. If the onset of the first episode is before the age of fourteen, these children are at the greatest risk for recurrence. Likewise, as other problems exist in the home, such as divorce, major conflict, and chronic physical illness, these factors increase your child's chances of having future recurrences. Every time there is a recurrence it increases the likelihood for even more.

Theories of Depression

Much work has been done to determine why children become depressed, and there are several groups of theories that have been developed. Understanding these theories allows you to understand how and why your child is depressed. No single theory can answer all of your questions about your child's depression. Therefore, it becomes important for you to know a little about each one so that you can start developing a plan of attack.

Biological/Chemical Theories

These theories of depression examine how the brain's chemistry, hormonal changes, and a family's history of mental illness contribute to the development of depression. In other words, it really takes a close look at the family and child's body to see if the depression is affected by physical factors. While this sounds quite simple, the biology of the brain and body is complex.

 **Fact**

Identical twins develop from a single fertilized egg. Two separate eggs create fraternal twins. Genetically, identical twins are the same. If one twin suffers from depression, the other is much more likely to become depressed, too. Fraternal twins share only half the same genetic material, so the rates for both having depression are not as high.

When there are factors within your body that you have little control over, feelings of helplessness and hopelessness make you believe you will never be okay again. It is not true. If a child has certain biological components that predispose him to depression, it is not a sure bet that he will become depressed. What it does mean is that you will have to be vigilant in watching for warning signs and also help your child develop other skills that can help reduce the effects of biology.

Attachment Theory

Psychologists have long studied child development and how a child's evolving personality affects this early period of life. The attachment theory focuses on how the mother, or another central caregiver if the mother is not available, and the child bonded from the start. It is thought that this is the child's most influential relationship during this time. Generally, if the bond provided the child with physical and psychological security along with consistent love, the child would be more immune from mental illness. You can see why it is so important for this particular caregiver to be emotionally healthy and prepared to take on the challenges of parenting.

Essential

Different psychologists have their own theories of when the attachment phase ends, but they do agree about two things. First, it is crucial for the child's development that attachment happens during the first year. Second, it is during the first two years that a child learns about independence and dependence and finds a healthy balance between the two.

As a result of the child's relationship with her mother, there are three kinds of attachment that may develop: secure attachment; avoidant attachment; and resistant attachment.

Secure Attachment

Obviously, all mothers or major caregivers strive for their children to have secure attachments. This means that the child knows she is loved and that that person protects her. Her caregiver is always there, waiting to provide that sense of comfort as she needs it. You have experienced this as you have watched your child wiggle from your arms, anxious to be free to crawl or walk around and explore her little world. Then, just as quickly as she wandered off, she was back, craving to be in your arms where everything was okay. As a child gets older, if she has had a secure attachment, she develops a strong core of trust and confidence that prepares her to meet future challenges. In addition, her adult relationships are apt to be healthy and happy.

Avoidant Attachment

If a child develops an avoidant attachment, she may avoid closeness with her caregiver. The interactions between the caregiver and the child likely have been inconsistent and have often neglected the child's emotional needs. The resulting view of this child's world is that the attachment cannot be trusted, and she feels safest when disengaged from others.

Resistant Attachment

Much like the avoidant attachment, the resistant attachment also has its roots in an inconsistent, unreliable bond between the caregiver and child. This is a more angry attachment, so to speak, because this child will more aggressively resist the caregiver's attempts at closeness. Whether the attachment is avoidant or resistant, both types make an individual more vulnerable to depression.

It should be stressed that the major caregiver is not solely responsible for making sure the healthy attachment is achieved. Just like adults, children have characteristics that influence how they interact with others. As a baby, if your child was sensitive to touch, you may have had more trouble bonding because of his avoidance of touch. Or perhaps your baby was high-strung. This child might not have been able to tolerate a lot of closeness due to his anxiety. Feelings and behaviors can be contagious. In other words, if you sensed that your baby didn't want to be held or nurtured, your feelings may have been hurt or perhaps you thought you needed to work harder at it. However you responded was a perfectly normal reaction, but you can now understand how you couldn't be completely in control of this process.

**Fact**

Your parenting and your child's temperament are not the only reasons that poor attachments develop. A divorce that takes away the major caregiver can interfere and disrupt the attachment process and cause tremendous harm. If a caregiver were to die, the loss would wreak havoc on a child's emotional development.

Behavioral Theories

Behavioral theories of depression look at outside causes of behavior and their influence on the development of symptoms. You have probably heard of Pavlov, who studied dogs' behavior. He offered dogs powder that smelled of meat and measured how much saliva they produced. As the days passed, he learned that the dogs would start salivating as soon as he entered the room. He coined the term "classical conditioning" and hypothesized that animals and people learn by watching and responding to what the environment presents.

Pavlov tried another study where the dogs were taught they'd get meat if they could recognize a circle presented to them. If an oval shape was presented, however, the dog would receive an electrical shock. As the trials of the experiment progressed, the circles and ovals were changed such that the two shapes were barely distinguishable. The dogs couldn't tell the difference either, so at the prospect of getting meat or a shock, rather than salivating they became very anxious and even bit at themselves. Pavlov concluded that psychological discomfort or distress was a direct result of not knowing what was going to happen along with a lack of control over situations.

In the context of depression, if a child has a parent that is sometimes loving and at other times physically abusive, he learns that he cannot predict what is going to happen to him, and as a result he becomes skittish when the abusive parent enters the room. If this pattern continues, his nervousness can develop into depression.

Social Learning

Albert Bandura came up with the theory of social learning. He hypothesized that children learn by watching others and modeling their behaviors. Behavior, or in this case depression, is the result of the interaction between the child and others in his world. For example, if you cope with frustration by hitting your fist against the wall, chances are pretty good your child will have plenty of opportunities to see you doing this. You may have heard "He acts just like his mother!" So don't be surprised if your child picks up on some of your less desirable behaviors!

 Essential

According to social learning theory, children and teens have probably seen thousands of examples of people who handle life's upsets in unhealthy, ineffective ways. These children model what they see and find themselves frustrated, helpless, and depressed. You need to look for opportunities to turn ordinary experiences into teachable moments because your child really is watching you!

Likewise, your child will learn appropriate ways of managing his behaviors and feelings if he has healthy models to watch. If you are angry about your day at work and you say to your child "I am feeling angry right now. I am going to take a few minutes and calm down before we play," you have taught him three invaluable lessons. First, you avoid taking your anger out on him. Second, you have labeled your emotion so that when he feels angry he is able to express it in a healthy, nonaggressive way. Third, you also taught him that there is something he can do to get himself under control. Bet you never thought two little sentences could do so much!

Cognitive Theory

"You are what you think." Theorists who came up with this view of the human condition would have told you that depression was a state of mind. According to Albert Ellis, there is a very strong relationship between thinking, feeling, and behaving. He believed that if you could change either how you thought, felt, or behaved, the other two operations would change. Cognitive theorists focused on the act of thinking as being the conduit to changing feelings and behavior. Depression and other negative states were the result of irrational thoughts, and if these thoughts could be replaced with rational ones, the depression would lift and self-esteem would increase.

 **Fact**

Martin Seligman introduced the concept of "learned helplessness." How a person navigates hardships and setbacks determines whether she will become depressed. If a child feels helpless and lacks a positive view of self, she is more likely to become depressed than the child who is more persistent in the face of difficulty.

As you can see, there are many ways to view depression. If you are worried that you should adopt one theory or another in order to get a handle on depression, resist that urge. Theories are just that— theories. More models of how depression occurs are being produced every year. The focus of this book is to help you learn about your child's depression, how it might have come about, and what you can do about it. Having an understanding that many factors contribute to depression gives you a better ability to recognize what your particular child is experiencing.

What Is Depression Exactly?

Anyone who treats depression has in her arsenal of resources the *Diagnostic and Statistical Manual of Mental Disorders, Fourth Edition (DSM-IV)*. It contains descriptions of every psychiatric disorder along with diagnostic information. Depression for adults is clearly explained, but not so for children. The *DSM-IV* lists the following symptoms necessary for a diagnosis:

A. Five or more of the following symptoms have been present during the same two-week period and represent a change from previous functioning; at least one of the symptoms is either (1) depressed mood or (2) loss of interest or pleasure.

> **1.** Depressed mood most of the day, nearly every day, as indicated by either subjective reports or observations made by others. Note: In children and adolescents, can be irritable mood.
>
> **2.** Markedly diminished interest or pleasure in all, or almost all activities most of the day, nearly every day (as indicated by either subjective account or observation made by others).
>
> **3.** Significant weight loss when not dieting or weight gain (e.g., a change of more than five percent of body weight within a month), or decrease or increase in appetite nearly every day. *Note:* In children, consider failure to make expected weight gains.
>
> **4.** Insomnia (sleeplessness) or hypersomnia (getting too much sleep) nearly every day.
>
> **5.** Psychomotor agitation or retardation (slow physical movement) nearly every day (observable by others, not merely subjective feelings of restlessness or being slowed down).
>
> **6.** Fatigue or loss of energy nearly every day.
>
> **7.** Feelings or worthlessness or excessive or inappropriate guilt (which may be delusional) nearly every day (not merely self-reproach or guilt about not being sick).

8. Diminished ability to think or concentrate, or indecisiveness, nearly every day (either by subjective account or as observed by others).

9. Recurrent thoughts of death (not just fear of dying), recurrent suicidal ideation (thoughts) without a specific plan, or a suicidal attempt or a specific plan for committing suicide.

B. The symptoms do not meet the criteria for mixed episode (of depression and mania).

C. The symptoms cause clinically significant distress or impairment in social, occupational, or other important areas of functioning.

D. The symptoms are not due to the direct physiological effects of a substance (e.g., a drug of abuse, a medication) or a general medical condition (like hypothyroidism).

E. The symptoms are not better accounted for by bereavement, such as the loss of a loved one, the symptoms persist for longer than two months or are characterized by marked functional impairment, morbid preoccupation with worthlessness, suicidal ideation, psychotic symptoms, or psychomotor retardation.

Doesn't this list make your head spin? What's even more frustrating is that this is a list for adults with only two mentions of how the symptoms manifest themselves in children.

 **Essential**

Remember that the *DSM-IV* is a manual for professionals to use in making their findings and treatment recommendations. It is not a book for a parent or another layperson. Your interpretations of the *DSM-IV* may lead to an inaccurate diagnosis and could slow down the treatment process.

While this is the official list of symptoms for depression, there is much more to making a diagnosis than just reading this list. More symptoms and their manifestations will be discussed later.

Depression Versus Sadness

How do you figure out if your child is depressed versus just sad? The biggest thing you can watch for is whether the symptoms you are observing are causing a substantial amount of interference in his day-to-day functioning. Children do not always have the two-week rule where the symptoms have to be present constantly. In kids, the symptoms can come and go, but watch for them to frequently pop up over that time frame.

Another way to see if your child is in a funk or really depressed is to take the HALT test. Ask these questions about your child:

- Is he **H**ungry?
- Is he **A**ngry?
- Is he **L**onely?
- Is he **T**ired?

If the answer is yes to any of these, it may be the blues. Easy ways to treat it are for your child to grab a snack, take a nap, or get some exercise.

Childhood Versus Teenage Depression

The symptoms of depression manifest themselves in very different ways at varying ages. What is important to remember is that you are looking for signs or behaviors that are out of character for your child. If you are thinking, "he never acts like that," pay attention. It does not necessarily mean he is depressed or suffering from anything extraordinary. He just might be having a rough patch. Following is a more general explanation of symptoms in children as they age. As you read about them, you will begin to see just how hard it is to make an accurate diagnosis of depression.

Symptoms from Birth to Age Twelve

At a glance, the following are symptoms of children before the age of three: feeding problems, tantrums, and lack of emotional expression. In ages three to five: fears; enuresis or encopresis; frequent crying and oversensitivity; lack of interest in others, including children; and decreased attention and increased distractibility. At ages six to eight: vague somatic complaints, resistance to activities, changes in school performance, social withdrawal. At ages nine to twelve: excessive anxiety, loss of self-esteem, social isolation, a lack of interest, anger, and suicidal thoughts.

Adolescent Symptoms

Adolescence comes with its own set of problems. Symptoms may include moodiness, extreme irritability and anger, appetite disturbances, sleep problems, overreactivity, lack of interest in activities and friends, substance use, delinquency, body image issues, and suicidal thoughts.

About half of depressed teens exhibit a sad mood, while the other half presents as irritable or angry.

Behavioral Symptoms

Symptoms of depression can usually be broken into two types—behavioral and emotional. Having this distinction might help you organize your child's symptoms in a way that lets you communicate it easily to a professional. Deciphering what emotions your child is experiencing before the age of five is difficult at best because he does not have the verbal tools to label his emotions, so most of his complaints will be behavioral.

Before the age of three, there are a few problems to watch out for. Feeding problems are typical with children who have depression. With babies and small children, there is a failure to thrive, an inability to keep up with the changes in normal development. Things that should interest them don't. Tantrums, in the form of constant crying, are common.

Ages Three to Five

As children reach the ages of three to five, they do what is referred to as "acting out" as a means of communicating what is happening to them emotionally. Although it is not a total surprise that a once-loved book can quickly become boring, what you're looking for is a lack of interest across the board in most activities that a child of a certain age should enjoy. Children who are quiet and reserved may become hyperactive, unable to control their excessive activity. An outgoing child may become shy or disinterested in being around other children. He will be resistant to new activities such as attending preschool or going to a party. Previously potty-trained children may begin to have accidents both during the day and night, or there is the chance that they become constipated. Often, a child will begin to experience a decrease in the ability to handle frustration.

Alert!

Resist the urge to grab onto a couple of behaviors that seem abnormal for your child and automatically assume there is trouble brewing. These behaviors could be attributed to just about anything. Children find a way to talk when you least expect them to, so with some patience and a little time you should have your answer.

While some of these symptoms may seem normal for your child, if they are causing him significant discomfort, there is a problem.

Ages Six to Twelve

As children reach the ages six to twelve, the behaviors become a bit more pronounced. The resistance to new activities seen earlier begins to extend to just about everything. A child will announce she doesn't want to go to school, and in fact, doesn't want to do anything that she used to enjoy. She might complain of a tummy ache that ends up having no root cause. Some will develop a vague physical pain such as a hurt elbow or a pain in the leg. School performance may decline. Socially, a child will become withdrawn, avoiding contact with friends. Unfortunately, even at these early ages, some suicidal gestures occur. They typically take on some form of self-destructive behavior such as scratching to the point of bleeding, cutting, or dangerous behaviors such as jumping from a roof.

Adolescence

Adolescents also become socially withdrawn from friends and family. They will experience a decline in their grades and performance. Those interested in sports or a particular school activity will suddenly announce they are quitting without offering much of a valid explanation. Many either begin to overeat or have a loss of appetite, and others will be preoccupied by how they look to the point of obsession Although teenagers are notorious for sleeping a lot, they may start sleeping even more. If they typically sleep from 10:00 P.M. until 7:00 A.M. and then take an hour's nap after school, you may notice the nap extending until dinner or later to the point that sleep is your child's major activity outside of school. Other adolescents cannot sleep and will be walking the floors at night.

Depressed teens often turn to drugs or alcohol as a way of self-medicating what is happening to them. Others begin to make poor choices that get them into trouble with the legal system. The scariest behavior a teen might exhibit is an increasing fascination with anything related to death. An artistic child who likes to write music may create songs about death and suicide. What they read or watch on television may change to more morbid topics. You may find notes written to friends about suicide or even a suicide note. Also watch for a teen that begins to give away his prized or meaningful possessions.

Emotional Symptoms

In order to explain why it is important to detect the emotional symptoms of depression, you need to understand the three main functions of emotions. First, emotions provide children, and adults, with the ability to adapt and survive. Without emotions, you wouldn't know how to interpret events around you and how to react to them. A second function involves regulating information. For example, if a child perceives that he is liked, he will seek positive affirmation from others. A child who perceives himself negatively will tend to behave in a negative fashion. Communication is the third function. Emotions express feelings and needs.

Birth to Age Three

Before the age of three, crying jags are an expression of either anger, anxiety, or dissatisfaction. Some theorists believe that this type of crying also can be an expression of fear and insecurity. When not crying, look for a lack of interest in others, especially other children, and little to no facial expression. Since this is an age where emotions cannot be expressed verbally, you'll need to fine-tune your ability to interpret the body language of your child.

Ages Three to Five

Between three and five, emotions are still expressed primarily through acting out. A child might refuse to go to day care or to another place they previously couldn't wait to attend. Extreme clinginess and a refusal to interact with others indicate some sort of problem, and again, you may not always know what it is. Again, you may hear about frequent tummy aches or another ailment. Some children may voice vague emotional complaints such as being sad or being scared. That might be all the explanation you get, which can be frustrating to decipher further.

Ages Six to Twelve

Those kids between six and twelve are finally getting to where they can actually tell you that they are sad because of a certain event or circumstance. If they are mad or scared, they can label the emotion and provide more of a specific explanation. They will express feelings of poor self-esteem and negative thoughts. Many times, a child will say that she believes "something is wrong" because she is feeling badly. In this case, probing further is crucial to determine just what is happening. Other red flags are either excessive questions about death or the actual verbal expression of wanting to die.

Adolescence

If you have an adolescent, you know personally the extreme anger a teen can inspire when you ask him a question. The response? A shrug, a roll of the eyes, or the ever-popular "I don't know." When he does talk, he might verbalize feelings that are overly critical of himself and others or say that he hates himself. Another teen will say he feels guilty, but when asked why he won't have any reason. Again, discussions about death or comments about suicide and wanting to die should be taken seriously.

 *Question?*

Are these behaviors or comments depression or just random things? Remember, two important factors must be present for a diagnosis of depression. If these symptoms persist or are frequently present during a two-week period, and if the symptoms are significantly interfering with the child's day-to-day functioning, then the possibility of depression needs to be considered.

Although teenagers are supposed to be able to communicate their emotions, you are risking disappointment if you think your teen is going to routinely come to you and tell you he's feeling badly in a direct way. The majority of teens do not wish to bring attention to themselves and often have no desire to talk to their parents, believing them not able to understand what they are going through.

Watching for out-of-character and extreme changes in behavior in your children and adolescents will be critical to determining whether they are depressed or are actually just being kids.

CHAPTER 2

Causes of Depression

I n Chapter 1, the theories of depression hinted at what the actual causes might be behind this puzzling disorder. As you realize by now, children really do have the ability to become clinically depressed. However, there is no doubt that our children experience stress and other circumstances that they perceive in their own unique ways. While some of these situations are things that they can control, more often than not they are helpless over most of these happenings. There are many factors that can contribute to depression's onset and recurrence.

Genetics

There is bad and good news about genetics. The bad news is that there are certain illnesses that you, as a parent, run the risk of passing on to your offspring. The good news is that if you or another family member has suffered from depression, you are a great expert on the topic. This means you can see the symptoms in others much more clearly, which will allow you to attack your child's depression sooner and more effectively.

Where Is the Exact Cause?

So far, no one has been able to identify the exact gene responsible for the onset of depression. Studies have been successful at showing that there is a genetic

bond between parents, siblings, and even twins. Whatever part genetics plays in the occurrence of childhood depression, it is not the entire reason for it. You may not pass on this disorder at all. A genetic family history of depression merely gives you more information to draw from, with your goal being prevention, early detection, and quick treatment.

Alert!

If a child has a parent or sibling who has had depression, he has about a 25 to 30 percent chance of developing depression sometime in his life. When both parents have had depression, the chances rise to 70 percent.

Brain Chemistry

Think of the brain as a complex machine. If it is well oiled and all the components are working properly, then presumably the machine will roll along without any problems. The machine has different components that do different tasks. In order for the machine to move efficiently from task to task without missing a beat, communication between those tasks is critical.

The Brain's Duties

In the brain, these components are called neurons, and they have to be able to communicate with each other just like the machine. The communicators between neurons are neurotransmitters named serotonin and norepinephrine. When these two chemicals move from one neuron to the other, they have to jump through what is called the synapse. If the brain is doing its job effectively, these chemicals move within the brain and the mood remains stable. If there are not enough of these chemicals or they are not being transported adequately, depression can pop up.

Essential

Aerobic exercise, such as walking or running, has been reported to have a great effect on the production of the neurotransmitters responsible for causing changes in mood. Still other patients insist that slow exercises, such as yoga or Pilates, help, too. For the most part, exercise should be seen as part of a more comprehensive treatment plan.

If your child is lacking the appropriate amount of these neurotransmitters, it is important for you to know that neither you nor he can magically make those chemicals appear and bring things back to normal. This is where antidepressant medication can be a lifesaver, and Chapter 11 will explore that more in depth.

Physical Illness

Depression is often associated with some physical illnesses and disabilities. Children often have chronic physical sicknesses that are very difficult for them to endure. It is painful enough to be ill, so you can imagine why depression is related to some illnesses. In making an accurate diagnosis of depression, don't forget to mention to a professional any condition that your child has or has had. You never know exactly how an illness has affected your child emotionally.

Medical Conditions

The following are some of the illnesses that depression might coexist with:

- Vitamin B$_{12}$ deficiency
- Mononucleosis
- Postconcussion syndrome
- Anemia

- Asthma
- Epilepsy
- Chronic allergies
- Diabetes
- Cancer

 **Question?**

How do I know my child's illness hasn't caused her depression?
You can't always tell. Even if you think your daughter's recent or chronic sickness is no big deal, you should always mention it to the professional working with your child. It just might be the key to getting at the perfect diagnosis.

The list of illnesses that might cause depression could go on and on. The point here is to think about the whole child. A diagnosis of depression has to be made by considering all of the factors that might have affected your child in one way or the other.

Physical Disabilities

When a child has a physical disability, she is more likely to become depressed unless she has a healthy set of coping skills at her disposal. A wheelchair-bound child, or one with a visible deformity, is singled out and attention, a lot of it unwanted, is drawn to her. Other children can be cruel, and the world is not always kind to people who are different. If a child does not know how to handle her special set of circumstances, then she is apt to suffer a loss of self-esteem and a self-image is created where she believes she is unloved, that she is a burden, and that she is even more different from others than she believed in the first place.

Another way her disability may set your child up for depression is due to a loss of experiences. If your child's problem limits her ability to move, walk, see, or hear, she is missing out on many of life's teachable moments and joys. As she realizes that she cannot do what others can, she may become depressed. This is especially true of children who are not born with a disability but have something happen to them that drastically changes the way they live their lives.

The Family Environment

The environment around a child, namely her family, has the ability to cause depression in children and teens. In the family, abuse almost always causes depressive symptoms in children. Poverty, neglect, and family conflict can also lead to depression. Parenting skills and substance abuse are two other factors.

Abuse

Physical and emotional abuses are horrible events for a child to observe or to have happen to them. Adults who are abused somehow believe they deserve to be treated badly and it is their fault that they are being hurt. If a grownup has that irrational belief, why wouldn't a child? Unfortunately, what happens is that a child doesn't possess the skills necessary to negate those beliefs, so a pattern of self-worthlessness begins to develop. The child is sure that he doesn't deserve any better. Aside from the lack of self-esteem, a child does not know how to get his emotional and physical needs met, so they simply are not met. It adds up to a very negative sense of one's self and the unit that should have provided unconditional love, the family.

Alert!

Do not underestimate what your child is watching at home. Just because he is not the victim of the abuse, he *is* suffering. Abuse does not have only one target. It affects every member of the family. A child cannot defend himself. If you can't protect yourself from abuse, at least try to find a way to protect your child.

Poverty and Neglect

Poverty and neglect contribute to a child's feelings of insecurity. Not getting enough attention from a parent makes a child feel unloved and unwanted. These emotions lead to fear, uncertainty, and inadequacy. Being bombarded by all of this negativity continues to have an effect on the child, and it's a miracle if he doesn't escape without depression.

Poverty in and of itself does not cause depression. However, if a family is experiencing severe financial troubles, the parents are often obsessed with how they will pay their bills or buy the groceries. This can cause an incredible amount of stress for the parents, and their attentions are not typically focused on their children's emotional needs. They may love their children, but they simply don't have enough physical time and emotional reserves available for their kids.

Drug and Alcohol Use

Substance abuse among parents is also a predictor of depression in children. Many parents overlook the amount of influence they actually have on their kids. Drinking too much or using drugs teaches children that there is a way to cope—and that's by *not* coping. It's an easy way to medicate and not have to feel. Not giving your child other coping skills leaves them feeling vulnerable, and it's quite easy for depression to creep in.

Loss

There is nothing you can do to shield your child from loss. Pets die, people die, and relationships change. For a child, loss comes in all shapes and sizes, from something as seemingly unimportant as not getting invited to a party or feeling neglected to more serious concerns such as having an absent parent or a death in the family.

Rejection

Adults understand that rejection occurs for many reasons, and that it isn't always their fault, but a child is particularly sensitive to it. For a child, rejection is a loss—a loss that feels extraordinarily huge. Because children are more apt to view things in terms of black and white, they perceive rejection as a loss from which they cannot recover. Not getting invited to a party suddenly seems like a major deal.

You as a parent, even if you know better, must honor your child's feelings. Help her to see that these setbacks are just that—temporary bad moments that promise to pass. Encourage her to focus on more positive experiences that she is having as a way to combat her feelings of loss.

Death

The death of a parent or sibling can be devastating. Losing a parent can mean the destruction of the child's entire world, and it is hard to rebuild it without the child suffering some long-term impact. Like the loss of a parent, the death of a sibling is tragic, too, but sometimes even more damaging than the loss of a parent. The child who is left behind often feels a lot of pressure to help the parent heal or to be everything the other sibling was to his parents. Kids also don't always know how to handle their parents' grief, which can take over the family and never leave. When this happens, the surviving child doesn't get the attention he needs to heal from this loss. In addition, surviving children report that they can't live up to their parents' memories of the dead sibling because everything is about preserving that child's memory. It is not surprising that these children develop depressive symptoms.

Divorce

Divorce also creates a loss for children even though there is no actual death. The child's world is turned upside down when routines are altered or a beloved parent no longer lives in the home. If a child is particularly close to the parent who leaves the home, he might feel sad, angry, and confused. He will often blame himself as being the cause for the divorce, although he is assured that is the farthest thing from the truth. Often divorce makes children fearful of intimacy because they perceive that people leave, and thus they shy away from relationships that might have the potential to hurt them like the divorce of their parents did.

Essential

A good indicator of whether a child will become depressed during a divorce is how the parents handle the changes and transitions. It is up to both of you to set aside your own feelings about the other and try together to present a united, loving, and secure world for your child.

Parental Conflict

Conflict between the parents steals time away from the children, too. Adults who are too busy trying to navigate their own troubles often don't have the time or emotional fortitude to deal with their children's emotional development. This is not to say they don't love their children. They do, but they are spreading themselves thin trying to make everyone happy. The children are usually the first to suffer. In addition, children learn how to cope by modeling what they see. If a child only knows how to be loved through fighting, screaming, and yelling, he tends to adopt the same skills. This sort of loss leads a child to develop negative or poor coping skills. This inability to cope, much like his parents' difficulties, can lead to depression.

Single Parenting

If you are a single parent, you have to work doubly hard to lessen the occurrence of depression because you are keenly aware that your child is experiencing the loss of having two parents. In addition to your possible guilt about this, your time, energy, and resources are pulled much tighter than the traditional two-parent unit. Thus, it makes sense that you have to work extraordinarily harder to give your child what she needs. If you feel you aren't living up to your own expectations, take an honest look at yourself. Most kids say they remember and cherish the time spent with a parent doing something together rather than seeing the house clean or having a home-cooked meal. Give yourself a break, and you might end up being an even better parent!

Parents too often get blamed for their children's troubles. However, there are aspects of parenting that are essential to the healthy emotional development of a child. Too much or too little structure can be damaging. The same is true for being too critical. Parenting is really a fine art, and one that you need to master to give your child a loving, depression-proof life. If you are at loose ends and don't know what needs to be done, buy a book on parenting. Better yet, don't be afraid to ask for help.

 **Fact**

A parenting style that treats a child as if he were perfect is putting him on the same path toward depression as quickly as if his parent was abusive. These are the children who never learn to be accountable for their behavior and their lives. Depression is the result of learning that they have unrealistic expectations of themselves.

Television and Other Influences

You and your kids have seen and maybe compared yourselves to the idealized images of presumably perfect people on the television and in print. What happens when kids are constantly pressured to be thin, beautiful, successful, and happy? They see commercials for smoking or using alcohol where everyone appears happy and carefree. Movies tout the riches and happiness that can be bought through wrongdoings. Songs promise true love. These influences are strong and obviously make lasting impressions.

What's Wrong with an Ideal World?

There's certainly nothing wrong with a child wanting to be the best or desiring happiness. But what happens when kids realize that life is not that easy, and that these things are not the absolute predictors for happiness? Typically they respond by blaming themselves, believing that they are failures or just not good enough. Other kids work harder, convinced that if they do, happiness is right around the corner. Using the outside world to create a secure self-image has the tendency to backfire. These are the kids who succumb to many types of pressure, and when things do not work out, they become depressed. They simply lack any internal sense of self, so when the external world disappoints them, they have nothing to fall back on for support.

Influences on Teenagers

How could your teen not be exposed to all of the things going on in the world today? War, post-9/11 issues, and natural disasters are on TV and in the papers. They have the Internet for communicating and getting involved in things they shouldn't or that they are not prepared to handle. If that's not enough, they are experiencing the coming of age in an era where there are more sexually transmitted diseases that ever before. There are more drugs to experiment with, and they have more freedom than you might have had as a teen. It's no wonder that they feel much more unsafe, hopeless, and uncertain than their parents. Your teen's reactions to these added stressors can easily contribute to depression.

Stressful Life Events

What about other stressful life events? You've seen how chemistry, genes, and a child's environment can help cause or prevent depression. As if that's not enough, what happens when a child experiences major life stressors? These are the events in a child's life that, as they add up, can put a child at greater risk for depression.

Coddington Life Stress Scale

A physician named R.D. Coddington devised a rating scale, the Coddington Life Stress Scale, which measures how much emphasis a major life event has on a child and thus the amount of stress a child is really under. While it was never meant to be a diagnostic tool for depression, research did find a correlation with high scores on the Coddington Life Stress Scale and depression. The following reproduction of this scale may give you a better idea as to how children are thought to perceive stress and why they might become depressed if they are involved in one, two, or several of these events. It may also surprise you to see what value or "life change units" are attributed to certain circumstances. Also of interest is how your child might rate an event as stressful depending on his age.

Under your child's age group below, circle any of the events that your child has experienced.

Coddington Life Stress Scale

Life Event	Preschool	Elementary	High School
Beginning school	42	46	42
Change to different school	33	46	56
Birth or adoption of a sibling	50	50	50
Sibling leaving home	39	36	37
Hospitalization of sibling	37	41	41
Death of sibling	59	68	68
Change of father's job requiring increased absence	36	45	38
Parent's loss of job	23	38	46
Marital separation of parents	74	78	69
Divorce of parents	74	84	77

Hospitalization or serious illness of parent	51	55	55
Death of parent	89	91	87
Death of grandparent	30	38	36
Marriage of parent to stepparent	62	65	63
Jail sentence of parent for thirty days or less	34	44	53
Jail sentence of parent for one year or more	67	67	75
Addition of third adult to family	39	41	34
Change in parent's financial status	21	29	45
Mother beginning work	47	44	26
Decrease in number of arguments between parents	21	25	27
Increase in number of arguments between parents	44	51	46
Decrease in number of arguments with parents	22	27	26
Increase in number of arguments with parents	39	47	47
Discovery of being adopted	33	52	64
Acquiring a visible deformity	52	69	81
Having a visible congenital deformity	39	60	62
Being hospitalized	59	62	58
Change in acceptance by peers	38	51	67

Outstanding personal achievement	23	39	46
Death of a close friend	38	53	63
Failure of a year in school		57	56
Suspension from school		46	50
Pregnancy of unwed teenage sister		36	64
Becoming involved with drugs or alcohol		61	76
Becoming a member of a church/ synagogue		25	31
Not making an extracurricular activity he wanted to be involved in (team, band)		49	55
Breaking up with boy- friend or girlfriend		47	53
Beginning to date		55	51
Fathering an unwed pregnancy		76	77
Unwed pregnancy		95	92
Being accepted to a col- lege of his choice			43
Getting married			101

Results

According to Dr. Coddington, between the ages of four to six, the average total life stress score is about 75; between nine and twelve is about 100; and between fourteen and sixteen, about 200. If your child's scores are higher than what is presented here, it does not mean that your child is certain to become depressed. It just means he has a greater likelihood to become depressed, so this is another way for you to quantify for a professional what your child has experienced and the effects these events have had on him.

 **Fact**

Studies show that if a child experiences major stress, she will have a greater likelihood of developing a depressive episode. If at least two major events have occurred within the last year, a child has a 50 percent chance of getting depressed.

Parents, do not be scared! The comments about parents and their parenting skills are not meant to alarm anyone but to provide necessary information. Parenting is not for the faint of heart, and all parents have plenty they can learn. One thing *is* sure. There is no way every single cause of depression could be enumerated. By the time you factor in the causes with all kinds of different people, you'd be overwhelmed—and exhausted! By providing your children with a relatively stable, secure foundation while fending off life's hard times and setbacks, you will be doing your best to prevent depression from getting its grip on them. It is definitely the biggest challenge you'll ever meet!

CHAPTER 3

Predictors of Depression

B y now you have learned that depression and its detection is tricky at best. Now that you have some working knowledge about the theories, causes, and some symptoms, you need to know the predictors of depression. Predictors may look the same as the causes of depression, but there are some differences. While you should certainly be on the lookout for some of the things discussed in the previous chapters, the following is a more comprehensive look at issues that can foretell a depression.

Family History

In Chapter 2, the factors of genetics, the child's environment, and other stressful life events served to show you just how vulnerable kids can be to depression. Obviously, one of the most important groups that will influence a child is her family. When talking about predictors of depression, it does not mean that if these items are present in your family that your child will automatically become depressed. These predictors should serve as red flags for you to consider when trying to decide whether your child is depressed and if she needs help.

Essential

Every family, no matter how healthy, has some level of dysfunction in it. To deny this is where the real trouble can begin. Take off your blinders and honestly evaluate how what is happening in your family could be a foreshadowing of depression for your child.

There are almost as many predictors of depression as there are families. In other words, your family is unique and will never completely match another in its complexities and problems. This is not the time to compare yourself with your neighbor or your neighbor's child. It requires honesty and a true willingness to face your family's troubles, but the payoff can be huge.

Mood Disorders

Depression is often predicted when mood disorders, personality disorders, or alcoholism are present. To be identified as a mood disorder, two things must be present. First, there is a significant change in mood that affects day-to-day functioning over a specific period of time. Second, there must be a loss of interest in pleasurable activities. Symptoms include problems with thoughts, feelings, behaviors, and physiology, such as physical complaints with no apparent cause. The *DSM-IV* lists a number of symptoms that have to occur for adults, and these symptoms must be present for at least two weeks. In children, the symptoms should affect at least two areas of functioning, but they will not always be present for the whole two-week time frame. Depressive, dysthymic, bipolar, and cyclothymic disorders make up the category of mood disorders and will be explained more in depth later. For now, just know that there is a direct correlation between these problems and depression.

Personality Disorders

According to the *DSM-IV*, the general diagnostic criteria for personality disorders are an "enduring pattern of inner experience and behavior that deviates markedly from the expectations of the individual's culture." This pattern is exhibited in two or more of the following areas:

1. Cognition (ways of perceiving and interpreting self, other people, and events)
2. Affectivity (the range, intensity, ability, and appropriateness of emotional response)
3. Interpersonal functioning
4. Impulse control

This pattern of interacting with one's world must be pervasive and inflexible across a broad range of situations. In addition, the pattern leads to significant impairment of functioning in social, occupational, or other significant areas of functioning. Individuals with personality disorders have had this pattern since at least adolescence or early childhood. Last, the pattern of behavior being exhibited cannot be accounted for by some other mental illness, substance abuse, or a medical condition.

Alert!

Do not attempt to diagnose a personality disorder in your child! It is a complicated problem and one that must be tackled by professionals. Labeling this in someone will have lifelong consequences as it is felt he will never completely be free of it and therefore sees himself as damaged goods.

Personality disorders tend to be difficult to treat and do not ever fully go away. With that said, you can see why this category of disorders is predictable of depression.

Alcoholism

By now everyone knows that alcohol abuse among teens is prevalent. But did you know that children as young as eight and ten are beginning to experiment with this substance? Alcohol is everywhere, even in our homes. Do not think that you must rid your home of alcohol to prevent the problem, however. Children generally learn about alcohol use in what they observe and pick up at school.

What happens when you come home at the end of a particularly horrible day and say out loud "Boy, I sure could use a drink. This day has been a killer!"? There is a chance that if a child witnesses this enough he will learn that this is a sure-fire way of medicating stress and trouble. An adolescent is particularly vulnerable to what he sees his parents and peers doing. If it works for them, he thinks, it surely will help me. It's not an altogether false impression.

No one is suggesting that you call a halt to your intake of alcohol. What you need to remember is that alcohol is a depressant, meaning that for the most part you wind up feeling worse after a few drinks than you'd imagined. If a child sees this as a coping resource for his parents, he is more likely to try it himself. Using a substance that acts as a depressant over a period of time is very likely to cause depression.

 **Essential**

Have you heard the saying that "misery loves company"? Unfortunately, when looking at these predictors, the saying is quite accurate. If both parents and then a sibling have a history of mood or personality disorders, or alcoholism, the chances that your child will become depressed will increase.

Loss

As discussed earlier in Chapter 2, loss is something everyone will have to grapple with, and some children experience more of it than others. Loss takes on many forms. It may be the death of a parent, sibling, loved one, or a pet. Divorce or the absence of a parent in the home is a loss. It may be leaving the first grade and a favorite teacher to go to the second grade with a teacher that doesn't click with your child. A child who gets rejected by another child or who doesn't make the team has experienced a loss. Do you see how quickly the amount of losses could add up to depression?

Childhood Loss

Children perceive loss in a fundamentally different way than do most adults. A child's concept of time is different. For a child, a loss might last from a few hours to a few days to a few weeks. Adults have the ability to understand that the feelings following a loss will ultimately go away. Why? Because adults have learned with time and experience that the pain from loss does heal. Children don't have that knowledge.

Adolescent Loss

Loss for a teenager can include the more traditional types such as the death of a loved one or a divorce. However, teens also suffer other kinds of losses that are equally as devastating.

The breakup of a relationship can often thrust a teen into depression. He thinks that this was the only girl he ever loved. He'll never meet anyone like her again. Life, as he knows it, is over. He may also begin to develop a more negative view of himself. "If only I had been good enough, more handsome, nicer, more athletic." A teen is typically going to turn this kind of loss inward and cannot process all of the feelings that he is having.

For a female, the loss is interpreted in much the same way, but she is usually going to be even harder on herself given the amount of pressure girls are under these days. Perhaps she couldn't juggle the time commitments that a relationship and her studies warranted. While she may have decided to wait, she ended up having sex with her boyfriend who then dumped her for another girl. Maybe she became pregnant. Her desires to please her parents, her teachers, and her boyfriend led her to make choices and do things she never would have considered doing. The breakup with a boyfriend and any ensuing consequences can then be seen as immense losses, and if she is not adequately prepared to deal with these issues, she can become depressed.

Alert!

Do not be quick to assume that a child who suffers only a few losses is more protected from getting depressed than a child with multiple ones. Every child is different, and their reactions to loss will vary, too. Be on the lookout for children whose skills for coping with loss appear to be stretched to their limit.

Another kind of loss for a teen that is translated differently from children is the loss of hope. Adolescents, as they begin to experience more of life, begin to realize that bad things *do* happen. When enough horrible things happen to a teen, he begins to believe that there is no hope for a brighter future. He starts to see events and people in absolute terms rather than realizing there is good and bad present in almost every situation. The longer a teen feels this loss of hope, the more vulnerable he will be to depression.

Sleep and Appetite

You're probably wondering why sleep and appetite are predictors for depression. Plenty of studies have been done on what happens to a human being both physically and emotionally when they are deprived of sleep or their appetites are disturbed somehow. They become less immune to illness and more reactive to stress. Stress is easily converted to other problems such as depression.

Sleep

If your child is not getting the rest he needs to repair his body and mind, he may become depressed. If you think back on it, has there been a time where you were much more emotional, irrational, and upset about something when you hadn't been getting your rest? The same thing happens with a child. The difference is that, again, you have knowledge and experience on your side. If your child has been up late studying for exams for several nights in a row, you will notice he is more irritable and edgy than usual. If this lack of sleep lasts for much longer, his emotional reactions are likely to escalate and you will wonder who the beast is standing before you!

Give a child a chronic lack of sleep, and he may get depressed. The same goes for too much sleep. Children at different stages of growth and development need more sleep than at other times. That is different from the child who is sleeping more than usual for longer periods of time.

Consider the story of Amy. Under ordinary circumstances, Amy is not a morning person! However, after hitting her snooze button once, she is up by 7:00 A.M. and out the door for school in forty-five minutes. After school, when she isn't practicing for the tennis team, she likes to chat on the computer, shop, and has even been known to do her chores without having to be asked. Occasionally, she might take a short nap for thirty minutes. She's routinely in bed by 10:00 P.M.

Now let's look at Amy in a different set of circumstances. For some reason, now Amy cannot get out of bed unless her mother physically shakes her, pulls the covers off the bed, and threatens that she'll be late for school. As soon as she walks in the door in the afternoons, Amy is in bed, sleeping soundly. She might miss dinner altogether, or she will make a brief appearance at the table and then go right back to bed. She might get up long enough to do some homework, but she will sleep the whole night through, even though she slept pretty much until her bedtime. This is not the teenager who is having a growth spurt and needs a little more sleep to accommodate it. Amy is becoming depressed and her body is trying to alert her to that fact.

Appetite

Just as too much sleep or too little may predict the occurrence of depression, so do changes in the appetite. An occasional lapse in your dietary functioning is normal and expected. There may have been times when you ate the dozen doughnuts or the half-pint of ice cream when you've experienced some sort of terrible event. That's not out of the ordinary. What you should look for in your child is a *significant* change in appetite. To be considered a predictor of depression, you must look at the overall picture. Is your child medicating herself with food? If she tends to overeat in times of emotional stress, and can't seem to control herself, she may be getting depressed.

 **Fact**

When children are experiencing growth spurts or are engaged in more physical activity than normal, they tend to eat more. Like adults, children don't eat as much in the summer when it is hot and will often eat more in the winter. Watch for changes in your child's appetite as a predictor of depression, but don't use it as the only measuring stick!

Likewise, if your child quits eating or the amount she eats is substantially less, it could be a warning that she is depressed. Of course, if a child is dieting, this is different. You should be on the prowl for eating behavior that deviates significantly from what is normal for your particular child.

The other troubling issue with appetite is that of eating disorders, which will be discussed later. Obsessions with body image and control are quite prevalent. Depression and eating disorders almost always go hand in hand.

Behavior

Actions often speak louder than words. Children have a way of communicating what is happening in their own little worlds. Whether they realize it or not, whatever they say can be filtered through what it is they are doing. Behaviors such as social skills, academic performance, and self-destructive gestures are often clues that a child might develop depression.

Social Skills

Social skills in childhood are vital to building lasting relationships and leaning to navigate the world. Children with poorly developed skills feel inferior, insecure, and vulnerable. This inability is setting them up for depression as they discover they don't fit in like the others. They stand out, and not for a good reason.

As the child becomes a teen, if he has experienced enough social traumas, he's going to be at risk for developing depression. Again, as teenagers are prone to think in absolutes, periodic rejection is interpreted as constant rejection. If he is turned down for one date or from one sport's team, he believes he will never be able to get a date or play any sport. He begins to see himself as a loser and as someone who doesn't fit in with his peers.

Academic Performance

It doesn't make sense that academic performance, on its own, is a predictor for depression, and on its own it isn't. But many children and teens feel a lot of pressure to be the best and to make good grades. Young children are taught that good grades are a sign of success and that they are smart. For teens, they are reminded that without stellar grades, their futures may be in jeopardy. If a child simply cannot do as well as his peers, he automatically assumes there is something wrong with him! Feelings of inadequacy can set in due to school experiences and set a child up for depression.

For academic performance to be seen as a predictor of depression, remember that what you are looking for is a significant change in performance, usually a decline. As children begin to experience negative feelings in their lives, it is hard for them to set those feelings aside to handle other tasks such as schoolwork. The bigger the feelings become, the more difficult it is for them to block those feeling out. A child may appear to not be studying or might be characterized by his teacher as lazy or as a child who is deliberately choosing not to do his work.

When a decline in school performance is present, it is best to consider the whole child before making a judgment. Many times, this performance is a cry out that a child is hurting and depression is not far behind.

 ## Essential

If your child is not performing up to par in school, consider the following: Has the range of difficulty of the work changed? Is there a learning disability present? How is his physical health, his home life, his social life? Just one of these is enough to predict symptoms of depression may follow.

Self-destructive Acts

Self-destructive behaviors can take many forms. If you notice any of the following, take heed. These behaviors almost always have a degree of self-destructiveness in them: substance use, head banging or cutting, suicidal gestures, and delinquency.

Younger children will usually act out their feelings through banging their heads repeatedly against a wall, the floor, or a piece of furniture. They may also slap their heads. Cutting behaviors include excessive scratching, picking, and using objects to cut on their arms or legs. For some, this behavior is so severe that it can cause significant injuries.

Teens have many more resources to use if they wish to be self-destructive. The use of alcohol and drugs is an easy way to numb their pain but can also be dangerous. Cutting is typically done by female teens, and they usually hide this behavior. Suicidal gestures, when the teen might not wish to really die, can result in death or terrible bodily harm. Oppositional, defiant, and delinquent behaviors are other ways some teens try to hurt themselves.

Children have a much more difficult time explaining to you what they are feeling if they have acted in these ways. When you ask them what is wrong, they will typically shrug or say, "I don't know." Their frustration about what they've done is apparent, but they can't express it. Teens who engage in these behaviors will tell you that they don't care or that they don't know how to feel about something. For some reason, they believe that doing *something* is better than nothing, even if it feels bad.

Depression cannot be overlooked as a resulting illness when a child responds to his world this way. Look for children who simply have no idea how to express themselves but in a calamitous way. This is the child who needs your immediate attention but cannot ask for help.

Comments

"I'm not good enough." "Nobody likes me." "I'm too fat." "I'm not smart enough." "I wish I were dead." "If only . . . , then . . . ." Most children make these dramatic pronouncements at one point or another in their lives. When they do, parents tend to respond by telling them how they are wrong or ignoring it. You are smart not to fall into the "poor, pitiful me" syndrome.

When to Take Comments Seriously

But can these comments be predictors of depression? They can be if you are hearing them repeatedly and frequently. Again, all kids like to invoke sympathy whenever they can. A child who constantly has negative things to say about herself is ripe for depression's grip. Depression is often the result of negative thinking about one's self and one's world.

 **Fact**

When your child begins to utter negative statements about himself, listen and be supportive. If your gut tells you he isn't buying what you're selling, there's a chance he really believes what he is saying. That's when you should consider depression as a possible outcome and seek help.

The Risk of Minimizing

Parents are often quick to minimize what their children do and say. Likewise, when a child seems depressed, you want to believe that it's just a passing event. If a child says that he is unhappy or even says, "I feel depressed," it's worth taking at look at it. Also, don't belittle or make fun of his comments even if he is just trying to get attention. Depression often begins with self-deprecating remarks and may be your child's way of asking for help.

Helplessness

Think back to a time where you felt helpless. Did you feel you had no control, no options, no way out? If you are honest, you'll remember this as a time of extreme discomfort and perhaps fear. Children learn helplessness in two ways.

Lack of Control

First, the more a child experiences failure, the more he begins to feel he has no control over his world. He starts to think he may as well give up because what's the use. At other times, he won't even get out there and try something for fear he won't measure up. After a very short time, this is a child who sees himself as inferior and worthless. You can see how a belief system such as that is predictive of depression.

Observation

Second, children learn by watching. If a child sees her mother take an active role against her abusive husband, the child learns that she doesn't have to be a victim. If she sees her father fired from a job, only to watch him spiral into despair, she comes to believe that there are many things she cannot control. Both points of view are valid. There are, of course, situations that a child can control and where she can learn that she is capable of survival. Likewise, it's important to learn that life is unfair, and things *are* going to happen outside of her control.

Learned helplessness leads to hopelessness. With this mindset, a child believes that her abilities are few, her self-worth is low, and her future is dim. It's no wonder that learned helplessness is a predictor of depression when that belief system permeates everything she does and thinks. It is devastating.

Self-esteem

When a child has healthy self-esteem, he feels competent and adequate to meet the challenges that face him. He perceives that he has value and that he is loveable. This is healthy, and it is probably the hardest task that you, as a parent, will undertake in helping him to develop. The hopelessness discussed above sets in when this task is not mastered. The damage associated with poor self-esteem is contagious. Once a child feels inadequate and incompetent in one area, he feels the same in another and so on until the child feels so useless that he basically gives up and depression sets in. Because kids so easily find ways to disaffirm their self-esteem, it becomes mandatory for you to find ways to boost it.

Perception of Self

A child's belief systems about himself enable him to interpret the world in turn. If life events are interpreted in a positive manner, a child naturally feels more positive about himself and vice versa. As his perceptions about life become increasingly dark, negative, and forlorn, he in turn will begin to perceive himself in the same light. Thus this habit of looking at the world in pessimistic, bleak ways is a predictor for depression.

Question?

What's the difference between a healthy self-esteem and arrogance?
Think of a healthy self-esteem as a balloon. It can rise in the air and float successfully. Because it's not too full of air, when it comes in contact with another object it will gracefully bump against it, but it won't burst. Arrogance is like an overinflated balloon—it may rise and float, but it is full of hot air and cannot withstand much pressure before it pops!

Sometimes these perceptions of self are temporary. For example, if Joe fails a math test for which he studied hard, he might say, "I am horrible at math." This may be a temporary perception based on a single episode. However, it may or may not be true, and the only way to find out is to try again. Depending on what happens next, and next, and next—this is when a more consistent perception of who he is emerges. If a child stops this process prematurely, he may forever be stuck in the "I can'ts" and the "I'm not good enough's." What comes next? Depression.

Gender

The differences in gender as they relate to depression are readily apparent by grade school. While little girls are taught to study hard and learn all they can, if they fall short they believe they are unable to do well. Little boys will typically use the excuse that they just didn't try hard enough. But how quickly children begin to start thinking negatively about themselves.

Adolescent females are twice as likely to have depression as males. Factors such as the view of females by the public, hormonal changes, and more serious body-image problems are thought to be some of the culprits.

Sexual Orientation

Many gay and lesbian adults will tell you that they knew that they were different early on. Young children don't usually say it in words, but sometimes their actions will communicate it. But the false feelings of being a misfit or that something is terribly wrong with them are there from the beginning.

As they approach adolescence, teens begin to struggle with their sexual identities much more. Along with the painful awareness that they are different, they also fear being rejected by their parents, their friends, and the world at large. Aside from issues of rejection, this is when harassment by their peers will begin if a teen is thought to be gay or a lesbian. It's no wonder the suicide rate among these teens is about three times as high as other adolescents.

The factors described above might lead to depression in a child, but not always. When a parent sees a list, she automatically adds up how many characteristics her child possesses. If it's too many, she becomes worried sick that her child is destined to become depressed. If she finds only one or two, she lets out a huge sigh of relief that her child is okay. Both may be wrong or right. Nothing in our lives really happens in isolation from everything else. This list is not going to give you a guarantee as to whether your child is immune from depression. These are merely events, behaviors, and beliefs that are known to contribute to the illness. Just knowing that your child has experienced a loss, or has a history of depression, for example, is not enough to rush him to a doctor. Look at these as warning signals that depression is a possibility, not an absolute outcome.

CHAPTER 4

Is My Child Depressed?

Although you have learned about depression's predictors, causes, and definitions, uncovering the truth about childhood depression is still elusive. In this chapter, you will start to get a real grasp on whether your child is depressed or merely temporarily sad. Making this distinction requires time and focus. Again, buck the urge to compare your child with someone else's. It never works and it is a sure-fire way to make an inaccurate decision. Gathering information is the quickest way to find the answer.

A Look at the Depressed Child

At different ages your child's depression will look different, so you need to be familiar with the various phases of childhood development. Remember that kids express emotions in thousands of ways, so knowing your child's personality and temperament is crucial. Then look at the changes you are seeing to assess whether he is being affected only in discreet areas or across the board.

At Five Years

Anne is five years old. She is in kindergarten and normally cannot wait to get to school. She is an independent, exuberant child and gets along well with the other kids at school. Things seemed to be going along well until right before Christmas. When her mother mentioned going to see Santa, Anne showed little excitement,

even though before Thanksgiving she had talked of nothing else. She began crying at night before bed and refused to sleep alone. When her birthday rolled around, she seemed even less interested in her gifts than before. Her mother described Anne as a "watered down, sad version of herself."

At Twelve

Charlie is twelve years old and has always been a straight-A student. He gets along fairly well with others but is a bit shy. When Charlie's grades started slipping, his mother didn't make a big deal of it at first. When he brought home Bs and Cs, she began to worry. Charlie became more surly and uncooperative at school. His teacher remarked that she'd never seen him behave that way. At home, he bullied his little sister, the same one he'd always protected. When asked what was going on, Charlie shrugged and replied, "I don't know. I don't feel good."

At Sixteen

Shelly is sixteen. Socializing is more important to her than schoolwork and it shows in her average grades. She gets along well with her mother with whom she lives alone. At night, Shelly can hear her mother crying on the phone about what a louse Shelly's father is and how they have been abandoned. Shelly worries about her mother and about herself. With time, Shelly became more combative and angry with her mother, blaming her mother for the divorce and the financial predicament they are in. Normally a fairly conservative dresser, Shelly started wearing more provocative clothes and a lot of makeup. She began to date boys she'd never shown an interest in and became sexually active. When she wasn't going out, she was at home sleeping. After they'd had a particularly brutal verbal exchange, her mother found Shelly in her room cutting her arms.

Each of these kids is depressed, but you will notice that they look completely different. They are! They are different ages, have various temperaments, and are at dissimilar stages in their development.

Alert!

If you are seeing characteristics of your child in these depictions, put on your detective hat. Is your child asserting his independence by speaking up or is he out of control? Is she just not excited about Santa because someone told her he didn't exist? Is he bullying his sister because someone is teasing him at school?

Depressive Thoughts

Depression is thought to manifest itself in an individual's thoughts, feelings, behavior, and physiology. Thoughts have a wide range, and with depression they can even be totally irrational. A child may have a thought about herself that is completely false. For example, she might make straight As but think she is stupid. She may be thin as a rail but believe she is fat. These irrational or false thoughts about one's self can lead to depression. In order to fight the depression, the thoughts will have to be challenged somehow.

Included in the depressive thoughts are problems with concentration, guilt or feelings of worthlessness, and recurring thoughts of death and suicide. When a child is depressed, it is often difficult to focus on homework. One normally achievement-oriented child described her depressed brain as being "mush." She couldn't get out from under the fog of depression long enough to listen in class or finish an assignment.

Other children feel unworthy of what they have or what they have achieved regardless of the reality of the situation. They take on the blame for things they haven't done and feel guilty if someone else isn't happy. Recurring thoughts about death and suicide can also occur.

A child's feelings when she is depressed may be sad and tearful. Others report irritability and anger. Both can cause a significant decline in her enjoyment of the things she likes to do. It's typically easier to recognize the changes in feelings for an adult experiencing depression. Not so in children, so look for a change of emotion that lessens enjoyment of just about everything for a child.

Depressive Behaviors

Changes in behavior when a child is depressed represent an extreme slowing down or the revving up of bodily movement. Take a child who is typically laid back, slow to respond physically, and generally less active. When she is depressed, she may become restless, hyperactive, and fidgety. All of a sudden, an extremely active child may become still, reserved, and inactive. This is what the *DSM-IV* refers to as psychomotor agitation or retardation.

 **Fact**

Some children are active, and then suddenly they slow down a bit. If your child is experiencing a change in physical activity, check to see if he is tired, sick, or bored. For him to be depressed, this behavior must be significantly different from before and last at least two weeks!

Depression and Physiology

Energy, sleep, and weight are considered physiological changes. With depression, a child who appears to be getting the appropriate amount of rest and nutrition may begin to complain of being tired all the time for no obvious reason. Often, they will report physical symptoms that have no root cause. A previously motivated child might show declines in studying, trying new things, and socializing.

When talking about weight and appetite, remember you are looking for marked changes in what is normal for your child. With weight, if your child loses 5 percent of her body weight within a month and she isn't dieting, that is a problem. In smaller children, look for failure to make weight gains that are expected for her age.

Keep a Calendar

Diagnosing depression can be a tricky business, but early detection of depression is important for two reasons. First, the longer it goes on, the more damage that occurs to your child. Left untreated, depression can lead to setbacks in your child's development, academics, and social life. Second, the risk for a depression to recur is very high if the first depressive episode is left untreated.

Many parents say it's awfully hard to notice some of these changes when you see your child every day, particularly when you have busy lives and other children. Your child's symptoms may be in response to a medical illness or a side effect of a medication. There may be some event happening in his life that your child is experiencing that is causing some sort of distress. That is why keeping a calendar is a great way to measure your child's symptoms to see if you are on track or merely overreacting. In either case, it's good information for deciding whether your child is going through normal childhood changes or if it's something more.

Make a Chart

Documenting your child's symptoms does not have to be fancy. You can keep track on a calendar, computer, or PDA. Remember to keep your calendar private. For one, no child wants to have this sort of thing posted on the refrigerator for everyone in the family to see. Also, kids who are aware that they are being recorded tend to alter or hide the very symptoms or behaviors you are trying to observe.

You should keep this calendar for at least two weeks, but a month is preferable. Pick two to four depressive symptoms—trying to track more than that gets complicated and parents tend to quit using it. The table below is a sample that you may replicate or use as a guide.

Symptoms Chart

	SYMPTOM	SYMPTOM	SYMPTOM	SYMPTOM
DATE:	_____	_____	_____	_____
	_____	_____	_____	_____
	_____	_____	_____	_____
	_____	_____	_____	_____
	_____	_____	_____	_____
	_____	_____	_____	_____

COMMENTS:

_____

_____

_____

You'll be tracking symptoms twice a day, in the morning and at night. For each symptom, you can devise your own way to say whether the symptoms are present, absent, severe, or mild. You might use a plus (+) or minus (–) sign or a check mark. Put a slash (/) between your symbols indicating day versus night. If a particular symptom has been incredibly intense on a certain date, you might add an exclamation point (!). Do whatever is easiest for you. Keep it simple as possible so that you will actually use this tool and you will have something you can interpret for a physician if necessary.

 **Fact**

If you have a female teenager, it will be helpful to make some sort of notation to indicate when she is having her menstrual cycle. By doing this, you can determine if she is having monthly symptoms that are merely troubling and that mimic depression, an important distinction for diagnosis.

Keep a Section for Comments

The Comment section of the calendar needs to include any information you find relevant to consider. It's difficult to remember what was happening on a particular day in your child's life. If your child is not depressed, those notes might prove helpful in determining whether there is a pattern in a specific area of his life (school, social) that is causing him concern.

Glean Information from School, Family, and Friends

For the most part, unless you have a toddler, your child will spend a majority of his time in a school setting. This is why you cannot overlook how he is doing at school and whether the school has noticed changes. Children who are quiet and cause little trouble in the classroom will go unnoticed but may be depressed. Some children are boisterous and mischievous, which can get them into trouble. Is this a child who enjoys the social aspects of school or is it a sign of something else? Children at the other extreme are labeled as troublemakers and are usually penalized in some way. But they may be depressed, too. Still others may have problems with learning and find it hard to concentrate or get motivated. This information is vital in getting the whole picture of how your child is doing.

Working with Teachers

While teachers will sometimes resist getting involved in this sort of thing, you have the right to at least demand participation. If you can't get it, don't be quick to overlook the possibility that your child's behavior is more than what meets the eye. If necessary, meet with the school's guidance counselor and enlist her aid. See Chapter 19 for more on school issues and depression.

A teacher needs to know if your child is taking medication, especially if a dosage will have to be administered during the school day. You will need to know your school's policy for handling medication and work with the appropriate persons to assure that your child gets his medicine on time. You won't know if your child's medicine is really working if you have no information about how he reacts to it during the school day.

Alert!

Unlike medical records, school records are not always confidential. Be prudent about how much information to share with teachers and the school. Children become known by a label or reputation, and it typically follows them from year to year. Ask your doctor if you are unsure what to share.

Get Information from Loved Ones

Getting information from family and friends is another way to get good information about your child. If you work and your child spends the afternoons with his grandmother, aunt, or babysitter, you have two choices. You can say nothing and see if they mention any marked changes in your child. However, they might be hesitant to do so for one reason or the other. So your second choice is to express your concerns. Explain that there is no reason for alarm, but that you are worried your child is exhibiting some signs of depression. Sometimes the less information provided the better, because it will help to keep their observations less biased. If family members are unclear as to what to look for, give them a simple list of symptoms such as the following:

- Oppositional behavior
- Acting-out behavior
- Social withdrawal
- Decreased concentration
- Decreased interest in pleasurable activities
- Increases in fears
- Recurrent comments about death, suicide

Essential

Don't ask teachers and caregivers to look for only the symptoms you have noticed. Remember that these individuals may see different problematic behaviors that you need to know about. If they are looking out for only the few symptoms that you have mentioned, you might miss out on additional and essential pieces of the diagnostic puzzle.

The other reason why including others' observations of your child is so important is that you need to know if your child is experiencing the core symptoms of depression or something else. What if your child is having a problem at school with fighting but gets along perfectly well with his friends when not at school? He could be the target of a bully at school, or he may feel insecure to the point that he has to prove himself somehow. Likewise, a child may constantly act out and defy her parents at home but may be a perfect angel at school. This may indicate problems at home within the marriage, parenting style, and other environmental factors. Including important others in this process keeps it as objective as possible, which is helpful for an accurate diagnosis.

Get the Diagnosis Right

For a parent, the first and most important rule of getting a diagnosis right is to do your homework! Think of it as putting together a scrapbook of your child for your doctor. You'll want to have an organized method to keep information so you don't leave any stone unturned. You'll have your calendar and information from significant others.

Checklist of Changes

You might also want to make a checklist of any other changes that, for some reason, didn't make it on your calendar. While this may seem like overkill, you'll be glad to have too much information rather than not enough. Make note of changes in:

✓ Mood
✓ Behavior
✓ Negative comments
✓ School performance
✓ Health
✓ Eating
✓ Sleeping
✓ Socialization
✓ Family
✓ Traumatic events

A physician appreciates this information. Remember, he doesn't see your child nearly as often as you do, so you want to make him feel as if he has been living with your family and watching your child just like you have.

Tracking Adolescent Changes

For teenagers, you may want to track changes that would detect self-destructive behaviors. For example, if you are concerned that your teen may be using drugs or alcohol, you may want to keep a specific symptoms list like the one below. Make sure that the symptoms are present to a significant degree before you begin to worry.

✓ Eyes (swollen, bloodshot, frequent use of eye drops)
✓ Slurred speech
✓ Secretive attitude (not due to normal adolescent needs for privacy)
✓ Cravings for sweets accompanied by abnormal eating habits and weight loss
✓ Drug paraphernalia (cigarette papers, pipes, bags of substances) despite his excuse that he's "just keeping it for a friend"

✓ Money constantly missing from your purse or valuables missing from home

✓ Staying home sick from school but feeling fine by later in the
day (hangover?)

✓ Sudden memory and concentration difficulties

✓ Neglect of appearance and/or poor hygiene

✓ Unfamiliar items in the trash (cans used for huffing, hidden
bottles)

✓ Prescription drugs and/or alcohol missing from your supply

Using Depression Questionnaires

Questionnaires are another great way to get a handle on your child's
symptoms. Some parents are overwhelmed by having to keep a calendar and lists, as well as trying to talk with the other adults involved
with their children. Simple depression inventories might help to nar-
row the focus to the symptoms their child is experiencing.

Choate Depression Inventory for Children (CDIC)

An easy one to try is the Choate Depression Inventory for Children
(CDIC). It isn't a standardized or formal test, merely an adaptation
and expansion of other surveys and research studies. You'll notice
that most of the statements begin with "I." Parents can still look at it
and answer how they think their child would respond based on what
they have observed in their child.

Please circle True or False to the following statements based on what
you have felt, thought, or done in the last 2–4 weeks (for parents,
answer based on what you have observed or how you feel your child
would respond).

True	False	1. I feel sad lots of the time.
True	False	2. I have trouble sleeping.
True	False	3. I feel tired lots of the time.

True	False	4. I don't have many friends.
True	False	5. I cry a lot.
True	False	6. I don't like to play with other kids.
True	False	7. I'm not as hungry as I used to be.
True	False	8. Other kids don't like me.
True	False	9. I feel lonely a lot of the time.
True	False	10. I have lots of stomachaches and headaches.
True	False	11. I don't like school.
True	False	12. I have bad dreams.
True	False	13. Sometimes I think about hurting myself.
True	False	14. I worry a lot.
True	False	15. I don't like myself
True	False	16. Other kids have more fun than I do.
True	False	17. I don't do as well in school as I used to.
True	False	18. Sometimes I have trouble concentrating.
True	False	19. I feel angry lots of the time.
True	False	20. I get into lots of fights.

Routinely, if you or your child answers "True" to three or more items, depression may be present, or it might be developing. If he answers "True" to the question about hurting himself, take that response seriously and take appropriate measures to make sure he is safe.

 *Question?*

Is a questionnaire enough to detect depression?
Depression inventories and questionnaires are screening devices. They are not devised to answer all of the questions about your child's symptoms. They should be used as another method for gathering information. Using them alone may result in an inaccurate or missed diagnosis.

Use your common sense, though. A "True" response to some questions answered by your child may indicate temporary adjustment issues. For example, consider question sixteen. If your child is grounded, then naturally he is going to believe everyone else if having more fun than him. Or just because a "True" response is given to a question about liking school, you may have a child who has never loved school.

Questionnaires Are Not Foolproof

You may want to use this questionnaire as a starting place for the other adults and teachers with whom your child has contact. It may help them organize their thoughts such that you have useful information. The Choate Depression Inventory is by no means the only one available. There are other depression inventories listed in Appendix B, and they might be worth perusing to see if one fits your needs better than the others.

Psychotic Depression

The words "crazy" or "deranged" are often bantered about, as is the word "psychotic." But when parents hear the word "psychotic," especially when it is being used to describe her child, it can be a very scary prospect. Given our current culture, most people associate psychotic with being a schizophrenic, and this can really send a parent into a tailspin.

What Is a Psychosis?

Psychosis is a fancy word for a separation from reality. When the mind is severely impaired, an individual loses the ability to distinguish whether what he is experiencing is real or false. This loss of reality falls into two categories: hallucinations (auditory, visual, and olfactory) and delusions.

Auditory Hallucinations

If a child is experiencing an auditory hallucination, he will say that he hears voices. Although it is obvious to everyone else that there are no voices, for the child, the voices are very real. The scariest part of this is that a lot of patients with auditory hallucinations report that the voices are encouraging the individual to hurt himself or others. This is dangerous because at that time the child is unable to distinguish between real voices and the voices of her psychosis. Thus, the potential for harm is present.

Essential

You cannot talk your child out of his hallucinations. Remember, these visions, voices, and smells are very real and present for the severely depressed child. Arguing the absurdity of the situation is futile and may result in your child keeping that information a secret rather than risking not being believed.

Visual Hallucinations

Just like auditory hallucinations, those with a visual quality contain images that the child thinks are very real. She might report seeing a dead person, or a lot of people standing in a group. Others have said that the people they see are not recognizable. Having these hallucinations often makes people feel paranoid, as if someone is watching or coming after them.

Before you panic, remember that these symptoms occur only in the most severe cases of depression. It is frightening at the very least to watch your child answer a voice, respond to something he sees, or complain of a strong odor that just isn't there. The good news is that these symptoms go away with treatment.

Get a Physical Exam

Some parents are worrywarts, especially if they have had experience in some way or another with depression. They are quick to jump on the depression bandwagon without considering the possibility of a physical problem. A good diagnostician will ask you the date of your child's last physical exam. Given how long ago it was, she might request that you get an updated one.

Take Your File with You

Take the information you have been gathering through your calendar, checklists, teachers, and loved ones with you to the doctor. He may or may not want to look at it, but as you begin to describe what is happening with your child, he may have questions. Having that material with you might be helpful to offer him proof that you aren't being an overly worried, reactive parent.

Getting Collateral Data

Remember the partial list of illnesses that can mimic depression listed in Chapter 2? If a physician is concerned that a physical problem is causing emotional symptoms, he will want to get an updated history on your child since she was last seen and will do a thorough examination. This may require getting blood work and other routine lab tests. The proper treatment of an undiagnosed illness might also alleviate the emotional symptoms your child was experiencing.

For teenagers, if you suspect she is using alcohol or drugs, or that she might be sexually active, tell your doctor. He can test your child for the use of substances and can check for sexually transmitted diseases. This is the time to leave no stone unturned!

This sounds like a lot of work for a parent to do before making a judgment about whether a child is depressed. It is! But the effort has its rewards. The more you know, the more prepared you will be to communicate your concerns to the right professional. In addition, the more you know, the more prepared you will be to do the very best for your child's specific needs.

CHAPTER 5

Risk Factors

As you read this chapter, some of the risk factors may sound similar to the predictors that were already mentioned, but there's an important distinction between the two. Predictors indicate only that a child might be depressed if he is thinking, feeling, and acting certain ways. Risk factors are those known entities that almost always put children at a greater risk for developing poor self-esteem and depression. Many of these events or situations are outside of the child's control. Add to the lack of control the fact that many children have poor coping skills to manage such things and depression is likely to occur.

Problems with Social Skills

From a young age, poor socialization skills can put children at risk for depression. A young child who has spent very little time around other kids will not always know how to respond, play, and share. Despite their young ages, children are intuitive and they begin early to reject others from their crowd. A child without these abilities gets left behind. Perhaps the more she tries to include herself, the more she is ignored. If she initially tried playing nice, she may become more aggressive. When this doesn't work, she is left adrift. Feelings of shame, loneliness, and helplessness emerge.

Before your child reaches school age, it is crucial that you involve him in activities with other children his age. Play dates, church centers, pre-schools, parks, and parties are great places to slowly help your child develop skills for interacting with other children. In addition to developing the skills, he will also be able to ward off depression.

Many experts think that being the class clown, the rebel, or the bully is a response to depression, and they are right. But it can also turn the other way around. Children are typically desperate to fit in. They may see others as being more popular, smarter, or more athletic. In trying to compete, or at least get some attention for themselves, these so-called personalities are formed.

Class Clowns

At first glance, class clowns are fun. They make people laugh and they are great antidotes to a boring classroom. But some children behave this way as a sort of compensation for how they really are—shy, lonely, needy, and scared. Their needs for attention and to be liked are so great that this seems like a perfect way to get them met. And they do receive positive feedback. Kids laugh at them and invite them to participate with the crowd. Parents tell their friends what a clown their little boy is and how he can make them laugh until they cry.

Who wouldn't want that kind of thing said about him? What you need to watch for is the child who is trying so hard to fit in that he'll do anything to get that laugh or that momentary attention. When it doesn't come his way, this kind of child has no idea what to do. It doesn't occur to him that perhaps it's just his material that's not funny. He takes it personally and wonders what he is doing wrong. Having no other way to get his needs met puts him at risk for the development of depression.

The Rebel

The rebel is usually a combative, curious, and stand-alone kind of kid. When there are rules, he wants to know the "whys" and "how comes" behind them. He will debate with you why the rule is stupid and why no one should have to do it. In a classroom, he might encourage dissension among the students. He doesn't know it, but he has the need to stand out. Rather than doing it in a pleasurable manner, like his pal the class clown, he is in your face, disagreeable, and a bit angry. When called down for his behavior, he is often the child who cannot take any personal responsibility for his behavior. It is always the teacher's or another person's fault, but not his.

An inability to be personally accountable or to be able to honestly appraise one's self puts him in danger of becoming depressed. The more he blames others, such as his fellow students, the more unpopular he will become. Even though he is loathe to admit it, he secretly would like to have friends and be accepted. As his antics increase, the less he is liked and the more likely he is to have self-esteem issues. Low self-esteem opens him up for depressive symptoms.

Essential

If your child tends to be a rebel, help him to understand the difference between rebellion and healthy disagreement. It's okay for him to question authority and to debate issues in a respectful manner. Teaching him respect for himself, others, and his choices will help to protect him against depression.

Bullies

Much is being written and studied about bullies. For most children who aren't the bullying type, they will tell you they have a healthy respect for bullies and try to stay out of their way. Bullies interact with other kids through intimidation, physical force, and mental abuse. While they aren't very likeable, these children have learned to behave this way. Perhaps they are bullied at home by an abusive parent or a sibling. Maybe that's the only way he gets heard in his family, so he thinks he must be like a bull in a china shop with everyone else.

What you need to know is this: As much as you don't like them and as angry as you can become if your children are their victims, bullies are demanding attention. Unfortunately, for many of these children, negative attention is better than no attention. But having others view you negatively does take its toll. The bully is just as much in peril when it comes to developing depressive symptoms as the very likeable class clown and the more tolerable rebel.

Children who are socially immature or lack the skills to navigate their relationships with peers are at a distinct disadvantage. While being popular is not the goal here, you want your children to have as many positive experiences in friendships as possible. The skills necessary for building relationships are also fundamentally important to their self-esteem. A child who knows she is valued and cared for, by even just a few people, is at a much smaller risk for depression than the child who feels like a misfit.

School Problems

When a child is depressed, his academic experience can be altered, damaged, and in some cases, even ruined. Some risk factors seem obvious, while others are so subtle that parents and teachers usually miss them. A child's depressive episode can last anywhere from six to twelve months. Its course is somewhat unpredictable in that symptoms can come and go, while at the same time increasing or decreasing in intensity. It's no wonder that depression is going to affect a child's educational experience.

Teaching Speeds and Homework

Academically, if a child or teen is falling behind in his performance on a subject for any variety of reasons, he will likely respond in one of three ways: try harder, ignore it, or worry. For example, fifth grade is a year in which the teaching speed and expectations for the students accelerate. Your child may have done fine through the fourth grade and even for the first part of the fifth. As the requirement to learn more in shorter amounts of time increases, your child may start to show signs of frustration. His grades might drop a little, but nothing noticeable, and he may begin to have more trouble grasping concepts that his peers seem to be managing without difficulty.

The first response, that your child will ask for help and work harder, sounds like the perfect answer to the problem. But remember that most kids hate to admit they can't keep up.

A more likely scenario is the second response, that he just quits trying and lets his grade drop. For some reason, the homework load of our children is larger than ever before. Because they have virtually no down time, children are becoming stressed and burned out. Once they start feeling this way, the quickest method to alleviate their anxiety is to just ignore it, hoping it will magically disappear. It doesn't, of course, and other problems are then created.

The other likely response is to worry. The problem with this is that the more a child worries, the more his mind is unable to concentrate on what the teacher is saying. A vicious cycle begins that can affect not one of his classes but all of them if the worry is not contained.

Overscheduling

Like the issue of homework, kids have more on their plates in terms of activities. Parents seem to think that keeping their children busy is the way to keep them out of trouble. This may be true, but only to an extent. Kids who have a loaded schedule are tired, pressured, and overwhelmed. For teens, there is the extra pressure of perhaps preparing for college, entering college, having a job, wanting to spend time with friends, and dating. As they become wearier as a result of all this running around, they are at risk for depression.

School and Self-esteem

Once kids are in school, they cannot resist comparing themselves with their peers. They begin to wonder if they are attractive. Are they liked? Will they get invited to the party?

If they have negative experiences, the end result to this problem is a slap to a child's self-esteem. The child will likely begin to show a lack of interest in school and may even refuse to go. Children and teens may develop mysterious aches, pains, or illnesses as a way to avoid what they perceive awaits them. Teens may begin to skip school. Lack of interest can turn to mood and behavioral changes, and before you know it, a child can be depressed.

Learning Disabilities

Learning problems *can* be hazardous to your psychological health. Children who experience problems with learning are often overlooked and might become depressed. If a learning disability is not caught early on, the problems with learning can grow exponentially. If your child has dyslexia, for example, and no one notices, she will begin to have problems with spelling. Later she might not be able to write sentences correctly and cannot fully comprehend what she is reading. Ignoring this problem creates a great deal of frustration for the child and a sense of being a failure. Depression is then likely to follow.

In teens with learning disabilities, if the problem is not diagnosed early, they will have a low tolerance for frustration and often quit trying. They will ask, "What's the use?" and believe they are stupid.

On the other hand, there are parents and teachers who are very concerned about their children's problems with learning. A child can be tested and evaluated early to see if he's learning at an appropriate rate or level. Once a diagnosis of a learning disability is made, the focus shifts to treatment.

Treatment

If your child is diagnosed with a learning disability, what will happen next? Your child might be placed in a resource class. She might be given a tutor. Additional accommodations might be made for her in the classroom so that she can keep up with her peers. In other words, every effort is made so that this child can have a successful academic experience.

Children don't like to be singled out. Having a learning disability sets them up for teasing, name-calling, and rejection by their peers. Often, the child comes to believe what she is being told by others and her self-concept becomes negative. Once again, this negativity puts her in direct danger of becoming depressed.

Question?

Is it a learning disability or is she just lazy?
That's the million-dollar question, because the two can appear similar at times. Talking with your child's teacher is the first place to go for help. If necessary, an educational evaluation can pinpoint any learning deficits along with your child's strengths.

The school is an excellent resource for understanding your child's development, talents, and problems. Just like gardens, children need attention to grow. Arming yourself with the right information pertinent to your child's needs is an effective way to prevent depression from creeping in.

Chronic Illness

It's already been established that a child with chronic illness or a disability has the potential to become depressed. But what about the illness of a parent or sibling? When a parent becomes chronically ill, the entire family balance becomes out of whack.

For a young child, the family is his world. If a parent becomes chronically ill, a major player becomes absent in one form or another. For example, if a mother gets breast cancer, there can be time spent in the hospital and time spent at home recuperating. Then there are treatments and their aftermath. All of this spells absence from her responsibilities as a parent, and ultimately, to her children.

No one is to blame for this—no one asks for a major illness. Even a long-term illness or disability that takes a parent out of the game for a while takes time away from a child who is reliant upon parents for nurturing, attention, and other emotional needs. A significant interruption in this parenting can put a child at greater risk for getting depressed.

A Parent's Illness

You may think that a child ought to be able to understand that a parent is ill and that it's not voluntary that he doesn't get his needs met. In reality, this is true. But remember, children are basically egocentric. They think mostly about themselves, and that is perfectly normal. When their needs aren't met, however, there is a tendency in younger children to feel responsible for their parents' unavailability.

Alert!

If you or your spouse has a chronic illness, do not let your child become the nurse. Letting him help out occasionally is a great way to teach compassion and responsibility. Too much of that role prevents him from getting to be a kid and puts him at great risk for depression.

When one parent is chronically ill, the other parent is usually absorbed by the sick spouse's needs. Now there are two emotionally unavailable parents present in a child's world. Often, it's all the healthy parent can do to manage his spouse's sickness while taking care of the household.

Sibling Illness

Also placing your child in jeopardy is the serious illness of a sibling. Parents are normally worried, tense, and emotionally drained when this occurs. When one child's illness consumes so much of the parents' energy, the other child might feel left out. Although sad about his sick brother or sister, the healthy child may exhibit anger, jealousy, or other negative behaviors as a result. In turn, these feelings get redirected at himself. He blames himself for not being loved enough, or for being bad and causing the attention to be directed elsewhere.

Fact

A child who overly identifies with the sick parent or sibling is at an even greater risk for depression. When he spends all of his time involved in the illness process, he actually starts to think he can somehow make it go away or at least make it better. His self-esteem becomes hooked in with this mission.

Serious, chronic illness within the family is something no one can control. Parents usually try their best to spread themselves out and often end up worn completely down or become sick themselves. If you are one of these parents, it's often very beneficial to involve other people who love your child. While nothing can completely replace a parent's love, time, and attention, things happen. Leaning on others actually can help decrease your child's chances for becoming depressed.

Family Environment

The way a family operates and interacts makes up its environment. Like a machine, there are different parts that have specific jobs. If every part is working correctly, then the machine operates beautifully. But if one part breaks down, the machine cannot work.

Being a parent is a dirty job. You are the major operating part of the family's machine. You get all the credit when things go well and, unfortunately and often unfairly, you get all the blame when it doesn't. Children rely upon you for stability, structure, and nurturing. When there are parts of the machine that are broken or the process needs to be changed, a child can suffer. Consider the following three examples of family upheaval: the loss of a job, moving, and incarceration.

Loss of a Job

If a parent loses his job, the family's financial and emotional stability is likely affected. For example, Mom stayed at home with the children prior to the loss of the job. Perhaps she decides to get a job and let her spouse take over the homemaking responsibilities. It may take time to find a job, so resources become slim. Once she finds a job, Dad begins his new "job" at home. Unless Mom and Dad are Siamese twins, they are not likely to do everything the same! This can cause either tiny problems at home or a major upheaval. Routines may alter, rules may change, and the entire family operation may undergo complete reconstruction. Also, Dad may be so focused on trying to get a handle on his new job that the kids are left to their own devices.

 **Fact**

There are ways to help your child cope when a major change is about to happen within the family. Open communication is the best plan. Explain to your child, at an age-appropriate level, what is going to happen. Finding ways to reassure the child that everything will be fine helps make the child more immune to depression.

If there is a teenager in the home, she may be put in the role of babysitter or surrogate parent. And while there is nothing wrong with expecting your teen to help out around the house or with her siblings, remember that the key is to keep his duties age appropriate and to recognize that she is, after all, still a kid.

Children are not immune to these changes. No matter how hard they try, though, they are resistant to change and stress accumulates. Again, they feel left out. They might be angry at Mom for leaving them and resentful that Dad has taken over. When Mom comes home, she may still be trying to run the house and enforce her rules, while during the day things are operating differently.

It must be said that in this example Mom and Dad are doing the best they can. No one is intentionally forgetting the children. It's just that parents during this time are more fixated on making sure the family is back on track. This takes a lot of time and energy, and emotional needs of the children are not the top priority. If it does occur to them that they are not spending enough time with a child, or that a child needs extra reassurance during this time, parents think they can make it up to the child later. Often, later does not come soon enough, and a child is at risk for developing depressive symptoms.

Moving

Moving is another major change for a family, especially if it is out of town. There is a new home, new jobs, new friends, and new schools. The stress moving places on a family is huge. Parents are focused on settling in and getting re-established. There are bank accounts to open, utilities to turn on, and supplies to get. Everything is new and parents are pedaling as fast as they can to take it all in and get things back to normal for their families.

Essential

The best way to help your child make a smooth transition after a family move is to take care of his needs first. Show him where he will be going to school. Get him involved in activities as soon as possible. Meet your neighbors and their children. The sooner he can feel secure, the less likely he is to become depressed.

Moving is stressful enough for adults, so you can imagine how a child must feel. Don't assume that just because your child is caught up in the frenzy of the move and seems excited that this is the case. More often than not, your children feel anxious and afraid during this time. While they are busy trying to get control over this new world, their feelings may not emerge until later. Encouraging your child to talk about what he misses from the old house, as well as what he thinks about the move, will get him engaged in his feelings and you will have a better clue as to how to help him.

Alert!

Children who have a sick brother or sister are likely to feel invisible within the family. Becoming visible often entails behaving in extreme ways—either positive or negatively—in order to get their parents' attention. Make sure you carve out time to spend only with the healthy child so that she feels her importance in the family.

Incarceration

In terms of family upheaval, a parent's incarceration is not as common an occurrence. But when it does happen, the family dynamics change drastically. If a parent is in jail, he is absent from the family and usually has limited contact. The responsibilities he had at home are now someone else's. Rules may change now that Mom is in charge. Mom may have to work, or maybe she was working before and now she has to get a second job to make ends meet.

A child needs to be aware of what is happening, again at an age-appropriate level. When no explanation is offered, she is quick to assume that she is somehow responsible for Dad leaving. Did she make him mad? Was she bad? Did he leave because for the third time that week she left her bicycle in the driveway when Dad told her to pick it up? Like many adults, a child worries, and that worry can become excessive and turned inward.

In addition, having a parent in prison is embarrassing. Children are often at a loss as to how they can explain a parent's absence to others. The humiliation and disappointment a child may feel about and toward an incarcerated parent makes her feel ashamed. Left unnoticed or unaddressed, she will become depressed.

These are but three examples of family upheaval, and there are hundreds more. Change within the family is guaranteed to happen. Too much change and chaos is going to have a significant effect on even the healthiest of families. Whether or not you have any control over the changes, you have to be on the alert for how your child is handling the pressures of family upheaval before it gets out of hand.

Sibling Troubles

When other children in the family are in trouble, it can be contagious to the healthy child. Just like a major move or chronic illness, a troubled child can take a lot of time and attention from the rest of the family. The serious illness of a child has the same impact on the other child as the illness of a parent. What about emotional illness?

Siblings with Mental Illness

Children with mental illness have the same effect on the family as those with physical ailments. Parents must spend time with this child by taking him to appointments, helping him cope with the world, and trying to keep him stable. It is also their responsibility to aid the entire family in understanding and managing a family member with mental illness. The healthy child often feels that there is one set of rules in the house for her and a very different set of rules for the sick child. Sometimes this is true depending on the situation.

Reactions from the Healthy Child

Whatever the case might be, the healthy child senses, and probably correctly, that her parents are consumed with the sick child. The healthy child may have compassion for her sick sibling, but she is also apt to be angry, jealous, and resentful. While she obviously doesn't want to be ill like her brother, she resents that all her parents do is talk about, worry about, and spend time with him. Rather than realizing that her brother may need this attention, she may feel as though she isn't worthy of it and will begin to feel unwanted. These negative feelings, if not erased, will lead to depression.

Conflict Between Siblings

In the midst of being the "forgotten" child, conflict between the two siblings often occurs. A child does not always know how to feel about a sibling who is sick. Statements such as "I hate him because he's sick," or questions like "Why do you pay all your attention to him when he is acting that way?" are common. If you are hearing these sorts of things on a regular basis, the child is likely angry and depressed. She may not act like it, but she is internalizing what she sees and experiences, which in her perception is the fact that you "love him more than me." While you hope that she has empathy for what he might be experiencing, she needs the same empathy for what *she* is enduring. Conflict between them needs to be managed carefully in a way that doesn't further alienate the healthy child.

Siblings' Delinquency and Other Behaviors

The delinquency and other out-of-control behaviors by a sibling are factors that put a healthy child at risk for developing depression. If your child has gotten into trouble with the law, the news usually gets around pretty quickly at school. This can be embarrassing not only to the one who acted unwisely but also for the "good" child. If your child is habitually in trouble at school and with the law, a reputation forms.

The "good" child is almost always uncomfortable with her sibling's reputation for trouble. Teachers unwittingly begin to treat the "good" child as if she is going to be trouble, too. Parents might clamp down on the "good" child out of fear that she might start behaving badly, too. The more she is treated this way, the more likely she is to think, "there must be something wrong with me, too." The result can be disastrous. The "good" child will either try to make herself as different from her brother as possible or will start behaving just like him. In either case, she will continue doing whatever she must do to get attention, and when it doesn't work, depressive symptoms appear.

Preexisting Psychiatric Illness

A child with an existing psychiatric disorder is more likely to develop depression. The treatment of mental illness is a tall order, and for children it can be downright overwhelming. Attention deficit hyperactivity disorder (ADHD) will be discussed in depth later, but assume for a moment that your child has just been diagnosed with ADHD. His symptoms are moderately severe. He takes medication and is in therapy to help him learn coping strategies. In school, his ADHD has caused him to have behavioral problems, and his grades are suffering due to poor concentration.

In just about every area of his daily life, some attention is being paid to his ADHD and the difficulties it and he are causing. As a parent, you might think, "Well of course I am paying attention to it. I'm trying to help him!" A good treatment plan will include strategies for home and the classroom. What a parent tends to forget is how the child interprets the illness.

Too much focus on the ADHD and not enough on the child as an individual will lead her to believe she *is* the illness rather than she *has* the illness. At school, her peers may tease her because she has to sit in front of the classroom or by herself. At home, her study routine may be markedly different from the other children and she may have a more rigid schedule. Siblings are usually the first to throw out such names as "psycho" or "crazy" at this child.

A child does not want to be different from her peers. In her mind, having a mental illness makes her stand out even more. She may feel as if people think differently about her, and in turn, she may begin to see herself as different. The combination of family, teachers, and peers is powerful, and their opinions matter to a child. If those opinions are negative, she is in peril when it comes to depression.

Essential

Even mental illness can have a bright side. For example, children with ADHD are typically intelligent and very creative. Their energy and focus has to be managed so it can be used productively. If your child has a mental illness, spend some time helping her understand the good parts and how it makes her special in a positive way.

Remember that depression can occur along with a preexisting mental illness, so the impact can be even greater. When there is a mental illness already present, if it is not being treated properly, a child's relationships, her self-esteem, and just about everything in her world can be affected. If that damaged self-image is not challenged, there's hardly a way to prevent depressive symptoms from taking over.

CHAPTER 6

Depression as a Part of Other Psychological Problems

W hen a child is depressed and is experiencing any of the psychological problems described below, his depression is likely to last longer and cause more difficulties in his day-to-day functioning. The fancy clinical term is *comorbid*. All that really means is that certain behaviors and disorders coexist with depression. Of course, it makes the diagnostic process even more baffling. Failing to address these problems has a tremendous impact on whether the treatment of the depression will be successful.

Anxiety Disorders

Unfortunately, the presence of anxiety disorders is higher in children and adolescents who have clinical depression. Included in this group is separation anxiety disorder, panic disorder, phobias, obsessive-compulsive disorder, and generalized anxiety disorder. Although some of their symptoms may look alike, anxiety disorders have specific characteristics that are unique and different from depression. How do you differentiate between normal anxiety and an anxiety disorder? Look for symptoms that are excessive or not appropriate for your child's age. For example, if your child is sucking her thumb at the age of nine, this is not something that a child her age would normally do.

Generally, look for the following symptoms: stuttering, clenched hands or jaws, nail biting, avoiding others, shaking, muscle tension, physical complaints such as

headaches and tummy aches, and fears of loss. In addition to these symptoms, adolescents with depression run away more often than their peers. This act is seen as a way to avoid dealing with what is happening. Seldom is there a teenager who has not felt misunderstood! An adolescent with anxiety is more emotionally reactive than usual. When any of these symptoms coexist with depression, the behaviors appear even more pronounced.

Separation Anxiety Disorder

In early childhood, anxiety disorders arise from stages of development that have normal anxiety issues, such as separation anxiety. Actually, this type of anxiety is normal to a point. During the toddler years, a child is learning about her world and beginning to navigate her journey independent of her caregiver. Anxiety and fear may be experienced as a child ventures out on her own. What makes her anxiety normal is that the feelings typically fade away as soon as she returns to her mother or another person with whom she has a very strong attachment.

 **Fact**

The most common anxiety disorder among children is separation anxiety. Roughly 35–40 percent of small children have a larger than normal fear of separating from their major caregivers. If your child is experiencing separation anxiety, the chances are very good that she may have depression, too.

The *DSM-IV* defines the separation anxiety disorder as:

A. Developmentally inappropriate and excessive anxiety concerning separation from home or from those to whom the individual is attached, as evidenced by three (or more) of the following:
   1. Recurrent excessive distress when separation from home or major attachment figures or is anticipated

2. Persistent and excessive worry about losing, or about possible harm befalling, major attachment figures
3. Persistent and excessive worry that an untoward event will lead to separation from a major attachment figure (e.g., getting lost or being kidnapped)
4. Persistent reluctance or refusal to go to school or elsewhere because of fear of separation
5. Persistently and excessively fearful or reluctant to be alone or without major attachment figures at home or without significant adults in other settings
6. Persistent reluctance or refusal to go to sleep without being near a major attachment figure or to sleep away from home
7. Repeated nightmares involving the theme of separation
8. Repeated complaints of physical symptoms (such as headaches, stomachaches, nausea, or vomiting) when separation from major attachment figures occurs or is anticipated

Additionally, the anxiety should be consistent for at least four weeks and be exhibited in a person under eighteen years of age. However, separation anxiety is rarely diagnosed in children under the age of two. Anxiety is a necessary and critical part of this particular developmental stage when a child is forming his attachments. Distress during this time is both common and expected.

Panic Disorder

A racing heart, dizziness, sweating, feeling choked or smothered. If you have ever experienced these symptoms, you know what it feels like to have had a panic attack. Typically, a panic attack pops up without warning and can last from just a few minutes to several hours. When a child has more than one episode of panic, she is diagnosed with panic disorder. A child can have any of these symptoms, but she may also think she is dying. A panic attack is traumatic to say the least, and the attack can lead to more problems, such as a huge fear of having more attacks or the avoidance of whatever the child thinks was the cause of her attack. For example, if a child has a panic attack at school, she may fear going back to school for fear she'll have another attack. She may avoid the classroom in which she had the attack because she thinks something about that particular room somehow caused the attack. In the extreme, if she has depressive symptoms along with her anxiety, she might generalize from her school experience that other places may also cause a panic attack to occur. In extreme cases, some kids become fearful to leave home.

Question?

How can I help my child if she is having a panic attack?
One of the most important things you can do is to calmly reassure her that she is not dying and will be okay. Second, help her slow her breathing by taking measured breaths with her or placing a paper bag over her mouth.

The symptoms of a panic attack, according to the *DSM-IV*, include:

A discrete period of intense fear or discomfort, in which four (or more) of the following symptoms developed abruptly and reached a peak within ten minutes:

1. Palpitations, pounding heart, or accelerated heart rate
2. Sweating
3. Trembling or shaking
4. Sensations of shortness of breath or smothering
5. Feeling of choking
6. Chest pain or discomfort
7. Nausea or abdominal distress
8. Feeling dizzy, unsteady, lightheaded, or faint
9. Derealization (feelings of unreality) or depersonalization (being detached from oneself)

10. Fear of losing control or going crazy
11. Fear of dying
12. Paresthesias (numbness or tingling sensations)
13. Chills or hot flashes

Phobias

A phobia is an intense fear of things or places that provokes severe anxiety. A child doesn't even have to come in contact with something in order to develop a phobia. If a child has repeatedly heard her grandmother's stories of being afraid of heights, she can become extremely afraid of heights. She may avoid getting into elevators or anything else that will put her at risk of being high up and unable to get down. Or perhaps a child had a chronic illness that necessitated many trips to the doctor along with shots or medicines. As a result, she may become extremely upset and scared at the mention of going to the doctor even for a routine appointment.

 *Essential*

Don't respond to your child's phobias with statements such as, "There's no reason to be afraid," or "You are overreacting, get a grip." Unlike grownups, a child believes her phobias are real. Minimizing her fears or trying to convince her they are irrational will only serve to make matters worse.

Social phobias result in a child avoiding circumstances where she might be judged or embarrassed. If she is forced to be involved with whatever is making her so anxious, she is likely to become even more anxious. At other times she might go ahead and persist, participating in an intensely stressful situation even though she is extremely uncomfortable.

Obsessive-compulsive Disorder

This is a disorder involving either repetitive thoughts or behaviors, or both. The thoughts and acts are not just excessive worry. The *DSM-IV* defines obsessions as recurrent and persistent thoughts, impulses, or images that are experienced as intrusive and inappropriate and that cause marked anxiety or distress. The thoughts, impulses, or images are not simply excessive worries about real-life problems.

Compulsions are defined as:

> repetitive behaviors (e.g., hand washing, ordering, checking) or mental acts (e.g., praying, counting, repeating words silently) that the person feels driven to perform in response to an obsession. The behaviors or mental acts are aimed at preventing or reducing distress or preventing some dreaded event or situation; however, these behaviors or mental acts either are not connected in a realistic way with what they are designed to neutralize or prevent or are clearly excessive.

These symptoms must be not only mentally stressful, but also are time consuming in that they take up more than one hour a day and cause significant impairment in day-to-day functioning.

 **Fact**

An obvious pattern of obsessive-compulsive disorder observed in children who also have depression is known as *folie du doute*. This means doubting mania, and it's when a child might repeatedly check to see if a door is closed, for example. So they actually doubt that they have done accurately what it is they have already done.

Obsessive thoughts create extreme anxiety. Compulsive behaviors are often a way to address the obsessive thoughts and are believed to reduce the anxiety. Coupled with depressive symptoms, a child can be emotionally and physically paralyzed by the thoughts and acts associated with this disorder.

Generalized Anxiety Disorder

Has anyone ever described your child as a worrywart? Every child worries about something now and again. Generalized anxiety disorder means a child worries, excessively, about a wide range of things. Children do not necessarily understand that their concerns are irrational. Teenagers can differentiate reality from fantasy but cannot control the worrying.

Generalized anxiety disorder in children is called overanxious disorder of childhood and is defined by the *DSM-IV* as:

A. Excessive anxiety and worry (apprehensive expectation), occurring more days than not for at least six months, about a number of events or activities

B. The person finds it difficult to control the worry

C. The anxiety and worry are associated with three (or more) of the following six symptoms (with at least some symptoms present for more days than not for the past six months). Note: Only one item is required in children.

   1. Restlessness or feeling keyed up or on edge

   2. Being easily fatigued

   3. Difficulty concentrating or mind going blank

   4. Irritability

   5. Muscle tension

   6. Sleep disturbance (difficulty falling or staying asleep, or restless unsatisfying sleep)

When anxiety and depression coexist, a child is on a never-ending cycle filled with discomfort, distress, and worry. The seeming lack of control makes children feel hopeless and scared. It doesn't matter which disorder is treated first, but getting at least some of the anxiety under control will help a child be able to more objectively address her depression.

Eating Disorders

When a child is suffering from depression, he or she is likely to have some sort of appetite disturbance. It can mean a failure to make expected weight gains that are normal for a specific age. It's not that uncommon for kids to eat too little or too much when they are depressed. The problem intensifies when a child becomes preoccupied with food. Depressed children typically have low self-esteem. Children often become preoccupied by food as a way to medicate themselves. Even though the resulting feelings are temporary, you can see how a cycle of unhealthy eating—either too much or too little—can affect a child's body image. Often, food is the *only* thing a child who is depressed can control.

Alert!

Eating disorders have been found in children as young as five. About 10 percent of children under the age of eleven have eating disorders, and almost half of eating disorders in children have an initial onset of before the age of sixteen. Be on the alert for any eating behaviors that are out of character for your child and her specific age.

Anorexia is marked by abnormal weight loss and an intense fear of gaining weight. Your child may refuse to eat even small portions of food. She may begin to exercise compulsively and see her body in a very distorted, exaggerated way. Bulimia combines binge eating and purging after eating. Often, these kids will abuse laxatives, diuretics, and diet pills. Compulsive exercise is also common with bulimia.

Children with eating disorders are typically female and have a perfectionist streak. Remember, eating is something that a child feels she *can* control. When depression hits and the world is an overwhelming set of challenges for a child, she will turn to an activity that will bring some sort of order to her life, even if it is unreasonable, irrational, and has unhealthy consequences.

 **Fact**

Occasional over- or undereating is nothing to be concerned about. Your child's eating routine becomes symptomatic when your child is either gaining or losing weight at a rate that is abnormal for the natural growth process. Watch to see whether your child is using food to soothe her emotions rather than addressing the root of her unhappiness.

Sexuality

Any child who has questions or doubts about his sexuality is bound to experience some level of depression. Your child faces many struggles in his young life. He yearns to have friends and to fit in with his peers. Imagine having questions or beliefs about your sexuality while you are just trying to be a kid! Even though times have changed and attitudes about sexuality have relaxed a little, homosexuality and bisexuality are still thought to be abnormal. Homophobia is everywhere, and unfortunately, kids can be extremely cruel. When a child stands out because of his sexuality, he is a perfect target for ridicule and rejection. Depression is not far behind, sadly, because he often lacks the skills necessary to fight off the judgment of others.

Despite your religious or moral beliefs about sexuality, a child who is struggling with these issues needs to be able to turn to his parents for help and direction. This is where keeping the lines of communication open is crucial to help him avoid developing depression.

Self-injury

Obviously, suicidal gestures and attempts are a sign that something is seriously wrong with your child. However, depressed children often engage in other self-destructive behaviors that are just as dangerous. Self-injury is often not as noticeable because children become very adept at hiding it. Acts such as biting the nails to the quick, cutting one's self with any object, persistent picking at existing pimples or scabs, and excessive scratching are but a few cries for help when a child is depressed. If you have a child who is engaging in such behaviors, you already know that trying to make sense of it is nearly impossible. Most of the time, even the child who is doing the act that is causing him harm can't tell you what is wrong.

The best explanation of what self-injury does for a child is to think of a pie. Pies have a crust on the top, and in order to keep it from bursting and overflowing, small slits are made in the crust. Just like those marks made on the crust let the air pressure out before the pie explodes, a child often injures himself as a way to let the pressure out when he is experiencing emotions he cannot handle. Most kids who engage in self-mutilation say they feel an immediate sense of relief upon injuring themselves. The pain is secondary, and if they do experience pain, it is a welcome distraction from their emotional pain.

Self-injurious behavior needs to be addressed as soon as it is discovered. Just because a child promises to stop, resist the temptation to believe him. This behavior can become habitual and addictive, so a child often finds he can't stop it by himself.

Learning Disorders

You already know that children who have problems with learning are at risk for developing depression. There are also children who already have depression who experience difficulties with learning because their symptoms are interfering with their ability to learn. This interference can put a child behind in his studies and in mastering critical academic material.

A problem with learning is said to exist when a child's performance in a specific area of learning is way below his potential. This is not about being lazy! As a child experiences a decline in school performance, his self-esteem is bound to suffer. Children with learning problems begin to feel they are not as bright as their peers, or that they are incapable of doing better. It becomes a never-ending cycle when a child experiences more failure and his depressive symptoms increase.

 Essential

> Learning disabilities are very treatable. Often, however, the coexisting depression gets overlooked. When seeking help for your child's difficulties, you may need a specialist who treats learning disabilities and a different professional to address the depression. Make sure you are honest with each person who treats your child so that everyone is on the same page.

Some problems with learning are very obvious, such as the child who reverses letters or numbers, or the child who cannot master reading, writing, or arithmetic. Also look for problems with your child's coordination, such as his fine-motor skills (holding a pencil, buttoning a shirt). Problems with learning can occur when your child has a short attention span and can't follow directions. If a child cannot comprehend what he is hearing, then problems with learning are bound to occur.

Behavioral Problems

First, understand that kids will be kids. You can't protect them totally from making mistakes, nor should you try. Behavioral problems associated with depression can be hard to spot. The key is to understand the difference between what is normal behavior versus an out-of-character or exaggeration of normal behavior. Also look for behavior that is out of sync with a child's developmental age. If a child has begun having temper tantrums but she is eight years old, she may be regressing and showing signs of depression. Maybe your child is normally a fairly laid-back kid who lets just about anything roll off her back. If she becomes very irritable and anxious for no obvious reason, she may be depressed. If her behavioral changes are readily apparent to others and are having a negative impact on her, consider depression as a cause.

Low Self-esteem

Which comes first—depression or low self-esteem? The answer really doesn't matter because they are so closely related that you can't have one without the other. When a child is depressed, he has a negative view of the world and himself. Children and teens compare themselves with their peers in just about every area—school performance, physical appearance, athletic ability, peer relationships. If their self-esteem is low and they see themselves as inferior to their peers, it's easy for depressive symptoms to creep in.

Other issues that can create the double monster of depression and low self-esteem are the loss of a loved one, feelings of helplessness and hopelessness, and fear. A child who fears making mistakes or disappointing his parents can carry this to an extreme. You may know that a kid can't be perfect, but he doesn't always realize this. How he processes his feelings says a lot about whether he will be resilient against developing depression or whether he will fall victim.

If it seems like just about anything can trigger depression, you are right. The key to helping your child is being vigilant, alert, and nurturing. It's a tough job, but it has tremendous rewards!

Chapter 7

Dysthymia and Bipolar Disorder

J ust to make the detection and diagnosis of depression a little more complicated, there are two disorders that have depressive symptoms as an integral part of their course: dysthymia and bipolar disorder. A better way to understand it is to think of these two disorders as subtypes of depression. While many of their symptoms are exactly alike, there are distinct differences that separate them. A definitive diagnosis should be left to a professional. For now, you need to understand the differences to help that process along.

Defining and Diagnosing Dysthymia

The easiest way to categorize depression and dysthymia is to think of depression as the flu and dysthymia as a cold. Dysthymia is like a low-grade fever that you can't get rid of, and it's more chronic in its course. This means that it lasts longer but the symptoms are less severe. Many children have described it by saying that until they got treatment, they thought feeling dysphoric was "just the way it is." It became part of them to the extent that they had forgotten feeling any other way.

An Important Distinction

One of the most important differences between depression and dysthymia is the length of time the symptoms have been present before a diagnosis can be made. In depression, the symptoms have to be present

for at least two weeks. For dysthymia in children, the symptoms have to be present for a year, more days than not, and the child cannot have had a major depressive episode during that time. The *DSM-IV* dysthymia diagnostic criteria states that the child must exhibit two or more of the following symptoms:

1. Poor appetite or overeating
2. Insomnia or hypersomnia
3. Low energy or fatigue
4. Low self-esteem
5. Poor concentration or difficulty making decisions
6. Feelings of hopelessness

You can see why it may be hard to distinguish whether your child is suffering from major depression or dysthymia. The easiest way is to consider the length of time your child has shown signs of feeling depressed. Although depression is difficult to endure, dysthymia is no less ravaging, especially since it lasts so much longer.

 **Fact**

Dysthymia and depression have as a component dysphoria. Dysphoria comes from the Greek word that means "poor attitude." In dysthymia, it means a poor mood. A child with dysthymia often describes herself as sad or down in the dumps. For depression, the mood is more severely unhappy, hopeless, and blue.

Depression That Becomes Dysthymia

For many children and teens, the symptoms of depression will go away with treatment. Sadly, for others, some of their symptoms will linger and remain long after the major depressive episode is over. At that point, they are diagnosed as having dysthymia. So don't be alarmed if your treating professional changes the diagnosis of your child. The diagnostic label might float between these two disorders.

What Does a Dysthymic Child Look Like?

As explained earlier, dysthymic children often think the way they feel is a normal way of life. Therefore, often they don't report having any symptoms, so your observations and those made by others becomes critical. Still other dysthymic children know something is wrong but don't know how to describe it so they keep it to themselves.

Alert!

A child with dysthymia has fewer and less severe symptoms than a child with depression. A dysthymic child is ultimately more impaired by his symptoms because the episode lasts so long. Do not overlook treatment because you think he is merely unhappy or reacting to something. It's worth it to get him professionally evaluated.

It is true that dysthymic children are sad. But even more common is anger. For some reason, anger is a very common depressive symptom in children. The anger might also manifest itself in an irritable mood.

Dysthymic Teens

The healthiest of adolescents can be unpleasant little creatures! Deciphering what is normal teenage angst and reactivity from what is dysthymia can be a very difficult task. Irritability and anger are common, but if they seem to be absent more often than not or out of reason with the current situation, you need to be watchful.

When the anger and hostility that teens are feeling becomes out of control, they become rebellious. They may be openly defiant, refusing to obey your rules. Fights and juvenile delinquency can occur. High-risk behaviors such as unprotected sex or substance use might be present.

 **Fact**

A child can be angry for no reason and may not show any discernible pattern of anger. When this is the case, a child is more likely to be depressed. The anger is more likely to occur later in the day than the first thing in the morning. In other words, reactive anger toward a person or event is a sign of more normal angry response.

Where Dysthymia Ends and Depression Begins

Something else to remember is that dysthymia can in fact coexist with major depression. After the initial period of time (one year) necessary to make a diagnosis of dysthymia, a child can then develop major depression. This is sometimes referred to as double depression. So it makes sense to get your child evaluated sooner than later.

Teens

As a child reaches puberty and adolescence, it is easy to discount a child's moods as being hormonal. Sometimes the imbalance and surge of hormones that your child experiences during this time can actually exacerbate or even cause dysthymia or depression. Since puberty can last as long as a dysthymic episode, the distinctions become even cloudier.

Forget the Label

Trying to label your child as depressed or dysthymic should not be your focus. Both disorders are debilitating in different ways, and both will cause major disruptions in your child's academic, social, and, if older, occupational functioning. The focus needs to be on seeing the symptoms and seeking help to determine if they are just moods or something more serious.

Defining and Diagnosing Bipolar Disorder

If it seems that the diagnosis of childhood depression just keeps getting harder to make, you're right. Overlooking bipolar depression, however, would be a mistake, as it is a more serious form of mental illness. Formerly called manic depression, it still sounds scary no matter what you call it. Unfortunately, people with this disorder are unfairly labeled "crazy" or "out of control." In fact, children and teens with bipolar disorder are typically bright, creative, and intuitive. However, these characteristics can get lost when bipolar symptoms are present.

 Essential

When trying to define depression, dysthymia, and bipolar disorder, part of the diagnostic process must focus on how many times and how often a child's moods cycle. This describes the various degrees of the symptoms being exhibited and can serve as a way to fine-tune a diagnosis.

Mania

You know what a depressive episode looks like, but what is mania? If you are functioning normally, you can have moods that include extreme happiness that is different from your more natural level of functioning. Your extreme happiness usually doesn't last long, however. Mania is described by the *DSM-IV* criteria as:

A. A distinct period of abnormally and persistently elevated, expansive, or irritable mood, lasting at least one week

B. During this period, three (or more) of the following symptoms have persisted and have been present to a significant degree:

1. Inflated self-esteem or grandiosity
2. Decreased need for sleep (e.g., feels rested after only three hours of sleep)
3. More talkative than usual or pressure to keep talking
4. Flight of ideas or subjective experience that thoughts are racing
5. Distractibility (i.e., attention too easily drawn to unimportant or irrelevant external stimuli)
6. Increase in goal-directed activity (either socially, at work or school, or sexually) or psychomotor agitation
7. Excessive involvement in pleasurable activities that have a high potential for painful consequences (e.g., engaging in unrestrained buying sprees, sexual indiscretions, or foolish business investments).

Small children rarely experience an episode of mania, but the risks increase when a child hits adolescence. If your child has had several major depressive episodes, you are probably relieved when he is feeling better. Early signs of mania can often be ignored because he seems happy.

Cycling

In order to better understand bipolar disorder, you'll need to understand the role that cycling plays in bipolar disorder. Cycling refers to how often a depressive or manic episode occurs and how long it lasts. If a child does indeed have periods of mania, her episodes of cycling are very rapid and almost appear continuous without a return to normal mood. To be considered continuous, symptoms must be present at least four hours a day.

Alert!

Cyclothymia is another category of mood disorder that involves a continuous cycling of depressed and manic moods. Its difference from bipolar depression lies in its severity of the moods. The mood swings are there. It's just that the highs and lows are less extreme.

Types of Bipolar

Now that you understand cycling, let's look at the two types of bipolar disorder, called bipolar I and bipolar II. Bipolar I is more severe. The mood elevation, in either direction, is more severe in bipolar I. The cycling is continuous and lasts for at least one week.

Bipolar II involves less severe moods, but the moods still present themselves in the extreme. An easy way to think about it is that these extremes are not so obvious; you notice changes in your child's moods that are not quite right or out of character. The mania doesn't necessarily cause the problems that the mania in bipolar I does, and often, after you have nursed your child through a depression, you are hesitant to believe anything is wrong when she is more energetic, happy, or talkative.

Fact

You probably know that many famous people had bipolar disorder. Like Vincent Van Gogh, many artists have this mental illness and have used it to their advantage to increase their creativity. Unfortunately, this often means avoiding treatment since they believe it will somehow curtail their talents.

There's another reason not to ignore your child's changes in mood. Part of the management and treatment of bipolar disorder lies in early detection. The chances for successful treatment—that is, having fewer episodes of depression and mania—increase significantly if you catch the disorder during the first manic episode or the first few depressive episodes.

What Does a Bipolar Child Look Like?

Just like depression, mania manifests itself in problems with thoughts, feelings, behaviors, and physical changes. Problems with thoughts include what are described as racing thoughts. If a child is having racing thoughts, she might change topics of conversation rapidly or talk so fast that she doesn't even finish a thought. She may not be able to concentrate on anything and will seem to be easily distracted.

 Essential

A child with bipolar disorder can also experience what is called a *mixed episode*. This means that instead of the cycling between depression and mania, these two states are occurring at the same time. It can be frightening to observe, but it needs immediate attention in order to protect a child from potentially harmful or dangerous behavior.

Associated Behaviors

Behaviors that are associated with mania are described as grandiose. This means a child may have an overexaggerated self-confidence. What is wrong with this, you might ask? After all, isn't a good, solid self-esteem important? Of course it is, but in the course of mania, this self-esteem looks very different. For instance, a child might have a healthy respect for heights. In a manic state, he might crawl onto the roof and think that he can either fly or won't be hurt if he jumps. It's a feeling of invincibility without any regard for the reality of a situation. It can also be something as simple as a child who all of a sudden thinks he can be the top athlete at school when he hasn't even tried out for a sport.

Behaviorally, a child can have a number of problems when manic. He may be extremely talkative, something that is totally out of character for him. His speech might be fast or pressured. When told to be quiet, it is nearly impossible for him to honor this request. He might be extraordinarily active and cannot sit still. This increase in physical activity can be productive to a point. But this attention to goal-directed behavior can become obsessive and he may not be able to pull his attention from what he is doing.

 **Fact**

Often the hardest part of getting help for a child with bipolar disorder is the child's resistance. Many children say they love their highs and that these are the only times when they feel good. It makes sense they wouldn't want to give that up. It's easier to convince them that their moods are troublesome when they are depressed or not manic.

High-risk Behaviors

The scariest behaviors that children can exhibit during mania are high-risk behaviors. This can range from a child who thinks he can jump off a roof without getting hurt to pleasurable activities that can be harmful. He might experiment with drugs and alcohol or become hypersexual. Another child may become preoccupied with cutting herself. Still another may spend all of her money and steal more from her mother's purse, often buying things she doesn't need or necessarily want. It's the impulsivity involved in these activities without any regard for the consequences that makes them dangerous.

Physical Symptoms

Physical characteristics of mania include a lack of or a reduced need for sleep and excessive energy. For all of you exhausted parents, this sounds like a dream come true, doesn't it?

A manic child may sleep less than three hours a night, or not at all. Although he may report feeling rested, even as the amount of time he isn't sleeping increases, his mood becomes more irritable and impulsive.

Track the Symptoms

Keeping a chart like the one shown in Chapter 4 is usually adequate for tracking dysthymic symptoms. Keeping track of your child's bipolar symptoms can be much more of a tricky undertaking. You can use a variation of the chart in Chapter 4 to keep your child's moods in check and organized.

What to Track

Several things need to be tracked. When they occur, depressive symptoms need to be listed. The same goes for symptoms of mania. List the symptoms of each and assign a number value system with 1 being mild to 10 being the most severe and crippling. Doing this will give you an idea of whether the symptoms are normal or they are a reaction to something happening in your child's life versus symptoms that are out of control.

The other important things that you want to find a way to measure are the length of a depressive or manic episode as well as the length of time between episodes. The chart doesn't have to be pretty, just accurate for your particular child. Again, you will have a visual tool that either substantiates your concerns or alleviates them. It will also speed up the diagnostic process once your child is seen by a professional.

Treatment Options

The treatment of dysthymia is much like that used to treat depression, which is covered in Chapter 11. Because of the chemical imbalances that are part of bipolar disorder, its treatment almost always includes medication. For those parents who are hesitant about giving their children drugs to reduce symptoms, please think twice. This is not a disorder that will go away on its own. While other treatments will help your child cope with this disorder, medication directly attacks the chemical root of bipolar disorder and provides an opportunity for symptom stability. There are a number of mood-stabilizing drugs that attack mania.

Medications

There are four common drugs used to treat mania: Depakote (divalproex sodium), Tegretol (carbamazepine), lithium, and Trileptal (oxcarbazepine). You've probably heard of the first two if you know anyone who is being treated for a seizure disorder. Depakote is currently the preferred drug if your child has what was previously referred to as rapid cycling, or the scary mixed episode.

Alert!

Although commonly used, the mood stabilizers Depakote and Tegretol should not be prescribed haphazardly to children and adolescents because they have not received FDA approval for use with children who have bipolar disorder. Lithium has only been FDA-approved for children over the age of twelve. Make sure your physician is using caution in prescribing these drugs for your child.

Lithium scares parents because it continues to have a stigma of being used on really crazy people. On some level, you are right to be concerned if your child is being prescribed this drug. While it does attack the depressive and manic symptoms of bipolar disorder, it requires very careful monitoring. Lithium levels are monitored by blood tests because it has been known to cause kidney and thyroid problems. This drug is prescribed based on a child's weight and blood lithium levels, so you can see why frequent visits to your child's doctor are important.

Side Effects

Of course, there are side effects to all of these medications. Depakote can cause drowsiness, stomach problems, weight gain, dizziness, and some problems in liver functioning although rare, and even thinning hair. Tegretol may cause difficulties such as drowsiness and dizziness, stomach problems, headaches, problems with vision, and fluctuations in liver functioning, and lowered white-blood cell counts. Lithium's side effects might include frequent urination and dry mouth, weight gain, tremors, stomach problems, and muscle weakness. Kidney and thyroid problems are also on the side effect list.

Essential

Lithium acts a lot like salt. Just like salt, lithium can make you quite thirsty. You can avoid dry mouth syndrome by keeping a bottle of water, a roll of mints, or gum handy. Reducing this side effect will continue to help your child cooperate with her medication regimen.

There are other less commonly used medications that can be helpful in stabilizing the symptoms of bipolar disorder: Neurontin (gabapentin), Lamictal (lamotrigine), and Topamax (topiramate). If these are mentioned by your child's physician, get the complete lowdown on these medications and their possible side effects before giving your approval.

With regard to the treatment of bipolar disorder, how do you decide whether to give a drug to your child considering that there *are* side effects? It's a balancing act. Do the side effects outweigh the benefits that your child is getting in terms of symptom stabilization? If they do, then you will want to talk to your child's physician and discuss medication alternatives.

"I'm Not Taking That!"

You also need to consider whether the side effects are interfering with your child's willingness to take the medication. A teen will often refuse to take medication because he doesn't want there to be anything wrong with him. For him, having to take a drug means he's "crazy." If he's had mania before, he will remember feeling as if he can do anything and conquer the world! This is powerful, so it's quite understandable that he won't want to take a medication that will take that away from him. For example, many girls who are taking these medications and gaining weight become frustrated quickly. They feel fat and ugly, and quickly become disenchanted with taking medication. If this is the case, communicate this with your doctor. It's important to be sympathetic to your child's concerns to increase cooperation.

Medication Is Not a Cure-all

There are other ways to manage dysthymia and bipolar disorder in conjunction with medication. Not every symptom will be alleviated or erased by medication. Frequently, a child has learned maladaptive ways of coping to modulate his symptoms. Psychotherapy can be useful here to educate not only the child but also the parents about dysthymia and bipolar disorder. The more you and your child know, the easier it will be to keep his symptoms under control and prevent them from causing significant problems with day-to-day functioning.

 *Question?*

When is psychiatric hospitalization necessary for my child?
When nothing seems to be working and your child's symptoms are putting her at increased risk for harm, hospitalization may be the answer. There your physician can try new treatments while protecting your child from any harm.

There are support groups available to children who have bipolar disorder and depression and to families who have had one of its members diagnosed with bipolar disorder and depression. You can always find helpful information about dysthymia, depression, and bipolar disorder on the shelves of a bookstore or online. Often, your physician will have material available in his office that will be informative.

The diagnosis and treatment of dysthymia and bipolar disorder is complex. No single treatment is going to work on every child. That is why keeping track of your child's specific symptoms and behaviors is critical. Educating yourself is a powerful way to get control over what is happening to your child and find the best treatment options available.

CHAPTER 8

Depression-related Issues

Nothing is as easy as it seems sometimes, and this is certainly the case with childhood depression. Parents often say they feel overwhelmed by all of this information and how to use it correctly. You must remember that although you are extremely crucial in the diagnostic process, you are not alone. Professionals look to you to help establish a baseline, or a starting point, from which to begin. Educating yourself about these disorders will be tremendously helpful to your child in the end.

Depression's Link to Other Mental Illnesses

You've heard the old question, "Which came first, the chicken or the egg?" Many parents want to know the same about depression and other mental problems. Like the proverbial chicken-and-egg question, the answer doesn't matter. Recognizing that there is a problem and addressing it is the true dilemma.

Depression has a lot of "relatives." These related disorders manifest themselves in problems with thoughts, feelings, behavior, and physiology. Each disorder comes with its own unique set of symptoms. Each contributes to a child's problems with day-to-day functioning and can cause significant disruptions in his relationships.

The relatives in a family are intertwined with one another, each affecting the other in unique and special ways. Some of these relationships can be troublesome, however, and in turn, problems occur. The same is true with depression and the following disorders. In order to fully understand the problem, the "troublemaker," so to speak, needs to be discovered. Whether it's a depressive symptom or a symptom of another disorder doesn't matter, they must all be confronted.

As you read along, you may begin to feel anxious because the list of symptoms that you must be on the lookout for keeps getting longer and longer. Don't try to memorize specific symptoms of a disorder. Just be aware if any of them are showing up in your child. Like the disorders discussed in earlier chapters, keep and organize a list or a chart of bothersome symptoms and let the professionals take it from there.

Attention Deficit Hyperactivity Disorder

You'd have to be living on another planet not to have heard of attention deficit hyperactivity disorder (ADHD). It is a popular label used today both on children who are truly suffering from the illness and for the kids who are troublesome in some other way. Basically, this is a disorder that causes problems with inattention, impulsivity, and hyperactivity. All three categories can be present, or they can exist separately. They are generally present before the age of seven. Its link to depression is thought to be in the child's self-perception. All too often, children with ADHD are seen as troublemakers, problem students, and as kids who are out of control. When children hear themselves talked about in such a way, they can't help but internalize these comments. Once they see themselves as failures or unpleasant to be around, depressive symptoms can begin to appear. In fact, about a third of children with ADHD have depression.

Inattentiveness

According to the *DSM-IV*, inattention manifests itself by the failure to give close attention to details or carelessness in school, home, or other activities; difficulty paying attention or sustaining attention; not seeming to listen when spoken to directly; failure to follow through on activities; difficulties with organization; disliking, refusing, or avoiding activities that require sustained attention; losing things often; being easily distracted by extraneous stimuli; frequent forgetfulness.

 ## Essential

Too often the positive attributes of ADHD are not recognized or emphasized. Although they are characterized negatively, children with ADHD are typically very bright, creative, and have much to offer the world. Helping a child understand this and helping him develop his own unique talents will reduce symptoms of depression significantly.

Impulsivity includes blurting out answers before questions have been completed; difficulty awaiting one's turn; and interrupting or intruding on others, such as butting into conversations or games.

For a child to be diagnosed with ADHD of the inattentive type, six or more characteristics of inattentiveness have to be present for at least six months to a degree that is considered maladaptive and not consistent with a child's developmental level.

 ## Fact

ADHD is a bit of a misnomer; it is not a deficit of attention! Rather, an ADHD child's brain is bombarded with so much stimuli that his brain can't focus on just one piece of information. It is more like the child is over-loaded with information and can't decide where to place his attention.

Is Your Child Active or Hyper?

It is often hard to distinguish between normal physical activity in a child and hyperactivity. A hyperactive child is almost constantly fidgeting with his hands or feet, or is generally squirmy. When remaining in his seat is expected, he gets up and can't seem to stay put. A hyperactive child has difficulty playing quietly. He is usually described as "always on the go" and "into everything." Last, a hyperactive child can also be excessively talkative.

Impulsivity

For a child to be characterized as having hyperactivity with impulsiveness, six or more of those symptoms have to be present in the same way. In teens, the impulsivity can take on a much greater magnitude of problems. A teen that is now driving may exhibit impulsiveness by speeding, reacting angrily behind the wheel, or other dangerous behaviors. If he is using substances, the tendency to drink too much will occur without him giving much thought to what he is doing. Fights and arguments are common. The problem is that impulsivity is a result of acting without giving any thought to the consequences. With teens, this can be not only dangerous but also deadly.

Oppositional Defiant Disorder

When a child has a persistent pattern of negativity, hostility, and defiant behavior, there is a possibility that oppositional defiant disorder (ODD) is present. A child with ODD has trouble holding his temper and is characterized as being angry and resentful. He is argumentative with adults and will actively defy or refuse to comply with rules or requests. He will deliberately annoy people, and in turn he will be touchy and easily annoyed by others. When he is confronted with his behavior or a mistake, it will always be someone else's fault. He will often be spiteful and vindictive.

ODD in Adolescence

While teens will exhibit many of the same ODD symptoms as a child, this is another disorder where teens can get into even bigger trouble. For one thing, there is more for them to get into as compared with younger children. Again, there is substance use, driving, sexual activity, and more. The stakes are higher and the consequences more dire.

Essential

There's a fine line between a child who is seen as independent and questioning of authority and a child who has symptoms of ODD. A child who thinks for himself and asks questions in order to understand typically does not suffer the negative consequences that a child with ODD does. A child with ODD is not happy and has a tendency to make others around him feel the same.

It is easy to see how depression may exist along with this disorder or how this disorder can create symptoms of depression. These children are often seen as difficult to like. When they are this way, it's easy to forget there may actually be an underlying problem. Unfortunately, this is mild compared to the more serious conduct disorder, which can be a result if ODD is left untreated.

Conduct Disorder

Kids who have conduct disorder (CD) often started out with ODD, but CD is much more devastating. These are the children who consistently violate the rights of others and disregard the rules of not only their parents but also of society. The seriousness of this disorder cannot be overstated.

The Diagnosis

Consider the *DSM-IV*'s list of symptoms for CD. Only three or more of these symptoms have to be present in the past twelve months, with at least one symptom being present in the past six months. There are four areas of concern: aggression to people or animals, destruction of property, deceitfulness or theft, and serious violation of rules.

1. Bullies, threatens, or intimidates others
2. Initiates physical fights

3. Has used a weapon that can cause serious physical harm to others (for example, a bat, brick, broken bottle, knife, gun)
4. Has been physically cruel to people
5. Has been physically cruel to animals
6. Has stolen while confronting a victim (for example, mugging, purse snatching, extortion, armed robbery)
7. Has forced someone into sexual activity
8. Has deliberately engaged in fire setting with the intent of causing serious damage
9. Has deliberately destroyed others' property (other than by fire setting)
10. Has broken into someone else's house, building, or car
11. Lies to obtain goods or favors or to avoid obligations (that is, "cons" others)
12. Has stolen items of nontrivial value without confronting a victim (for example, shoplifting, but without breaking and entering; forgery)
13. Stays out at night despite parental prohibitions, beginning before age thirteen years
14. Has run away from home overnight at least twice while living in parental or parental surrogate home (or once without returning for a lengthy period)
15. Often truant from school, beginning before age thirteen

You can now see why this is a frightening and serious disorder. Our juvenile system is full of children with CD whose mental illnesses have not been detected. About 40 percent of children with CD have depression, too. This is not surprising given the negativity a child must feel about himself and how others feel about him when he engages in these behaviors. If intervention is not made early, these are the children who will often engage in more dangerous behaviors as they age and are likely to be in frequent trouble with the law.

Physical and Sexual Abuse

Children who are abused either physically or sexually often end up seeing themselves as bad. When a person in whom a child has placed her trust violates that, it is inconceivable to her that this adult has hurt her intentionally. Thus, since a child typically believes her parents or other loved ones don't do anything wrong, their abuse must not be wrong either. She may see herself as to blame for the abuse she receives.

 Essential

> Hard as it may be to believe, adults who were sexually or physically abused do not realize that they are repeating the same behaviors that damaged them as children. Often the pattern of abuse becomes so ingrained in their experiences that they see it as a natural part of their worlds, thus making it hard to break the cycle.

Abuse as Love?

Sadly, some children equate abuse with love. As they age, they expect all adults to treat them this way, and unfortunately, they will approach relationships with the feeling that "You hurt me because you love me." If they are treated well in a relationship, often they won't know how to react as this sort of relationship does not feel normal.

The scars of physical and sexual abuse often last a lifetime. Abuse has the potential to strip a child of all his feelings of self-worth and dignity. It's no wonder that these children have symptoms of depression.

Seasonal Affective Disorder

Have you known anyone who seems to become depressed during the fall and winter, only to have those symptoms disappear with the return of spring? Many people, adults and children, feel more "blah" during these months and tend to hibernate more than usual.

Seasonal affective disorder (SAD) not only includes depressive symptoms, but also excessive sleep and appetite, decreased physical activity, and even an increase in craving for carbohydrates. SAD is thought to be caused by a lack of sunlight during these months.

SAD is probably easier to spot in a child than in an adult. Because children still go outside during winter months to play, they are exposed to more sunlight than adults. If your child is indoors a good bit and her mood, sleep, appetite, and activity level changes significantly, the presence of SAD must be considered. The good news is that this disorder can be managed quite effectively by getting exposure to the sun or light that mimics the sun, such as a specially designed lamp and bulb.

Alcohol and Drug Abuse

Many children medicate their feelings of depression by using drugs and alcohol. While it is bad enough that teens engage in this behavior, the prevalence of substance use in younger children is on the rise. One reason for this may be the peer pressure that children feel on a daily basis and their desire to fit in. Another reason may be that they see adults using substances to feel better. Still others feel so bad that they will try just about anything to make those feelings disappear!

Alert!

Inhalants are popular substances for kids to abuse. Kids call it "huffing," which is described as inhaling the fumes from things like glue, spray paint, nail polish, and gasoline. This is easy for a child to hide, so you need to be on the lookout for inhalants in your child's possession that are not things he typically uses in other activities.

The list of substances that are available to children is ever growing but consists primarily of alcohol, amphetamines, cannabis (marijuana), cocaine, hallucinogens, opioids, phencyclidine, and sedatives (hypnotics or anxiolytics). Caffeine and nicotine, though not considered necessarily dangerous, are included in this list.

Is My Child Using?

What does a child look like who is using substances regularly? A child who normally makes good grades may stop studying or become disinterested in school altogether. She may have trouble getting up in the mornings when she used to jump out of bed at the first ring of her alarm clock. She may be more reactive than usual, bursting into tears or a rage over something seemingly trivial. Questions about her whereabouts might be met by an overly defensive stance. When she returns from a social activity, she may avoid being in close contact with her parents for fear they might smell alcohol or other substances on her breath. She will be careful not to make eye contact lest her parents notice her glazed or bloodshot eyes.

Other Clues

There is another set of clues that you need to be watching for to determine if your child is abusing alcohol or drugs. Often a child's set of friends will abruptly change and he will begin to hang out with a very different crowd. He may show a decrease in activities that he used to enjoy so that he can spend more time indulging in substance use. He may engage in increasingly risky behaviors such as driving under the influence or getting into fights. Despite getting caught, he may continue to use and may not be able to stop.

Teenagers are famous for wanting their privacy, so it is normal for them to want to be in their rooms and to not want you to invade their space. If the amount of time your child is spending in his room becomes more excessive than usual, he may be actually using substances in his room or spending his time trying to get a substance. He may be using a fan that he normally doesn't in order to diffuse odors, or his window may be always open even when it is cold or really hot.

Question?

What's the difference between abuse and dependence?
Abuse is recurrent use of a substance despite problems with day-to-day functioning, the law, or physical harm. Dependence is marked by a tolerance for a substance such that more of it is needed to get the desired effect and despite efforts to cut back. Symptoms of withdrawal are also present.

Start Educating Early

Children are naturally focused on the present and rarely see their current behaviors as having potential consequences later. They are not aware of their own morbidity, so when they are told that these substances can seriously harm or kill them, they ignore your warnings. The conversation about substance use needs to start early in grade school. Without lecturing, there are ways to educate your child about the dangers of substance use. If your child is actively using, don't pick that moment to confront him. Instead, you'll have better luck if you will let him sober up and then calmly try to address the situation.

To Search or Not

Parents typically ask if it's okay to search their child's room. Obviously, you do not want to invade anyone's privacy, and that is the first thing your child will holler if you search his room. If you have a suspicion that your child is using alcohol or drugs, you have every right to search his room. Your responsibility is to protect him and guide him. A child rarely becomes completely distraught and angry if he has nothing to hide. Excessive defensiveness and anger may be a sign that you are right on track with the search.

Drug Testing

No parent wants her kid to feel like he is living in a jail. However, if he has repeatedly been caught using alcohol or drugs, you are perfectly within your rights as a parent to have him randomly tested. Random drug testing is better than telling your child beforehand, as they can be quite crafty in finding ways to fool the test. Again, most kids won't like the idea, but if they are clean, they are usually cooperative.

Alert!

Many parents are reluctant to address their child's use of substances because they think "I did it when I was young, too and I'm okay." Resist the urge to identify with your child's use. Remember that you are the parent and it is your job to protect and monitor your child's involvement in things that are harmful and illegal.

Because many drugs and alcohol have a depressive effect, it's expected that kids who use will be depressed. Also, those substances that act as stimulants cause a rebound effect, meaning that the high feeling goes away and a person may become more down as a result. If a child is medicating his depression by using alcohol and drugs, his use will only make the condition worse. If he is not depressed, regular and frequent use of substances is likely to create depression.

Posttraumatic Stress Disorder

When you hear about posttraumatic stress disorder (PTSD), you probably think of war veterans who have returned and are somehow psychologically impaired. In fact, many people don't believe in the existence of PTSD. This disorder deserves attention here because it is clearly associated with depression, and the results can be crippling. Without understanding these symptoms, you will likely miss the existence of this disorder in your child. To gain an insight into PTSD, here's the definition from the *DSM-IV*:

A. The person has been exposed to a traumatic event in which both of the following were present:
1. The person experienced, witnessed, or was confronted with an event or events that involved actual or threatened death or serious injury, or a threat to the physical integrity of self or others
2. The person's response involved intense fear, helplessness, or horror. Note: In children, this may be expressed instead by disorganized or agitated behavior.

What Is Considered an "Event"?

With regard to the event itself, your child may have observed severe physical abuse toward a parent and was afraid she was next. Perhaps the child was the victim of either sexual or physical abuse, or both. If you and your child were involved in a car accident in which someone was seriously hurt or even killed, this can cause PTSD. Another example is the death of a loved one.

Basically, any event that is out of the range of normal, everyday happenings that threatens your child's sense of security can be a trigger for what the *DSM-IV* calls a posttraumatic stress response, which is characterized by the following:

B. The traumatic event is persistently re-experienced in one or more of the following ways:
1. Recurrent and intrusive distressing recollections of the event, including images, thoughts, or perceptions. Note: In young children, repetitive play may occur in which themes or aspects of the trauma are expressed.
2. Recurrent, distressing dreams of the event. Note: In young children, there may be frightening dreams without recognizable content.
3. Acting or feeling as if the traumatic event were recurring (includes a sense of reliving the experience, illusions,

hallucinations, and dissociative flashback episodes, including those that occur on awakening or when intoxicated). Note: In young children, trauma-specific re-enactment might occur.

4. Intense psychological distress at exposure to internal or external cues that symbolize or resemble an aspect of the traumatic event.

5. Physiological reactivity on exposure to internal or external cues that symbolize or resemble an aspect of the traumatic event.

 Essential

Adults take in information and process it differently than children. Just because you don't believe what your child experienced isn't traumatic, do not assume she is interpreting the event in the same way. Doing so will cause you to miss your child's distress and increase her chances for depression.

Avoidance and Arousal

Along with the posttraumatic response to the stressor, a child will persistently avoid things that remind her of the trauma. She may refuse to think about it or to talk about it. She may report an inability to remember a critical piece of the trauma. She is likely to avoid anything that reminds her of the experience. You may notice your child seems detached from others and her own emotions.

The other set of symptoms include increased arousal that was not present prior to the traumatic event. These include difficulties falling or staying asleep, irritability or outbursts of anger, problems with concentration, hyper vigilance, and an exaggerated startle response.

Now you can see how ravaging PTSD can be. Symptoms of depression almost always accompany this disorder. Much of the symptomatology can be avoided or minimized by getting help for your child as soon after the traumatic event as possible. Even if your child claims to be fine, it's better to be safe than sorry.

 **Fact**

Just because your child appears symptom free immediately after the traumatic event, don't assume that she has gotten over it. Symptoms can appear as late as six months or more after a trauma. While this makes PTSD harder to recognize, it is nevertheless just as devastating.

Medical Illness

In Chapter 2, medical illness was cited as a cause of depression, so there's no need to go over that in depth again. But there is one thing that you may want to watch for in your child when it comes to illness and depression.

When Illness Is Depression

Children and teens often express their feelings through somatic complaints. A child who has recurring stomachaches or headaches with no obvious physical cause may be trying to tell you something. Some kids have even more vague symptoms such as a pain in their leg or a stiff back. If you cannot find any reason for these complaints, such as an injury, the flu, or a stomach bug, you might want to consider an emotional cause.

Is He Really Sick?

Parents often remain conflicted as to when a child's complaints need to be taken seriously. A quick trip to the doctor will help you determine if there is something truly wrong, if your child is merely seeking attention, or if there is an emotional problem manifesting itself in physical problems.

Hopefully, you aren't completely overwhelmed by the barrage of information to which you have been exposed. Now that you know so much about depression and related issues, congratulate yourself. But you have another job ahead of you—making the decision to get help.

CHAPTER 9

Seeking Professional Help

As time goes on and your child's symptoms worsen, inevitably the decision to seek professional help will have to be made. Just like deciphering what is truly going on with your child, you will have plenty to learn before approaching treatment. Although the task can be daunting, you owe it to your child to get him the very best treatment you can provide. And, as with everything else, the more you know, the better decisions you will make.

When to Intervene

Now that you've become quite educated about childhood depression, related disorders, and other related issues, it's time to decide if your child's problems are going to go away on their own or if your child needs professional intervention.

The problem here is simple. Even the best of parents have, at best, an amateur assessment. You have your knowledge, your observations, and your instincts that tell you something may be wrong with your child.

You also love your child. This is a good thing, but it can make you biased in many ways. You may be overly worried about symptoms that are in fact normal feelings and behaviors your child is experiencing. You may overlook others, believing they will pass. This is why, despite how much you have learned, the next step is to get confirmation of your findings. Professional

resources will be able to tell you whether your concerns are real or whether your child is just passing through an abnormally difficult time or a developmental stage.

Parental Reservations about Getting Help

You wouldn't be a good parent if you didn't have at least some concerns about getting help for your child. This is a completely new territory for you and for your child, so it's normal to feel anxious. How much will it cost? How do I hire a qualified professional? You may question whether your child is just merely changing as he passes from one developmental stage to another. Are his behaviors a response to something happening at home, such as your impending divorce? Another very common reservation parents have is that they expect their children to talk to them, not some stranger.

Why Won't He Talk to Me?

"Why wouldn't he want to talk to me if something is wrong? He should be able to talk to me instead of a perfect stranger." This is a common lament from parents, but one that may not be fair here. Children can be good at acting out their feelings rather than describing them. Often this is because they don't know how to label their feelings and thus describe them with accuracy.

 **Fact**

Professionals trained to treat children and adolescents have many resources for helping them define their emotions, describe them, and therefore address the ones that are troubling. This is one of the most important parts of treating depression, and it is a coping skill that will last a lifetime and help your child through many other situations.

When a child is asked how he feels about something or what is wrong, the typical answer is to either shrug or to say, "I don't know." Often, the more you push, the more resistant the child becomes to talking. It's important not to take this personally. Often a child believes that his "bad" feelings will somehow upset you and make you unhappy, and so he keeps quiet. At other times, the child is feeling hopeless and figures no one can help him, not even you. Deciding to involve a professional lets your child know that you are not afraid to seek help, and he shouldn't be hesitant either.

Cost

Another reservation parents have is cost. Obviously, you have to consider the cost of something when making a decision. The same is true for medical care. Part of parents' denial about their child's problems leads them to believe they can't afford to hire a professional. But perhaps you should consider this: not seeking help will cost you more in terms of money and your child's happiness than getting it. You may think nothing of paying money for a cell phone, cable TV, and other luxuries. Why wouldn't you spend money on getting help?

A parent might also be a bit intimidated about the entire treatment process. Putting your child in the hands of a complete stranger can be scary. It is perfectly understandable that you have reservations about how to secure the most appropriate treatment for your child. This chapter should help answer many questions you may have and give you some guidance for seeking help.

Educating Yourself

While you probably know more about depression now than you did before reading this book, it is time to learn about what treatments are out there and available to meet the specific needs of your child. The medical jargon associated with treatment is enough to send your head spinning! The best place to start is to understand the difference between practitioners, treatment regimens, and how insurance works.

Mental Health Practitioners

Mental health professionals that you might want to seek out or that you might be referred to include pediatricians, family practitioners, psychiatrists, psychologists, social workers, and counselors. The first three professionals just listed have been to medical school and completed extensive residencies in order to earn their degrees. Many of these have also obtained further training in order to become specialists in a particular area of medicine, such as a pediatrician who is specifically trained to treat children and adolescents.

Psychiatrists

Psychiatrists (John Doe, M.D.) specialize in diagnosing and treating mental illness. They prescribe medications if necessary, and some provide therapy. However, most psychiatrists focus their practices on diagnostic and medication issues.

Question?

Who is best equipped to make a diagnosis?
The best choice is either a psychiatrist or psychologist. The biggest difference is that psychiatrists can prescribe medication if necessary. But a psychologist can just as easily make a diagnosis and refer to a psychiatrist to determine if medication is an appropriate option for optimal treatment.

If you are considering going to a psychiatrist, it is best to find one who specializes in child and adolescent psychiatry. He is more likely to understand the unique differences in children versus adults, and he will know how to handle medications at an age-appropriate level.

Pediatricians and Family Practitioners

Pediatricians and family practitioners cannot be overlooked as good alternatives for medication issues. Often they have had plenty of experience with depressive patients and prescribing medications with good results. Some will be more comfortable than others in doing this and will only treat those patients with symptoms that are very specific and mild. Others will immediately refer you to a psychiatrist. If you are considering using these physicians for the treatment of your child, you can be fairly sure they will tell you if this is something they routinely do or if they would prefer to give you a referral.

Psychologists

Psychologists (John Doe, Ph.D.) have a doctoral degree, which typically means they have a master's degree in addition to the doctoral education that includes more schooling and internship training. In terms of education for mental health, psychologists have more extensive education than medical doctors. They are capable of making a diagnosis for your child but cannot prescribe medication, although there is a movement to change this. They are capable of performing evaluations and treatment (therapy). Like medical doctors, they often have a specialty, such as child psychology.

Fact

If you can't find a specialist in your area, don't give up on the hope of getting good treatment. Ask around, and chances are you will find a doctor or other mental health professional that may not be specifically trained in the area of children but has experience anyway and can handle the issues you present.

Social Workers

Social workers (John Doe, LCSW) typically have master's degrees and are able to make diagnoses and provide therapy. In some areas, social workers are just as capable of providing the same quality of treatment as a psychologist. But psychologists will almost always have more in-depth training across a broad range of treatment methods. If you would rather employ a social worker, the best thing to do is to research his education, experience, and reputation.

Essential

You've heard that no question is stupid. In the case of making a decision as to where to take your child for treatment, research is key. Ask questions, and then ask more! Don't stop until you are satisfied that you know everything you can about a particular provider or treatment process.

Some psychiatrists and psychologists employ social workers to do screenings with new patients. They will often perform what is called an "intake evaluation" to better determine what services might be needed. Less serious cases may be referred to social workers, and more complex issues get passed on to psychologists and psychiatrists.

Counselors

Last, you may encounter what is called a licensed professional counselor (John Doe, LPC). Their training can be obtained in several different arenas, but most have a master's degree. Depending on the severity of your child's problems and the amount of training a counselor has, this may be the perfect treatment provider.

Types of Treatment

Treatment for your child will primarily be either medication, therapy, or a combination of the two. These treatments will be discussed more in depth in Chapter 11. For now, in making the decision to get treatment, you will need to suspend your beliefs and or your suspicions about both. The reason you are seeking help for your child is because you are not the expert here when it comes to treatment. While you may be an expert on who your child is and what his problems are, a mental health professional will provide a much more objective, unbiased opinion about your child.

Medication Issues

Medication issues will include your child's specific complaints, his age, weight, and other factors. A doctor will work to get the medication best suited for your child. A good doctor will address with you any concerns you may have about your child taking medication. He will explain the benefits of medication as well as any possible side effects. His goal should be to make an accurate diagnosis and determine whether medication is necessary. In addition, he should provide education not only to you but also to your child at an age-appropriate level.

Alert!

A physician who gets offended or defensive about your wanting a second opinion is not likely to be sympathetic to your questions and concerns. He should be more than willing to do whatever you feel is necessary to feel comfortable about your child's treatment. As a general rule, if he balks at getting a second opinion, move on.

Therapy

Therapy may be on an individual basis with your child, or it may include other members of the family. The type of therapy will depend on your child's specific problems and needs. It will also take into account other factors that might need to be addressed, such as family problems, parenting issues, or school issues. For it to be most effective, a therapist should try to address all the issues that may be contributing to your child's depression.

When considering therapy for your child, if he is also on medication, make sure you have a therapist and physician who are willing to collaborate with one another and with you. The best treatment will be one in which everyone is playing on the same team and where no critical information slips through the cracks. Your participation in the process is important as well, but try not to bombard them with phone calls. Unless it's an emergency, you will have better luck if you make a list of your questions and concerns as they arise. One phone call with several questions is better than four different contacts. It's also okay to ask for a few minutes before or after your child's appointment with the therapist or doctor if you need it. Doctors and therapists may have certain rules about this process, but they do understand that you are a worried parent and that you will need some attention, too. Consider changing doctors or therapists if they are uncooperative with this process.

Insurance and Payment

A quick word needs to be said about insurance and payment for treatment. Take the time to review your health-care plan carefully or call your provider. You need to know which type of treating professional is covered by your insurance and what your payment will be after insurance pays its portion. If you have a particular professional that you wish for your child to see, make sure she is included in your plan. You've come this far in deciding to get help for your child. Skipping the insurance step is apt to result in unnecessary frustration and misinformation.

 **Fact**

Every moment counts when trying to get your child help. This is because children change constantly and quickly. A failure to stay one step ahead of your child's problems will result in missed symptoms. Often, the later the treatment comes in the course of the depression, the harder it is to treat successfully.

Finding a Diagnostician

Before you pick a diagnostician, get a current and thorough physical evaluation of your child. This will take care of two things. First, any physical illness that mimics or can cause depression will be detected. Second, a good mental health practitioner will ask you to get a physical exam for your child in order to rule out illness, and you will be one step ahead of the process. If you can, get your doctor to write a letter for you providing the state of your child's health.

When Your Pediatrician Is Hesitant

If your pediatrician does not wish to treat your child's depression, he is still one of the best referral sources for a good mental health professional. He relies on these professionals to work with him and usually knows their work. Because he is a trusted part of your family, so to speak, his referrals are typically sound and appropriate.

 *Essential*

A good source of mental health recommendations is to contact a local university, if available, and ask for their psychology program. For a psychiatrist, call the closest medical school's psychiatry department. These institutions often graduate students who go on to live in the area. They will know of several acceptable places for you to start.

Family Physician

If you don't have a pediatrician or he doesn't have a referral for you, try a family physician. Like pediatricians, they are used to making such recommendations. Your insurance company can give you a referral, but the names on their lists are on what is called "preferred providers." There is no reason to refer you to anyone who isn't on their lists, but this doesn't necessarily mean it's a bad referral. Schools also have a list of professionals they like to work with, but you have to be careful about this if you aren't ready for the school to know what is happening with your child.

Other Sources for Referrals

The best referrals, other than from your pediatrician, usually come from other parents or friends. Mental health professionals will tell you that their biggest source of referrals comes from word of mouth. In other words, satisfied "customers" are usually more than happy to give you the name of the person who helped them out. Don't be embarrassed to ask. Remember, the reason they know the name of a good mental health professional is because they or their children have been to see one.

The one place from which to avoid picking your treatment source is through the Yellow Pages. That does not mean there aren't good professionals listed here. Everyone who lists in the Yellow Pages pays for their advertisements. Unfortunately, not everyone who is listed is qualified to care for children, and like every other profession, some are not even reputable.

Preparing for the First Appointment

You've finally got your child's first appointment scheduled. Now what? You realize that the appointment will only last somewhere between an hour and an hour-and-a-half. Like all parents, you feel like you won't have time to get it all out. The easiest thing to do is to make a list of concerns regarding your child. Do not assume that what you have to say is trivial or nonessential. You don't know that, and a good professional would rather have too much information than not enough.

Get Organized

Take your file of information with you. Start with a record of your child's last physical exam, along with a history of your child's development. Also note whether any stressful events have occurred within the last year.

Remember the mood chart that recorded your child's symptoms you were advised to make? Now is the time to share that mood chart. It doesn't have to be pretty or especially presentable. But it needs to be easy to read and somewhat organized so that the professional can understand it.

Last, be prepared to answer questions about your child's sleep, appetite, behavior, school performance, and any information that may have been reported to you by others, such as teachers.

At the Office

Arrive a few minutes early so that you can complete any paperwork that is required. Resist the urge to chat with the other parents who may be in the waiting room. Everyone has a story to tell, but listening to others at this time is apt to make you even more nervous and uncomfortable. In turn, your child will pick up on your anxiety. It is best that you and your child remain calm so that you will be ready when your time comes.

You can expect that the professional you see will come up with what is known as a "working diagnosis." This merely means that your professional has some sort of idea about what is wrong with your child, and this gives him an initial idea of what direction to take next. Depending on what happens through the next few appointments either with him or someone else he recommends for treatment, the diagnosis may change.

How to Pick the Right Therapist

Whether your child has been given a working diagnosis by a physician or if your first appointment is with a therapist, the relationship between the child and therapist is going to be critical in your child's treatment and its ultimate success. There are several things to consider when picking the very best therapist for your child.

Ask Questions

Remember that you are basically interviewing a therapist who will potentially be treating your child. You are also paying for a service and you deserve to get the best. That is why you should interview several therapists until you find the one who is just right for your child. Ask about her education, her licenses, and her work experience. You should also ask if there are any complaints lodged against her by patients with her licensing board.

Alert!

Just because a therapist has a complaint against her does not mean you shouldn't employ her. Patients complain for all sorts of reasons, and licensing boards are required to look into all of them no matter how baseless the complaint. Ask questions—you'll be able to tell if your therapist is being open and honest with you.

Ask about Therapy

Next you should inquire about what kinds of therapy are going to be used with your child. Cognitive therapy looks at a child's beliefs about herself and her world and how those beliefs contribute to the way she sees herself and, ultimately, her depression. For some children, this is a very effective way to treat depression.

If the therapist says she plans to use behavioral therapy, she will use techniques aimed at helping a child behave differently in the face of depressive symptoms. Troublesome behaviors are targeted because they are believed to be part of the causes of a child's depression.

Family Therapy

Family therapy may be a part of your child's treatment and you need to be prepared to cooperate. In no way is a therapist who recommends family therapy saying you are to blame for your child's depression. As you will read about later, the family who has a child with depression is also affected by the depression. Other problems within the family, such as parenting, your marriage, or an illness, may have contributed to your child's depression. The family may need to have a chance to work through some issues as a way to help the depressed child, and in turn, the entire family.

Additional Concerns

If you decide to employ a particular therapist, the next thing you should do is address how therapy will be structured. Aside from discussing the cost of therapy, you will want to know how long your child's sessions will last and how often she needs to be seen. In addition, ask how often you will be allowed to talk with the therapist about your child. Setting some goals for therapy will give you some security that your child really is going to be helped and that there is a workable plan.

Essential

Children under the age of sixteen do not have the right to privacy, which means the therapist can talk with the parent if she chooses. Adolescents have the right to privacy, but that confidence can be breached with a parent if the therapist believes the child is a threat to himself or others.

If your child is prescribed drugs in conjunction with therapy, make sure the therapist has some working knowledge of the prescribed medications. She will be unable to offer advice about taking the drugs, but she can spot side effects or signs that the medicine is working. She can then work in collaboration with the doctor prescribing the drugs in order to optimize the treatment.

Is It a Good Fit?

The therapist you have picked for your child can be the most reputable in town, but she might not be the best match for your child. Initially, your child may say he doesn't like the therapist. Frequently this is a response born of fear and reluctance to open up to a stranger. If it is a good fit, then these comments will cease.

It isn't necessary that you like the therapist in the same way as your child. Look at the rapport between them and how your child responds to her feedback. As long as you feel confident about the therapist's credentials, if your child seems to be getting something out of his time with her, leave it alone.

Last, a good therapist will know if she and your child don't jive. If she recognizes this she will likely refer him to another therapist. Don't take offense at this, because actually she is doing you a favor.

The Importance of Honesty and Full Disclosure

As a parent, when picking professionals to help your child, now is not the time to hold back any pertinent information. If there is a history of mental illness, addiction, abuse, or suicide, tell the professional. Even if your child hasn't been directly exposed to anything that may have occurred in your family, tell it anyway. The professional is the one who will be able to take that information and decide whether it is relevant for your child and his treatment.

Be an Open Book

Treatment is only as effective as the amount of honesty provided. This should include your being able to share your fears and concerns about your child, no matter how inconsequential they might seem. Every detail a professional can glean from you gives her a better, more whole picture of who your child is and how to help him.

Seeking professional help is a very difficult, personal choice you may be forced to make on behalf of your child. Once you have found the right professionals who can give you back your child without depression, you will realize it was worth it!

Chapter 10

The Decision to Undergo Treatment

Okay, you've been to your initial appointment with a physician or therapist. Perhaps medication, therapy, or a combination of the two has been recommended. If you are like most people new to the psychological world of treatment, the extensive medical terminology may have overwhelmed you. Many parents leave this appointment feeling somewhat relieved but are still confused about whether their child should undergo treatment. If you are worried about making that decision, and wonder how it will affect you and your child, read on.

Do Your Homework

You already know to ask about a professional's credentials (licenses, professional organizations). You've checked into your insurance benefits and have some understanding about payments (what's covered and what's not). But there's still a bit more you need to check into before making the decision to proceed with treatment.

Some Considerations

Chapter 9 discussed picking the right therapist. There are a few other things you might want to consider. You may have found what you consider to be the perfect therapist or physician for your child. You are excited that you will be able to provide what you feel is the best option for your child.

You then call the office of this particular professional to set up a series of appointments. What you hear next is quite unexpected. "I'm sorry, the doctor doesn't work on Fridays." "You can have an appointment, but it will be six weeks before we can get you in." In other words, your schedule, your child's schedule, and the schedule of the professional are not in sync at all! You could try begging, but it probably won't work.

Essential

If you can't use the professional you originally chose, ask if there's someone else in that office that is available who can meet the needs of your child. Also, professionals tend to have a list of other therapists or doctors that they respect and use for referrals. Picking from that list should get you another good fit for your child.

You'll have to decide how important it really is to have this particular individual treat your child. Can you change your or your child's schedule to fit in? Can your child wait for six weeks to get an appointment? If you can accommodate this professional's office hours and availability, then it may be worthwhile to do so. However, if you were successful in finding one professional whom you believed was a good fit for your child, you can probably find another. Whatever you decide, don't give up on treatment altogether because then no one wins, especially your child.

Don't Rely on Insurance Company Referrals

On another note, when making the decision to send your child for treatment, try to refrain from asking your insurance carrier to give you a referral. Often, insurance companies contract with professionals to offer their services and pay them at a discounted rate. There's absolutely nothing wrong with this practice, but carriers hardly ever thoroughly check out the providers on their lists. Typically, little is known about the quality of care these people provide. Also, don't use those referral services that advertise in your area. Professionals have usually paid a fee to be on those lists. There's nothing wrong with that, but again there's a lack of knowledge about how they really perform in practice. Using these methods is like trying to shoot at a moving target!

Just because your child likes the professional you have chosen may not be enough. Check out the surroundings in which your child will be getting treatment. Is it kid friendly? Are there toys, crayons, or books in the waiting room and the office? Is the staff friendly and accommodating to children? Are they patient in the face of a waiting room full of active kids?

Alert!

Even though you have confidence in the professional you have chosen, your child might still be a bit hesitant. Help your child pick a favorite stuffed animal, book, or game to take to the first appointment. This will give your child something easy to talk about, and it will help break the ice between her and the therapist.

Remember that although trust, a safe environment, and warm communication are the hallmarks of a good therapeutic relationship, it will take more than one appointment to make that happen. Have patience and try not to force the process.

Discussing Treatment with Your Child

How exactly do you go about discussing your decision for your child to undergo treatment? Three answers come to mind: carefully, gently, and confidently. Being careful and gentle means that you consider where your child is developmentally. A four-year-old understands a lot less than an eight-year-old. Explain why you are seeking help in such a way so that your child understands there is a problem.

Essential

It's easy to associate a child's personality and identity with their depression. Your child will pick up on this and begin to see herself as damaged and lacking in self-worth. Make sure you separate your child's identity from the disorder and help her do the same. The depression is *not* your child!

What to Say

For younger children, an explanation might go like this: "Sometimes we get sad and we don't know why. I have arranged for you and me to go see a lady (or man) who talks to kids all the time about how they feel. There's nothing to be afraid of, and I will be right there with you."

For an older child, you can give more detail. Never, ever apologize for taking your child to treatment. You want her to understand that seeking help is a good thing. Try to answer her questions as best you can, and don't be afraid to say, "I don't know."

What if your child refuses to go? This is likely to make you second-guess your decision to seek treatment because "maybe it isn't that bad." Stop and think! This is where your confidence needs to kick in. *You* are the parent and you have done your homework! You might try gentle persuasion, but if she still refuses, then it's time for a different approach. Tell her that you can certainly understand her misgivings about seeing someone and that it is normal to be a bit anxious. You can even bargain with her, but only a little. You might say, "You don't want to go and I get that. But we *are* going. We'll talk about how you feel about it after you've tried it." The bottom line is that you are in charge, not her.

Your Child's Role

Aside from teaching your child about what she is about to do, it's important to help her understand her role in the process. She will be responsible for reporting to the doctor how she may feel on medicine or how she feels about a particular event. Encourage her to ask questions of the professional. Doing this will teach her two things. First, she will have an active role in getting well and will see herself as capable of doing so. Second, she will learn skills to get her needs met that will follow her through her life.

Who Else Needs to Know?

When your child begins treatment, there are two responses parents often have. Some will not want anyone to know, and others will be eager to share their story to get feedback or to compare their child's experiences with another child. Before you say anything, give careful thought to your motives for remaining silent or speaking out.

A Good Rule of Thumb

A good way to decide whether to share information with other family members or outside the family is to talk to the professional who will be treating your child. Immediate family members probably need to know. Siblings will intuitively know something's up. Your child's treatment need not be discussed in depth, but it is also a great way to teach compassion and educate other family members about depression.

School

It is important to discuss your child's condition with her school. She spends a lot of her time at school, and changes in your child will be noticed. The parents of her close friends may need to know about your child if she will be spending lots of time there, too. In these two areas are people who can look out for your child. They care about your child and her needs. Should she experience a side effect, or an improvement or problem is noticed, these are the individuals you can count on to keep you informed.

There seems to be no hard and fast answer as to who needs to know about your child's depression. Your therapist or physician can help you determine how much to share and who to tell. At the very least, err on the side of caution and refrain from telling too much. Your child doesn't need or want any negative publicity.

Alert!

Let's be honest. Though they may mean well, some people do not know how to keep things to themselves. If you choose to share information about your child's treatment, be careful whom you tell. Even in the twenty-first century, there's a stigma about mental health, and busybodies don't need to make things worse for your child!

Exploring Parental Feelings and Fears

All parents want their children to be happy and healthy. Naturally, they are discouraged when their child is diagnosed with depression. It's normal to wonder if you have done something to cause your child to be depressed. Did you not hold her enough? Did you yell too much? Did you neglect her somehow? Parents of depressed children say the questions can go on and on to the point of becoming irrational. The questions lead to guilt and shame, and often this prevents parents from seeking help for their children.

Your Role in Your Child's Life

As you have learned, children absorb and learn a lot from their environment, a large part of which is family. While there may be parental contributions to a depressive episode, no one causes another's depression. It is important to be educated about your role as a parent in your child's life because you do have influence.

The first thing that you will need to do when making the decision to involve your child in treatment is to let go of your self-blame. No matter what the circumstances are surrounding the history behind your child's depression, you didn't make it happen! Parenting is a responsibility that requires on-the-job training. You were not born knowing everything there is to know about rearing children. All parents learn by trial and error. Hopefully, you will learn from your successes and your mistakes, and you will be ready to learn how to help your child rather than to waste your energy feeling responsible.

Get Rid of Your Anger and Resentment

Some parents report feeling angry and resentful because their children are depressed. A child with emotional problems takes a lot of time from your regular routine. You may miss work to take her to the doctor. Your other children miss out on your time because you are busy helping the depressed child. Your marriage and social life may suffer. So why wouldn't you feel angry? You know your anger is not helpful, but you can't help it.

 *Fact*

If you are having trouble managing your own fears, anger, and other feelings about your child's depression, get some help. Some professionals who treat children have support groups for parents. Do not be afraid to share these feelings with others who understand. Taking care of yourself during the process has another reward—your child will benefit from a healthier parent!

You will have to get past it. Once again, what you're feeling is perfectly natural. But anger takes so much emotional energy, energy you can't spare because you have plenty of things on your plate requiring emotional involvement. Find ways to express your anger healthily and try not to take it out on those who don't deserve it, particularly your depressed child.

Let Go of Denial

Any parent, if he is honest, will admit that he doesn't want anything to be wrong with his child. Some things seem more acceptable than having a mental health problem. When a child is diagnosed with depression, a parent is often in denial. He would prefer to bury his head in the sand, hoping it will go away and his child will be fine. When this doesn't happen, he is confused and may think, "How did *this* happen?"

The best way to handle this is to get a grip! Your child's depression has been diagnosed and it is real. Quit denying it or making bargains with the man upstairs that it will go away. All children encounter one problem or another, and yours is not a superhero!

Accompanying denial is his cousin, fear. What if my child's depression never goes away? What if it worsens? What if it leads to other problems? Once again, your fears are normal. How you handle them, however, is critical.

You simply cannot give in to your fears, and you can't ignore them, either. Fear is often an emotion that warns you that there are other troubling emotions lurking inside you. Listen to your fears. What is it you are really concerned about? Are your fears legitimate or are they out of control?

Get in the Game

One way to eliminate some of the fear about your child's depression is to ask questions, get educated, and get proactive. This will give you back control over your emotions and put you in a better position to help your child through his difficult time.

Alert!

When you use insurance to pay for your child's treatment, you need to know that a mental illness diagnosis will follow them for a long time. That doesn't mean you shouldn't use your insurance, but you might discuss the possibility of using a diagnosis that might not hold as big a stigma as others.

Probably the biggest problem a parent faces is when her child diagnosed with depression or another mental illness is dealing with the stigma attached to it. While society has come a long way in accepting mental illness as being real and serious, "being crazy" is still how many people judge those who are unfortunate enough to have mental illness.

The Stigma of Mental Illness

You may know that depression is a common malady in today's world. You also know that there are plenty of others who say being depressed is just an excuse for not dealing with the trials and tribulations of life. People judge that which they can't understand, and there will always be people who have negative opinions related to mental illness.

 **Fact**

It is essential to prepare your child for the judgments she might face when others hear about her depression. She may want to be particular about whom she tells, but she should never be made to feel inferior in any way. Help her learn skills to not let the stigma of mental illness damage her recovery, and ultimately, her self-esteem.

Obviously, you'd rather your child not have a mental illness. A physical illness or a broken arm is much easier to explain, and it is much more acceptable to be ill in these sorts of ways. You simply cannot let yourself fall prey to feeling stigmatized. And, read this carefully, you also cannot completely protect your child from the stigma of mental illness. Children with depression typically become very compassionate toward others who are having trouble. Helping your child to understand that there are positive things that can come out of having depression will do wonders to decrease the stigma that others try to place on mental illness.

Trust Your Gut

Not only women have intuition—men have it, too. It's called trusting your gut. When you are making the decision to put your child into treatment, the doubts, fears, and insecurities about finding that right person can be overwhelming. It would be so easy to sit back and do nothing and just wait. Wishing this doesn't make you a bad parent, it makes you normal!

You've done your homework and you've picked a professional that you believe will be the most helpful to your child. You've checked into insurance and appointment schedules. You've done it all and you still don't understand why you don't feel good about your decision.

Why Am I Still Worried?

The answer is pretty simple: You don't want your kids to be hurting. When they are, you do what needs to be done to help them, to protect them, to take that hurt away. But there is absolutely no guarantee that everything will be okay or like it used to be. Just realizing that is enough to drive you nutty. This is when you must trust your gut. Your gut is that voice deep down within you that knows what is best for you and your child.

The key to trusting your gut lies in hearing it. Take some quiet time and listen to yourself. Take a few minutes to write down all of your fears, questions, and concerns about treatment. At some point, you will have to make a decision. Trust your gut—you are smarter than you know!

Getting a Second Opinion

You read about getting a second opinion earlier. Before picking a professional, it's a great idea, if you have the time and ability, to interview several people. Find out how they plan to treat your child, how they will measure the success or failure of treatment, and any other pertinent issues. Doing this will give you essential information to pick the best professional for your child's needs.

Essential

Think of getting a second opinion as finding a better model appliance. In other words, you are the consumer of psychiatric and psychological services. If you are not satisfied with the services you are receiving, you have the right to keep shopping until you find the right "model."

But what if you pick a professional and after a few appointments you are not pleased with your choice or your child is making negative comments about the therapist? You can either wait for a couple more sessions to make sure you aren't being premature in your suspicions or you can do something about it immediately.

Talk Directly with the Source

Discuss your concerns with the professional. Most are happy to listen to you, answer questions, and offer explanations as to why they do things a certain way. If you feel your worries have been alleviated, treatment can continue. The professional may offer to help you find another person to treat your child's specific problems.

If your professional becomes defensive and argumentative, this is usually a pretty good sign that he doesn't like to be questioned and, unfortunately, is going to do things the way he wants regardless of whether there is a better way. Depending on the seriousness of your concerns, this may be enough to send you running from his office to find other treatment.

CHAPTER 11

Treatment for the Mind, Body, and Soul

Most experts would agree that the treatment of depression is multidisciplinary. This means that the most successful treatment is usually a combination of medication and some form of therapy. That is because depression affects the mind and the body, and even the soul to an extent. Just as you would expect your child's broken leg to be fixed using all the techniques available, the same is true for depression.

Psychotherapy

Psychotherapy is just a fancy word for counseling or therapy. For purposes of simplicity, we'll use the word *therapy* here. Whatever jargon is used by your therapist, the goals are generally the same. The biggest goal of therapy is to help your child reduce his symptoms of depression while he is being helped to achieve his highest level of functioning. The emphasis is on whatever your child's highest level is, and this should not be compared to other children.

It is also important to realize that the therapies you are about to learn about need to be tailored to fit your child's developmental age and where he is emotionally. A child who is six years old will express herself quite differently than a fourteen-year-old. An extremely depressed child may need different attention than one who has less symptomatology. If your therapist is properly trained, he will know how to take a certain type of therapy and apply it

appropriately to your child. The way in which he conducts therapy might change as your child's symptoms improve.

 **Fact**

Before therapy begins, your child may be given psychological testing. Psychometric testing is used to detect particular symptoms of, for example, depression. Testing can also be used to pinpoint any other mental health problems that might exist. Testing is a great way to make sure the therapist doesn't miss anything, and it also provides him with evidence supporting his diagnoses.

There are generally three types of therapies used to treat childhood and adolescent depression: play therapy, cognitive-behavioral therapy, and interpersonal therapy.

Play Therapy

Play therapy is typically used with very young children who are not chronologically old enough to express their emotions. It is also used with young children who are having a hard time putting their experiences into words. Dolls, animals, puppets, games, drawing, and books are all used.

Dolls, stuffed animals, and puppets are great tools for having a conversation with a child. Often, the child *is* the doll, animal, or puppet's voice. It is easier for her to say tough things when she believes it is coming out of someone else's mouth. You have probably watched your own child with one of these objects saying something like, "No, no, you can't do that." She is probably mimicking what you have repeatedly said to her. The same is true here. She can report being sad, angry, or a myriad of other emotions. This technique is also helpful in determining whether a child has been sexually or physically abused. Over time, themes of play emerge and play therapy focuses on those issues.

Question?

My child's depression isn't that bad. Won't it go away on its own?
It might. Don't make a decision based on what you think, or even based on what you read here or elsewhere. You hire experts to handle other problems in your lives. A professional will be able to tell you whether your child needs expert help.

Drawing is also helpful for younger as well as older children. For older children, games and books may be used. Have you ever been driving down the street with your child and all of a sudden he brings up something that is bothering him? This is what drawing, playing games, and reading books do. These are avenues for them to casually bring up what is on their minds.

Adolescents don't usually engage in traditional play therapy. Books may be used, but they are for educating a child about his depression. Occasionally, Game Boys or other hand-held gaming devices are used. This can help break the ice as he may be apt to mention things that are bothering him while he is focused on playing his game.

Alert!

Typically a therapy session lasts forty-five to sixty minutes. Do not be alarmed, however, if your young child comes out in twenty to thirty minutes. With play therapy, a child can become anxious, especially when uncomfortable feelings emerge. He may not be able to handle any more time that day, and a therapist will not push him until he is psychologically ready.

Other therapists have been known to take a walk with a teen or even engage in some sort of physical activity like basketball. These activities put adolescents at ease with the hope that they will be comfortable enough to talk.

Cognitive-behavioral Therapy

Cognitive-behavioral therapy addresses a child's view of himself, past and present circumstances, and his beliefs about the future. When a child is depressed, these views are pessimistic, sad, and maybe even angry. This therapy helps a child to understand how his thoughts affect his mood. There is an emphasis on monitoring how a child feels and making him realize he has control over his thinking. If he can control his thoughts, he can thus control his mood. Negative thoughts and behaviors are replaced by more positive, productive thoughts.

Let's say your child has been bullied a good deal at school. Over time, he has come to believe he is what the others kids labeled him— fat, stupid, and psycho. Rather than try new things, he now withdraws because he knows the kids are right and he won't be able to do them. He quits studying that which is difficult because, to him, what's the use? You watch him as he becomes more and more depressed.

When he enters therapy, this approach will attack the negative thoughts he has about himself and his environment. He might be given homework, such as trying one new activity to see if he really will fail. He may be asked to make a list of all his good attributes. The therapist takes this new evidence to show him that he is not what he has come to believe about himself. New, more positive beliefs become substituted for the negative ones.

 *Fact*

Cognitive-behavioral techniques are not only great for treating depression, but they also have an excellent use outside the therapeutic relationship. Teaching your child these skills greatly reduces the likelihood that your child will become depressed, or if he is, lessens chances for a future relapse.

Self-control and the acquisition of problem-solving skills are other goals of cognitive-behavioral therapy. Armed with skills to restructure his thinking and ways to solve problems, a child can then begin to control his behavioral responses as well as his emotions.

Interpersonal Therapy

Interpersonal therapy is a newer approach used to help a child understand how certain events or problems have contributed to the occurrence of depression. Family and other social relationships are also explored as these have a tremendous impact on how a child interacts in his world and how he sees himself. Often, this is used in conjunction with cognitive-behavioral therapy. This therapy may include the family in some sessions to resolve conflicts or to help them learn better ways to communicate. It also helps a child to realize that he is not alone in what caused or contributed to his depression.

Parents often ask how long it may be before they see an improvement in the child's depression. The bad news is that a child might get a little worse before he gets better. The reason for this is twofold. First, remember, he is depressed. His energy level might be low and so he is not ready to address his problems yet; he is simply too tired. Second, depressed children have a lot of feelings inside that have not been expressed for a variety of reasons. As these feelings begin to pop out, their behavior may start to match the negative emotions they are now feeling.

Understand that teens are going to complain a good bit in the beginning of therapy. They are, in essence, being forced to talk, and most of them would rather have a tooth pulled! Give the therapist some time to prove your teen can trust her.

The good news is that these outbursts will eventually stop. Your role during this time needs to be one of patience and understanding rather than reproach and anger. If a child is in therapy once a week, you should start seeing some improvement in his symptoms and behavior in four to six weeks. Of course, this also depends on your child's level of depression, his cooperation with treatment, and other more ambiguous factors.

Medication

As you will recall from Chapters 1 and 2, the brain is a magnificent organ. While its chemistry is designed to run smoothly, often there are glitches in the neurotransmitter system. When this happens, an individual can experience all sorts of problems.

The neurotransmitters discovered thus far that regulate emotions and mood are called serotonin, norepinephrine, and dopamine. A decrease in one or all of these can result in depression. Medication serves to jump-start the manufacture of one or more of the neurotransmitters. It goes into the brain and helps to increase the natural production of neurotransmitters back to a level where they belong. Once this is happening properly, depressive symptoms are alleviated and your child's mood should return to normal.

Alert!

Warning: Tricyclic antidepressants should not be prescribed to children who have certain heart ailments, seizure disorders, or, at times, if there is a family history of cardiac disease or seizures. This is another good reason to give the physician that is treating your child a complete medical history.

There are three general categories of medications used to treat depression: tricyclic antidepressants, monoamine oxidase inhibitors (MAOIs), and selective serotonin reuptake inhibitors (SSRIs). You need not understand the chemistry behind them, but you do need to know the jargon so that you'll recognize it when you hear it. Your child's doctor can explain how they work.

Tricyclic Antidepressants

Tricyclic antidepressants are not used as often as they used to be because of their possible side effects, which will be explored later.

These drugs are slow acting, which means that a child will have to take them at least two weeks or more before any lessening of symptoms will be observed or reported. A child will start out with a small dose of the medication to see if he can tolerate it, and over a period of four to six weeks that dosage will be increased and tweaked until the right level for your child is achieved.

Waiting for a tricyclic antidepressant to work can be frustrating for the parent who is anxious for a quick fix. Older children and adolescents will also get impatient, and if they don't immediately begin to feel better will often refuse to take their medicine. Thus it is essential that your doctor explain this to your child and to you so that you will be prepared for a longer wait time.

Tricyclic antidepressants include Elavil (amitriptyline), Norpramin (desipramine), Pamelor (nortriptyline), Tofranil (imipramine), Sinequan (doxepin), and Anafranil (clomipramine).

The names sound complicated, but you need to know both the brand names and the generic names (the ones in parentheses above) so you can recognize them if the doctor mentions them.

Fact

Sometimes children who are depressed begin wetting the bed after they have already been potty trained. Not only is it frustrating for you, it is embarrassing and shaming for your child. If your child has been having uncharacteristic bedwetting accidents, some of the tricyclic antidepressants, such as desipramine or amitriptyline, can help.

Monoamine Oxidase Inhibitors

Here's another fancy name. Actually, you will hear "MAOIs" more often and it sure is easier to pronounce! While they work faster and work on symptoms that don't respond as well to other medication, this is not usually a physician's first choice of medication for your child's depression for two reasons. First the side effects, if they occur, are severe. Second, your child has to follow a diet that avoids eating any food that contains tyramine. This is an amino acid found in aged cheeses, bananas, meats, products that have yeast, alcohol, and some over-the-counter medications. Eating these foods while taking MAOIs can cause a heart attack, hypertension, and other serious complications.

MAOIs include Nardil (phenelzine), Parnate (tranylcypromine), Eldepryl (selegiline), and Marplan (isocarboxazid).

Selective Serotonin Reuptake Inhibitors

These are also called SSRIs. Doctors like to prescribe them because of their low risk of side effects. They are also very effective in their treatment of depressive symptoms. This is why they are probably the most widely prescribed antidepressants and the most popular. Parents and their children are more likely to cooperate with an antidepressant that has such a good success rate.

SSRIs include Prozac (fluoxetine), Paxil (paroxetine), Zoloft (sertaline), Lexapro (escitalopram oxalate), Celexa (citalopram), and Luvox (fluvoxamine).

Alert!

Do not rely only on the advice of a pharmacist about taking or stopping antidepressants. Check with your physician before starting or discontinuing your child's antidepressant medication. Some medicines require that you taper off of them, while some, if taken in conjunction with certain other antidepressants, can cause life-threatening side effects.

Atypical Medications

These are drugs that work well when other antidepressants don't work or can be used alongside SSRIs. Besides its use in treating bipolar disorder, lithium (lithium carbonate) is used in children, especially those whose parents have taken lithium and had good results.

Sometimes it is used with SSRIs when there are symptoms not being alleviated fully by the SSRIs alone.

Other atypical antidepressant medications include Remeron (mirtazapine) and Wellbutrin (bupropion). Cymbalta (duloxetine hydrochloride) and Effexor (venlafaxine) increase the production of serotonin and norepinephrine.

Deciding to allow your child to be treated with medication is a huge decision. The antidepressant medications are not addictive but may cause side effects. If a medication is working, a child will typically stay on it for nine to twelve months. Stopping the medication prematurely increases the risk of relapse. After this time has passed, you can work with the doctor to wean your child off of his medicine to see how he does without it.

Medication Side Effects

Even the most effective and popular antidepressants have side effects. A doctor tries to prescribe a medication aimed at ameliorating your child's symptoms. As he is deciding what medication to use, he tries to balance it with what sort of side effects might accompany the medicine.

Side Effects

The following is a list of each medication's potential side effects.

Type of Antidepressant	Side Effects
Tricyclic antidepressants	drowsiness, dry mouth, weight gain, dizziness, blurred vision, nausea, constipation, fatigue, mental confusion or problems with concentration, muscle twitches, excessive sweating
Monoamine oxidase inhibitors (MAOIs)	insomnia, nausea, shaking, excessive sweating, high blood pressure

Type of Antidepressant	Side Effects
Selective serotonin reuptake inhibitors (SSRIs)	nausea, headaches, nervousness, insomnia, weight loss or gain, dry mouth, excessive sweating, fatigue, agitation
Atypical antidepressants	check with your doctor as side effects can mimic those of other medications

 Essential

Don't let the possibility of side effects deter you from putting your child on medication if he needs it. Many side effects can be managed by switching medications or making adjustments to the existing medication. Sometimes another medication can be added. In any case, trust that your physician knows how to make the most of your child's medication.

Questions for Your Physician

If you are considering medication for your child, ask as many questions as you want of your doctor. The following is a list of questions you might want to ask:

- Why are you recommending this particular medication?
- What are the potential side effects? Which side effects are most frequent?
- If there are side effects, can I do anything to minimize them?
- How long will it be before you know if the medication is working or needs to be changed?

For teenagers, you might ask the following additional questions:

- How do I get my teenager to comply with medication?

- What if he won't take his medication regularly?
- Will any of these medications affect his ability to drive, play sports, or participate in other activities?
- What about the effects of taking these medications and drinking?
- What would be the risks of an overdose with these medications?
- Will growth and/or learning be affected?

The most important thing you can do as a parent when your child is prescribed medication is to follow your doctor's orders explicitly. Do not assume that a little change here and there won't matter. Remember, that is why you hire experts!

Alternative Remedies

Much has been made over the existence of nutritional or herbal supplements and how they can treat depression as well as medications. While some people will tell you that these supplements work wonders, not much is known about how these work with children. These supplements will be discussed, but a word of caution must be issued. *Do not* use these substances with your child unless you have talked with her physician first.

St. John's Wort

St. John's Wort is likely an herbal remedy you have heard about in magazines. In Germany, this is an extremely popular treatment for depression. The research is contradictory about whether this remedy is successful.

Vitamin B

Vitamin B has an important role in a well-running central nervous system. A deficiency in vitamin B can cause depression. That's why some people turn to taking vitamin B with the hope that their symptoms will go away.

Omega-3

Do you remember your grandmother touting the benefits of cod-liver oil? Yuck! But it just so happens that there is an element in cod-liver oil that actually helps develop and maintain brain cells. It's called omega-3. Again, the jury is out as to whether it really helps with depression.

5-HTP

Probably the most reliable alternative remedy is 5-HTP, which is short for 5-hydroxy-l-tryptophan. It is actually an amino acid found in the body that gets converted to serotonin in the brain. If the appropriate dosage can be determined, studies show that many report a significant lessening in depressive symptomatology.

Do not give your child 5-HTP if he is already taking an antidepressant. Doing so increases the likelihood of a severe reaction. If you insist on using unconventional methods to treat your child's depression, work with someone who is knowledgeable about alternative medicines, appropriate dosages, and other related issues.

Alternative remedies can work, but don't give them so much credit that you overlook the more traditional medicines available that are positively known to treat depression. Less is known about how these remedies work with children, so that is a reason to be even more careful when considering the alternative route.

Diet, Exercise, and Spirituality

Alternative remedies that are virtually free in terms of cost consist of diet, exercise, and some sort of "food" for the soul. These can be extremely beneficial in helping to treat and even prevent depression.

Diet

Much is made about eating healthy. Eating too many sugar-loaded foods and caffeinated beverages can cause a child to become irritable and his mood can become unstable. Food allergies can also cause mood swings. But can you force your child to change his diet? It may seem impossible, but the sooner you help your child develop healthy eating patterns, the better. With a teenager, educate him about how food affects mood and what he can do if he is willing to give it a shot.

Exercise

It's not exactly news that exercise is good for the mood and general health. But how do you get your child to exercise? Try to involve him in group activities such as a team or some sort of lessons, like tennis, where other kids are also exercising. Appeal to his talents. If he likes to swim, get him on a swim team or find a pool where he can regularly exercise.

Also, set a good example! Studies show that children whose parents regularly exercise are more likely to adopt that healthy habit.

Spirituality

Spirituality is a broad term and means many things to many people. Spirituality has been found to have a calming effect on depression. Activities such as meditation, prayer, or quiet time can provide your child with an inner strength that will benefit her all her life.

The Role of Advocate for Your Child

You are your child's biggest fan. You are her cheerleader, her nurturer, her supporter, and her leader. When there is a problem, she turns to you and expects that you will know how to help. When you don't know how to help, it is *your* responsibility to put your fears, your pride, and your frustrations to the side and focus on your child's needs. Some believe that asking for help makes them weak or needy, and that they have somehow failed. A healthy parent knows and teaches his child that asking for help and support is actually a very brave choice.

Of course, teenagers will sneer at your words of advice, your compliments, or your attempts to draw them out. This is to be expected, but rest assured. No matter how they appear to be reacting to you, they are nonetheless hearing and registering what you say.

How to Advocate for Your Child

Never forget what you have learned about modeling behavior. When your child sees you taking action to resolve issues, he learns to do the same for himself. One of the biggest ways to make an impression on your child about the necessity of treatment is to show that you are not afraid to seek help. Ask questions, do research, and ask more questions. Explain to your child that the treatment of depression is as foreign to you as it is to him, but that you are not going to stop until you get him the help he needs.

How to Be an Advocate When Your Child Is Resistant

Kids are quick to deny that a problem exists, especially when there is a stigma attached to it like there is to mental illness. Your role as an advocate is to dispel his denial. Often, denial is really a form of fear, and the longer you allow him to live under the pretense that everything is fine, the worse you may be making it for him. Teach him about mental illness and the unfair stigma associated with it. Help him see that both of you can educate others who are facing this illness.

The moral of the treatment story is this: There are many treatment options to consider for helping your child, but you are not alone in the decision-making process. Once you have found a competent professional, you have a partner in your child's treatment plan. This is the person who will be able to help navigate you and your child through the murky waters of depression treatment.

CHAPTER 12

Strategies for Children

The decision to seek help for your depressed child is yours. You have researched depression and how to get the best treatment available to fit your child's particular needs. The next step is to help your child learn strategies for managing her depressive symptoms, things that are under her control. Being proactive will not only teach your child ways to cope with depression, it will also give her skills that she can take throughout her life to deal with tough struggles.

Education

Obviously, you and your child need a solid education about depression. More importantly, she needs to understand her specific symptoms and how her depression manifests itself. This education will give her a foundation to work from and build on as treatment begins.

Step One

The first step in this process is for you, the parent, to listen, talk, and then listen some more to your child. In order to help your child understand what is happening to her, you need to hear how she describes her experiences. Listening involves more than just hearing, however. You have to try and put yourself in your child's shoes. See the world from her perspective and resist judgment. It's difficult not to give advice or criticize her choices, but this is the time to bite your tongue. Don't try to rescue her. You are actually helping more by letting her contemplate options and ways to change her life.

**Fact**

Your child is much more likely to confide in you if he associates you with pleasant interactions and experiences. Try spending time with him doing what he enjoys, not what you'd rather be doing. When he sees you entering his world, he will begin talking when you least expect it!

Step Two

Another critical task you should accomplish is to help your child develop a proactive approach to life. This in turn aids in the development of a healthy self-esteem. A child who knows that she "can do it" feels confident about herself and sees that she has the ability to make good choices for her life.

The way in which you communicate with your child can result in a child's negative beliefs about herself. For instance, many parents are guilty of having asked, "What were you thinking? What's wrong with you?" Repeatedly speaking to your child like this results in a child who thinks she is damaged or defective, or that she can't do anything right. You may be thinking that surely your child knows you mean no harm by saying these things, but it isn't always true. Over time, she integrates these comments into her view of herself, and a negative self-image begins to emerge. Those with negative self-esteem are more vulnerable to developing depression. So what you say does count!

When discussing depression with your child, the way that you present the information will make all the difference in the world as to how she approaches treatment. Although there is something wrong with her, she is not weird, crazy, or strange. It is up to you to prove that to her so that seeking treatment will be a welcome relief, not something she is dreading.

Cognitive Restructuring

Earlier, you learned that cognitive therapy is a way to treat depression that tackles thoughts and beliefs. Thoughts influence feelings, and thus feelings can cause depressive symptoms. Attacking those negative beliefs and thoughts leads to better management of feelings and therefore a decrease in depressive feelings.

Aaron Beck was a major force in the cognitive therapy movement. He explained depression through three concepts: the cognitive triad, schemas, and cognitive errors.

Cognitive Triad

The cognitive triad refers to the way a child sees herself, her world and her place in it, and her future. A depressed child is likely to see herself as worthless, incompetent, and unlovable. You can spot this self-image by listening to how your child describes herself. "No one likes me." "I never do anything right." "The teacher hates me." Obviously, these statements alone do not spell depression. But if your child is saying negative things about herself more often than not, it's something to consider.

 **Essential**

When your child talks negatively about himself, he may really mean it or he may be manipulating you to get what he wants. Don't give in. Rather, if he continues acting this way, pick a less heated moment and confront him about it. If he reacts defensively, he is probably trying to evoke sympathy rather than expressing true depression.

In this triad is also the way a child interacts with her world and interprets the way it communicates with her. It is negative and pessimistic. The same is true about the way a child sees her future. The depressed child believes that what she encounters will be nothing but bad. She sees her future the same way—dark and hopeless.

Schemas

Schema is a fancy word for perception. How a child perceives situations and people affects how she will interpret future events and people. When this is done in a negative way, a pattern of pessimistic anticipation occurs. It doesn't matter that the way a child sees things is not accurate. She perceives it that way, and that becomes her reality. It's easy to see then how depression is formed.

The thinking is irrational and distorted, but yet it continues. These irrational thoughts become beliefs and are called cognitive errors. Children begin to see things in terms of black and white, with absolutely no gray. For example, a child who has never made anything but straight As in school will respond to a B with "I never make Bs. What is wrong with me?" Perfectionistic thinking for children is a great way for them to develop depression.

Cognitive Errors

Cognitive errors also come in the form of expecting the same result from different situations. Generalizing a negative outcome leads a child to avoid certain opportunities and to believe nothing good will come out of anything. Even if something positive does happen, it gets discounted as a fluke or "no big deal."

Alert!

Never forget that your child is a sponge! He is absorbing how you act, react, and communicate. If you are behaving in a negative, pessimistic fashion, he is likely to model what he sees. You can be a powerful preventative against depression just by changing the way *you* interact with the world.

Depressed children jump to conclusions and overreact to negative outcomes. Rather than seeing a mistake or a bad experience as part of life, he will interpret this as something he should have been able to control or something he doesn't deserve. He will blame himself, and in turn a negative self-image is developed. And you know what that leads to—depression.

Cognitive Restructuring

So how do you battle this cognitive triad if it exists in your child? Cognitive restructuring is a technique that forces an individual to identify the negative, irrational, and distorted thoughts and to challenge them. Aaron Beck broke it into four techniques. The first requires that one look for the evidence that the thought or belief is true. The second technique is to ponder whether there is another way of looking at that thought or belief. When a child expects nothing but a negative outcome, the third technique can be useful. Challenging that negative expectation by asking "what if" questions can help a child see that the worst might not happen at all or might not be so bad. The fourth technique encourages testing the thoughts and beliefs and then replacing them with more reasonable ones.

 **Fact**

Cognitive restructuring works well with kids who don't believe they have any control over themselves or their world. As they get older, these are the children who cannot control their behavior and get into trouble. Teaching these skills whether a child is depressed or not can actually prevent future behavioral problems.

Let's take a look at John. He is ten years old. John is an overachiever in everything he does and has gotten a lot of positive reinforcement for it. So far, whatever he has tried, he has done well. He has been invincible!

All of a sudden, John starts having trouble with math. He gets a C on a quiz, a B on the next test, and at the end of the semester he is barely passing. John is devastated and his parents are a bit dismayed.

He continues to do well on his soccer team and makes straight As in all of his other classes. His father is an accountant and makes comments pretty regularly that it is impossible that a child of his cannot master math. His teacher says she doesn't know why he can't get with the program.

John hears this, and for whatever reason he still cannot overcome his problem with math. He even quits trying to do his homework, deciding there's no use since he will fail anyway. When it comes time to learn a new skill in English, John becomes paralyzed with the belief that he can't master this task either. In soccer, the goals that once were so easy for him to make don't happen. His teammates ridicule him for not taking the team to victory. He starts to see himself as what he calls a "loser," and believes he can now do nothing right. His mother tries to console him and negate his feelings. Nothing works and he becomes depressed.

In therapy, John is asked, "Where's the evidence that you are a loser and that you do nothing right?" John cites his problems with math and recent soccer troubles. Although there are some instances in which he is correct, that he can't do some things well, he is then asked about other activities. Didn't he just win the spelling bee? Doesn't he have one of the major roles in his school's play? What the therapist is doing is trying to get him to investigate whether his assumptions about himself are really true. It turns out that there *is* evidence that contradicts his feelings and thoughts.

The next task the therapist will have to accomplish is to help John come up with alternative interpretations about his math difficulties and soccer playing. John is in the fifth grade, a time where school often becomes harder. Perhaps he wasn't totally prepared for the skills he is learning in math. Or maybe not doing his homework, which is really practice for mastering a skill, is making it worse. Maybe there is a learning problem that is just now showing up and interfering with the way he acquires information. What if the way in which he studies needs to change?

There are many ways to help a child reinterpret his experiences, and they don't have to be negative. Perhaps John's soccer mistakes lately are due to an injury. Maybe there is a new goalie on the other team who is especially good at blocking the kinds of shots he takes.

It's also healthy for the therapist to help John develop a more balanced view of himself. In other words, he doesn't have to be perfect. Parents often overemphasize a child's strengths to the point that a child has a very unrealistic view of himself and expects that everything he touches should turn to gold.

 ## Question?

How do I boost my child's self-esteem without inflating his ego?
It's often a hard line to draw, but it can be done. Help your child understand that while he is good at certain things, he also has weaknesses and that is to be expected. Foster a sense of humor that allows him not to take himself so seriously.

Next, a therapist can get a child to explore possible outcomes that might not be so dire as the one the child has currently. For example, what if John doesn't make an A in math? John believes that his father will be disappointed and that he won't be a straight-A student, which is a horrible notion for him.

When pushed, John came up with some other scenarios. He was able to realize that making something less than an A will not undermine his other achievements. When he talked with his dad, he realized he wasn't really a disappointment. If he can't make a goal in soccer, it isn't up to him totally to make the team win.

Last, to test his beliefs, John is challenged to think these new alternative responses whenever he encounters negative feelings. For example, when faced with math homework, he is told to find a math problem that he thinks he might be able to do. He is also told that if he can't master it the first time, ask his dad for some help. He does this and finds that indeed, with some practice, he can get the answer! Discovering this leads him to try another problem, and then another.

He begins to develop some confidence, and while he still might not be perfect in math, he has much more confidence to try it.

Sometimes a child has trouble learning these skills. A therapist may then try to offer her own alternative thoughts to the child. The therapist can directly challenge a child's thoughts and feelings and debate alternatives with him. Then a child can see the technique in practice and learn to model it.

Problem-solving Skills

Teaching a child the skills for solving problems is pretty straightforward. It involves helping your child define the problem, come up with possible solutions, weigh the consequences, and pick a plan of action. After this is done, the child is encouraged to re-evaluate his choice of action to see if it was appropriate. If not, he is to pick another solution and try again.

How It Works

Here's an example of how problem-solving works for kids without depression. Savanah is eight years old and a notoriously disorganized little girl, especially in the mornings. She gets up late and often forgets to brush her teeth or make her bed because she is in such a hurry to get dressed and ready for school. Then she misses breakfast because she couldn't pick out what to wear. Her mother yells constantly from the time she is up until the second she is dropped off at school. This makes Savanah feel guilty and stressed.

Generating Options

Her mother decides that it's time to resolve this problem. She and Savanah sit down together. Her mother asks her what she could do differently to make mornings less chaotic. Together they generate several options and make a list. Savanah suggests that her mom not make her brush her teeth or make the bed. Okay, it's not a good option, but her mother puts it on the list anyway. Her mother asks how Savanah might choose her clothing more quickly. Savanah says her mother could just tell her what to wear. About breakfast, Savanah thinks going to McDonalds every day would be a good choice.

Savanah's mother reminds her that Savanah rarely likes what her mother picks out for her to wear. Savanah remembers that her friend puts her clothes out the night before and tells her mother this might work. When asked to think about eating breakfast at McDonalds, she agrees with her mother that it would take time to make the extra stop and that wouldn't be a good choice. Her mother also thinks Savanah needs to get up fifteen minutes earlier, and of course, Savanah disagrees with this.

Making a Decision

Together they make the decision to try the following. Savanah will put her clothes out every night before she goes to bed. Rather than sitting down to breakfast each day, her mother will provide her with a muffin or something else to eat in the car. Her mother would refrain from yelling, which only caused Savanah to be more anxious. A week later, they sit down to evaluate how their solutions were working.

Even though making these changes worked, Savanah was still running behind three mornings out of five. It turns out she moves slow in the mornings and trying to rush her does not work. Her mother said that perhaps she should get up earlier. Again, the child didn't like it but agreed to give it a try.

 *Essential*

> A depressed child is particularly negative and self-punishing if he cannot solve problems the first time he tries. It becomes critical to help him understand that solving problems is often a trial and error process, and that mistakes cannot be avoided. The beauty of it is that there is always more than one way to do things.

One week later, Savanah's morning schedule was running very smoothly and she was arriving at school unstressed and happy. And her mother had quit yelling!

Once children learn that there are alternatives to thinking negatively about one's self, their feelings, and their actions, the depression that has been looming can lift. Again, these skills can be a powerful preventative for depression, so it's never too early to begin teaching them.

Communication Skills

Knowing how to communicate effectively is a skill that affects so many areas of a child's life. Children that are depressed are typically withdrawn or have difficulties getting along with their peers, so they have few friends. They may feel uncomfortable about initiating contact with a potential friend for fear of being rejected. Once he gets a friend, he may be possessive and jealous, not wanting his new friend to focus any attention away from him.

Spend some time evaluating your child's social life. Who are his friends? Is he trying to fit into a group that clearly does not want him? Is he having problems with joining a group or starting a conversation?

Communication Skills Can Be Learned

Help your child understand that the ability to communicate is something that can be learned. Teach him about the importance of eye contact, facial expressions, and personal space. People, even kids, react more positively to someone who looks them in the eye. It conveys interest and confidence. Your child's facial expressions say volumes about how he is feeling or what he is thinking. Having a pleasant expression puts people at ease and usually receives a positive response. Many kids do not understand the notion of personal space. Children need to learn that everyone, including themselves, deserves some privacy and some space from others.

 **Fact**

A good way to teach a child about the need for personal time is to take some for yourself. Explain to your child that everyone needs privacy. Tell your child that you need some quiet time and that you expect not to be disturbed for a certain length of time. Encourage her to do the same.

Listening as a Communication Skill

Also important in the area of communication is to teach your child to listen to others. One of the best ways to begin a conversation or to get to know someone is to ask the other person about herself. Teach your child this skill as it will show interest in others and help him develop empathy.

Likewise, if your child is doing something that is apparently putting other children off, gently explain it to him. Children typically do not mean to be annoying. They simply may not realize how their behavior is affecting others. Describe the behavior to him and then ask him to put himself in another child's shoes. Usually he will be able to recognize what he has been doing. He may not know how to change the behavior, however, and so you may need to work with him to find other options for his behavior. Once again, you are accomplishing dual goals. He is learning to get a feel for what others are experiencing and he is developing good problem-solving skills.

Labeling Emotions

Humans are born not knowing what to call certain emotions. If you, as a parent, have not developed the ability to define an emotion, chances are that you won't be able to teach your child either!

There are a couple of good ways to help your child label what he is feeling and thus to find an appropriate way to express it. Depending on your child's age, make a list of emotions that you feel your child needs to recognize.

Here is an example:

Happy	Sad
Mad	Scared
Nervous	Excited
Confused	Rejected

You can come up with hundreds of words, but try to keep it simple. Have your child either act out how he thinks these emotions would feel or have him draw a face or picture depicting the feeling. Ask him questions along the way so that when he experiences that particular feeling, he can put a name with it and express it.

Analyzing Events and Statements

Another technique that is beneficial is to have your child tell you about an event. Make a list of what he says, for example:

I went to a party.
Susie wouldn't speak to me.
MaryAnn told me I was fat.

Once you have done this, go over each sentence with your child and ask her how she felt at that moment. Once she can identify her emotions, you will be able to help her cognitively restructure what she thought, if necessary, by using the steps outlined earlier in this chapter.

Seeking Outlets for Emotional Expression

Even though children can learn to identify their emotions, they may not know how to express them in healthy, appropriate ways. The more alternatives a child has for expressing what is happening to her internally, the more likely she will be to let those feelings out. Having many tools to do this lessens her chances for developing depression. Consider the following areas for providing your child outlets for emotional expression.

Alternative Outlets

Besides the physical outlet, exercise, there are ways to express emotions, especially negative ones, that do not hurt anyone. Beating on or screaming into a pillow is a great way to express anger or other negative emotions. Teaching your child to breathe deeply as a means of relaxing will take some of the intensity out of his emotions. Another technique is to have him clench his fists or tense his entire body, and then let the tension go.

Creative Outlets

Creative outlets include drawing, painting, putting on a play, and writing. Anything that calls on your child to express her emotions using creativity is healthy. Some kids like to play music or write poetry. Encourage what they enjoy as they will be more likely to do it when feeling emotionally out of control. Not only does it help the expression, it also enables your child to relax and perhaps get her mind off of unpleasantness.

Essential

No matter how your child chooses to express her emotions, she needs to understand that having feelings, even negative ones, is natural. However, she is *never* allowed to hurt someone intentionally or to hurt herself. If she is unsure how to communicate what she is feeling, a good alternative is to run it by someone she trusts before reacting.

Social Outlets

Social outlets encourage your child to interact. Some social outlets could include talking to you, a friend, or another relative. Or other options could include a formal group, such as scouting, that allows for the opportunity to share feelings, experiences, and seek advice from others.

Demystifying the Stigma of Mental Illness

It's easy to understand how your child having a mental illness is akin to his having a great big wart on his chin. It separates him from the crowd, and it provides others with an opportunity to tease, bully, and annoy him. While you certainly don't want your child to believe that having a mental illness should be a deep, dark secret, he does have a right to privacy. Tell your child that no one needs to know what he does not wish to tell.

 *Question?*

How can my child answer questions about his depression?
The best thing you can do is encourage your child not to be defensive but to elicit empathy, not sympathy. This may be the perfect opportunity for him to educate others about depression. The more people understand, the more supportive they will be.

If there is something good about feeling depressed, it's being able to understand how debilitating a mental illness can be for other kids. Your child is in a unique position to show that having a mental illness is not something to be embarrassed about. Without even realizing it, he may be the motivation for another child to ask for help.

Depression as a Teacher

Depression has a way of teaching its victim about empathy. Your child will have "walked in another's shoes" if he has suffered from depression. So once your child has experienced the discomfort and trauma of depression, he can be a fabulous mentor to other kids who have any sort of mental illnesses.

This chapter has focused on the development of proactive skills for preventing and fighting depression. But what if it isn't enough? Is your child at risk for suicide?

CHAPTER 13

Suicide: Is Your Child at Risk?

T he scariest part of having a child with depression is the ever-present concern of suicide. While traditional thought was that young children don't think about, much less try to commit, suicide, this is no longer true. In fact, children with depression are seven times as likely to attempt suicide. More often than not, that depression has not been treated. The good news is that with some careful vigilance along with knowledge about the risk factors and the warning signs, suicide can be prevented.

Prevalence among Children and Teens

According to an article published in *A Pediatric Perspective* (2000), 60 to 80 percent of children and teens who have depression will attempt suicide. Even more shocking, children as young as five years old can be suicidal. About 8 percent of teens with depression will attempt suicide. Girls make more attempts, but boys are four to five times more successful. To make matters worse, of those who made unsuccessful attempts, 40 percent will try again!

High-risk Groups

Two types of children with depression are thought to be at a higher risk for suicidal behavior. The severely depressed child who feels hopeless and worthless and children with accompanying eating disorders are the first group. When they attempt suicide, it is usually well

thought out and planned carefully. The second group consists of depressed children who are impulsive and in a fit of emotion try to hurt themselves.

 **Fact**

The reason boys are more successful than girls in completing a suicide is that they typically use more lethal methods that have little to no chance for failure. The three most common ways boys commit suicide is with firearms, hanging, and overdose or ingestion of some poisonous material.

Are Young Children at Risk?

Small children can also become suicidal. They start out with a preoccupation with death accompanied by some sort of feeling that they are bad. They lack the ability to understand that death is forever, and so their attempts or statements need to be addressed immediately. One of the most popular attempts a small child will use is to jump from a roof of a house.

Suicide is the second-leading cause of death among teenagers. For children, it is the fourth-leading cause. These statistics are not meant to scare you, but they should serve as a very serious wake-up call if your child is depressed.

Risk Factors

Of course depression is not the only reason children attempt suicide, but when coupled with other risk factors, the risk for an attempt increases. Research estimates that if a family member has attempted or committed suicide, a child is two to three times as likely to do the same. There are several reasons for this. First, if a child has lost a parent through suicide, he may experience guilt that he somehow caused his parent to commit suicide. Also, he may think that if his parent used this behavior as a coping skill, then he can do it, too.

Second, a child experiences emotional loss when a parent dies. That loss can be even more profound if it was through suicide. This sort of loss makes a child vulnerable to depression, and left unresolved, he may resort to suicide just like his parent.

Third, some research claims that suicidal individuals have a chemical makeup that makes them more prone to suicidal behavior. Thus some experts postulate that the tendency toward suicidal behavior is genetic.

Emotional factors such as hopelessness, worthlessness, and feeling as if he has no control over his circumstances puts a child at greater risk. Included here is the child who has attempted suicide before. Eating disorders and substance abuse can intensify feelings of depression and put a child a greater risk for harming himself. In addition, substance use lowers the ability to control impulsive behavior.

Alert!

Children who are psychotic have trouble distinguishing between reality and fantasy. Often their auditory hallucinations include voices telling them to harm themselves or others, and they have trouble controlling the impulse to obey the voices. If your child is psychotic, make sure you get a clear explanation from her as to what she is hearing and get help immediately.

School Performance

Believe it or not, poor grades or performance in school is a risk factor. The more failures a child experiences, the lower his self-esteem will drop. When this happens, a child believes he is a disappointment, a failure, and that there is no way he can improve. Dying is seen as a way to avoid having to deal with what he perceives is a hopeless situation.

In addition to these problems at school, many teens feel pressure from parents and others to meet expectations. When they do not or cannot measure up, their concerns that they are disappointing others further contributes to their feelings of being "less than" or "not good enough."

No One Likes Me

Everyone experiences the feeling of not fitting in or that someone doesn't like you. For a child, this can be devastating because they don't know how to handle this sort of rejection. Again, poor self-esteem creeps in, and depression often follows. Likewise, in families where there is a lot of conflict and tension, a child can quickly become overwhelmed by the chaos and discord. He will often report that if he were "better" somehow, things would improve at home. Of course, this isn't true, but for a child, this is his reality and one that sets him up for depression and possible suicidal behavior.

Essential

Handguns in the home, especially when loaded, are another risk factor for suicide. If a child is impulsive, and the thought of suicide pops into his head, heading for the gun is the first place he is likely to go. If the gun is loaded, he doesn't even have to think any further than pulling the trigger.

Loss

You may have a child who has recently lost a friend, a boyfriend, or a girlfriend. Too often, adults say that they remember how that felt and a child "will get over it." For the most part, this is true. Yet there are some children who have suffered multiple losses, and as these pile up, his resistance to depression weakens. As well, some kids just don't know how to cope with these losses. They can become overwhelmed by feelings of loneliness, despair, and worthlessness. Once again, they may be at greater risk for doing harm to themselves.

Abuse

Children who have been physically or sexually abused are at risk for suicide. Again, while you can rationalize that what happened to them is not their fault, a child simply does not see it that way initially. They feel as if they somehow caused the abuse to happen, that they deserved it somehow because they are bad. Left unaddressed, the self-blame often carries with it a good amount of anger, and as the anger fuels the negative esteem that is developing, the combination can lead to dangerous behavior.

Children who are unsure about their sexuality are two to three times more likely to attempt suicide. The reason for this seems to be the problem a child faces in coming to terms with his sexuality. In addition, the response from loved ones and the child's community has a tremendous impact on how he adapts.

Sharing the Secret

Parents often want to know if it is healthy for a child to know about another child's suicide or attempt. Generally, the answer is yes. The reason for this is because open communication, the ability to ask questions, and the willingness to address suicidal feelings will reduce the likelihood that your child attempts suicide. If a child knows he has a safe, confidential place to turn when he is feeling like he wants to hurt himself, he may be more willing to open up about his feelings.

Question?

Is suicidal behavior contagious?
You may have heard of instances where one teen commits suicide and others follow with gestures or attempts. What a teen sees is that suicide is now a real option, not just one he has in his head. It is a real phenomenon and one that must be watched carefully.

However, there is other evidence to suggest that if your child is depressed, hearing about another's suicide will increase his thoughts that dying is an option for him, too. Then there is the fact that in the immediate weeks following a child's suicide, the number of attempts by other children increases.

Antidepressants and Suicide

A lot has been made of the link between antidepressants and suicide. Do antidepressants increase the risk? The research is still out on a definitive answer. Obviously a child with depression is at greater risk for suicide.

Fact

One study conducted by a Seattle health-care system found that the incidence of suicide is, in fact, greater in the month before beginning a medication regimen than while on it. This is largely because many people don't get the treatment they need until they are at their worst.

Whether a child is at greater risk for suicide while taking an antidepressant should not be the first question a parent needs to ask. Instead, ask the doctor prescribing the medication about the possible side effects and if suicidal thoughts are among them. Also ask how your child will be monitored and how often. A physician who is well-educated in these medications will choose to be slow and deliberate in his prescription of antidepressants and will want to keep a very close watch on your child.

Warning Signs

Parents can be so worried about their children that they think just about anything can be a sign of something! While some of the following warning signs will seem obvious, others are not so clear. If your child is depressed, this is an appropriate time to worry about the "anythings" until you are comfortable that your anxiety is unwarranted.

The oddest warning sign is when a child seems to be coming out of a period of depression. It is a parent's natural response to be relieved and to begin feeling optimistic about her child's recovery. But consider this example even though it may sound far-fetched. You are told that the bucket sitting across the room from you is filled with one million dollars, and all you have to do is walk across that room to get it. Hardly a problem, wouldn't you say? Yet a depressed patient will tell you that making the trek across that room feels impossible, because just getting out of bed each morning and brushing his teeth zaps him of what little energy he has. In fact, two of the symptoms of depression are fatigue and lack of motivation.

A depressed child will often feel this way, but when the symptoms lift just a little, she starts to see that suicide may be a way to escape her suffering. This, in turn, gives her a feeling of control over her depression and she will appear to be feeling better.

Significant Withdrawal
Children can become quiet and withdrawn when they are depressed. They will shy away from social settings, their friends, and their families. The more isolated they become, the more prone they are to being depressed and possibly suicidal.

With teens, the differentiation between normal isolation in their rooms, for example, and a more pervasive withdrawal is often hard to detect. Adolescents like to be in their rooms away from others, and this is normal. What you should be on the lookout for is a teen who spends almost all of his time in his room, and the amount of time is significantly different from his normal routine. If he is usually outgoing, likes to be with his friends, and enjoys a lot of activities and then suddenly this stops, there is most likely a problem that you need to address.

Accidents

All kids have accidents. In children with depression, look for repeated accidents despite the known risks or consequences. In small children, it may be continuous head-banging or running in front of cars. For teenagers, it may be several car accidents caused by the same thing.

What you should look for are "accidents" that occur frequently over a close period of time. A lot of times, while these behaviors can be conscious, many are actually subconscious attempts to hurt one's self. It could be that your child's self-destructive behavior is a sign of suicidal thoughts.

Akin to frequent accidents is the involvement in increasingly risky behaviors. These are things such as using drugs, cutting one's self, and placing one's self in extremely dangerous situations such as playing Russian roulette. Less obvious is the child who doesn't wear a seat belt, or plays with matches, for example. Just because a child is not harmed if he engages in any of these behaviors does not mean he isn't self-destructive. It may be his attempt at crying out for help.

Rejection

Earlier you read about the notion of not fitting in or being rejected. For teens especially, the idea of suicide can often occur when they break up with a boyfriend or girlfriend. Her heartache feels endless, and in a moment of pure desperation she may attempt to hurt herself as a way of relieving the pain.

Just like the loss of a boyfriend or girlfriend, children are devastated by the loss of others in their lives, too. The death of a parent, a close relative, or a friend can be equally or more painful. An especially nasty argument with a parent can be interpreted as a rejection and put a child at an increased risk for suicide.

Essential

Parents tend to make light of their teen's breakup with the love of her life, which is actually more like her love of the moment! Don't tell her "You'll get over it," or "There's someone better out there for you." Your teen won't buy it at that moment. Instead, offer empathy and a good shoulder to cry on.

Obsession with Death

If your child has a preoccupation with death and dying, this isn't necessarily a warning sign of suicidal behavior. At certain ages, especially in younger children, there is a natural curiosity about dying and where people go after they die. You should become concerned, however, if your child is depressed and the preoccupation seems more like an obsession. Repeated questions or conversations about death may be a red flag. Drawing only pictures about death or writing poetry about death are behaviors that you should check out. Giving away prized or cherished possessions also falls into the "warning" category. A more obvious warning signal is if you find a note that signals your child is planning a suicide or is saying goodbye. Rarely is this someone who is merely being dramatic!

Related to the expression of suicidal thoughts through creative outlets, physical acts, and self-destructive behavior is the verbal expression about wanting to die. Every child at one time or another has hysterically said, "I wish I were dead" or "Maybe you'd be better off without me." These are manipulative statements aimed at generating parental guilt and sympathy. In a depressed child, however, it is important to really *hear* what your child is saying. If these comments come up frequently, without provocation, she may really mean them as opposed to just using them to get what she wants. Consider the following statements:

- "_____ would be better off without me."
- "Nobody would miss me if I were gone."
- "They'll be sorry when I'm gone."
- "I won't be around much longer to bother you."
- "Do you ever think about what it's like when you're dead?"
- "I can't take it anymore. I want to die."
- "If I could just go to sleep and not wake up" or "If a car hit and killed me that would be fine by me."
- "I'm going to end it all" or "I am going to commit suicide."

Usually you will see or hear something that alerts you to your child's suicidal leanings. However, remember that you are, after all, a human being. You are going to make mistakes and you may miss some of the cues that your child is communicating. Being too hard on yourself or having too high expectations for your parenting puts you at greater risk for missing what is obvious. Listen, observe, and be there. By doing these things, you should be able to help your child avoid a life-threatening behavior.

 **Fact**

When a child attempts or commits suicide, sometimes there just aren't any warning signals! Many responsible, healthy parents who were in tune and involved with their children have reported that they saw nothing troubling before their child's suicide. They live the rest of their lives deciphering every moment they can remember searching for the clue they missed.

Suicidal Ideation

There is a difference between merely thinking about suicide and planning it, and then attempting it. That doesn't mean you can take this piece of this puzzle less seriously though. With the exception of a very impulsive suicidal gesture, some thought and planning almost always goes into suicidal acts. This is called suicidal ideation. These are the thoughts about suicide and the game plan for dying that many depressed individual's experience. They do not always lead to suicide, however, but people who have suicidal ideation are more likely to attempt suicide. So these thoughts and plans cannot be overlooked or dismissed.

Question?

Is it true that children who say they wish to die never commit suicide? That is a myth! Children who discuss wanting to kill themselves are at just as great a risk as children who remain silent. Her statements might be a cry for help or something much more serious. In either case, check them out.

Although suicide is most rare in very young children, it does not mean they don't think about it! Again, it is normal for children to think about death. A depressed child, however, can become preoccupied with death and dying. This is why you must be on the lookout for risky, self-destructive behaviors and statements like those listed above. Talking to your child and getting help at this point is an excellent way to diffuse those feelings.

Should I Ignore It?

Many parents believe that giving attention to these thoughts and behaviors is likely to increase their frequency. Not true! The child who makes a vague statement aimed at trying to make you feel bad or to guilt you into something should not be allowed to get away with this behavior. Make it clear to her that you would be very sad if she meant what she'd said and that she will not gain anything from you if she is using it as a weapon. She needs to understand that you do not take these comments lightly but that you won't give in either.

Stay Alert

If your child is making these statements or engaging in self-destructive behaviors, particularly when there is nothing to gain, you should take her seriously. If she laughs you off and claims you are overreacting, resist the urge to believe her. Keep on the alert until you feel comfortable that she is okay.

In terms of suicidal ideation, it's sometimes hard to distinguish the idle threat versus a real one. If this is where you find yourself, then err on the side of caution. Talking to your child about suicide does not cause suicide!

The Plan

The other part of suicidal ideation, planning, becomes more dangerous. A child with a plan is one step closer to being able to commit the act. When a child is asked about his plan, it is often vague. "Oh, I'd drink something," or "I might take some pills." There are three hypotheses at work here. He may be crying out for help, and rather than ask straight out he will try this more emphatic approach. He may be in the beginning stage of making a plan and just hasn't gotten that far with it yet. Or he may be lying and may have a much more elaborate plan that he doesn't wish to share with you. Does it matter which hypothesis is true? No! If there's a plan, there's a problem. Even if it is a cry for attention, it is a pretty serious way to do it, and whether he is depressed or not, this behavior needs to be addressed.

Suicide-proofing the Home

The way a child kills himself is often dependent on what lethal means are available to him. As mentioned earlier, guns, hanging, and overdose or poisoning are the three top methods. It's pretty obvious that you should keep guns out of reach or locked up. But making your home a suicide-free zone is much harder when there are so many things a child can do to harm himself.

What Is the Method?

If your child is depressed and has suicidal ideation, get as much information from him as you can about his plan. If he plans to drink bleach or another poisonous substance, get them out of the house. The same is true with medications. If he mentions hanging himself, get rid of belts, ties, rope, and anything else that can be used. Like-wise, if your child has a history of cutting himself, get rid of the potentially harmful items such as knives and razors.

Alert!

Children planning a suicide can be extremely sneaky. Pay close attention to see if your child is hiding potentially deadly items or if something is missing from its place in your home. This can be especially hard since many common household items are not considered dangerous. Listen to your gut and follow it.

Searching Your Child's Room

Should you check his room? Again, this goes back to the belief that your child deserves his privacy and trying to balance that with protecting him. If you have reason to believe your child has suicidal ideation or has attempted suicide in the past, routinely doing a room check is not a bad idea. Remind your child that you are not looking at his personal things, but that in light of his behavior and/or statements, you will need to check his room for your own peace of mind. A child who has attempted suicide in the past will usually understand this and know that it is a consequence of his past actions. A defensive child may have something to hide.

Keep Him Safe

Last, if you are concerned that your child cannot control his suicidal thoughts, *do not* leave him alone. He may try to bully you out of it or try to convince you that he is fine. Don't buy into it. Take him with you, or leave him with another responsible adult (not a friend of his) until you feel that he is not a danger to himself.

Help Manage Suicidal Thoughts, Feelings, and Behaviors

If you are unsure whether your depressed child is suicidal, there are two very important questions to get out in the open. First, ask him directly, "Are you feeling suicidal or like you want to hurt yourself?" If the answer is yes, don't become hysterical. If you react too strongly, he is likely to withhold information out of a desire not to upset you or to protect you. Stay calm but firm and ask, "Do you have a plan?" Whether the answer is yes or no, take him seriously and run, don't walk, for help.

 **Essential**

> Therapists often get a suicidal patient to make an oral "no harm" contract. If he feels he cannot control his suicidal thoughts, he promises to tell a parent, call 911, or take some other action before hurting himself. This is effective in stopping the thoughts from taking over. Parents can use this technique at home, too.

There are several ways to talk with your child about his suicidal thoughts and feelings. First, tell him that when someone is depressed, suicidal thoughts can occur. Remind him that before he was depressed, he didn't want to die. Feeling suicidal is a symptom of depression and will go away with help.

Debating the Issue

While it is important to take his suicidal ideation seriously, it is often helpful to gently argue the point that he does have a future. For instance, say his girlfriend broke up with him. He might say, "There is no one else like her. I'll never have another girlfriend. I don't want to live without her." You could ask if it is really true that there is no one like her. You might remind him that there are plenty of girls out there with the characteristics of his old girlfriend. You may want to ask, "You mean this is it for you? There really will *never* be another girl for you?" It is possible that you can get him to see where his thinking is distorted and the option of suicide is not the way out.

Using Religious Beliefs

If your child is religious and suicide is seen as a sin, it is perfectly acceptable to remind him where he will be going if he does that! It may sound manipulative, and okay, it really is. But when you are fighting for your child's life, use what you can. Ask him if he wants to be on life support in case he botches his attempt. It's cruel, but it is often enough to jolt him back into reality and see that suicide is not the answer to his problems. Last, emphasize how his death would affect you. Tell him that even though you understand his despair, you hope that he won't do something that will ruin your life.

Helping manage suicidal ideation also means teaching your depressed child how to handle adversity and uncomfortable feelings. Suicide is permanent. If he can see other alternatives for alleviating his depression, he will likely be relieved and turn to those options.

Remember that the child who wishes to die needs two things: a method and the opportunity. While you cannot control every circumstance of your child's life, with treatment and hands-on parenting, you *can* make the option of suicide difficult, inconvenient, and avoidable.

CHAPTER 14

Inpatient Treatment

W hile most children and teens who suffer from depression do not need inpatient treatment, there are times when their symptoms are out of control and cannot be managed by the more traditional methods of therapy and medication. When a child presents a danger to others or herself, or when she is simply unable to function at all on a daily basis, treatment that takes her out of her environment and keeps her safe usually provides relief and improvement.

Is It Time for Inpatient Treatment?

If you think making the decision to get help for your child is a scary proposition, you can only imagine how terrifying it would be to consider removing your child from home for help. Sometimes, no matter how much treatment you have sought for your child, he simply cannot improve. Hospitalization or any other confining types of treatment are typically foreign entities to you unless you have actually been hospitalized for a mental illness.

Just because a child has been suicidal or is currently suicidal does not necessarily mean he needs to be hospitalized. Look for a pattern of such attempts. You'll know it's time to consider more extensive treatment if your child cannot be stabilized on medication, no matter how many times it has been changed or altered. If a child cannot control his behavior, or is regularly at risk

for hurting himself or voicing desires to hurt others, this is serious. If he is simply not making progress with his therapist, it's time.

Distorted Views

Adding to your fears and doubts about whether treatment away from home is the best option for your child is society's portrayal of mental health facilities. Think back to *One Flew Over the Cuckoo's Nest* or the more recent movie, *Girl Interrupted*. As compelling as they both were, each of these films probably left you with negative images of such places and rightly so! Most facilities are not like what you've observed on television, and if your child needs more aggressive treatment, you may find yourself having to choose this option. These facilities are safe, clean, and friendly. Typically, the employees are caring, empathic individuals who work very hard to make sure your child's needs are being met.

 **Fact**

Just because your child is not improving with traditional treatment methods does not necessarily mean she needs to be removed from the home. Talk with your treating professional to see if enough time has passed for improvement or if the treatment needs to be tweaked for better results. Out-of-home options should be a last resort.

Self-injurious Behaviors

Self-injurious behaviors that cannot be controlled are also a sign that inpatient care is needed. These behaviors include cutting one's self with:

- Knives
- Nails
- Razors
- Scissors
- Paper clips

- Safety pins
- Pencils or pens
- Scratching
- Picking at previous cuts that are healing

In terms of self-mutilation, know that kids can be tricky and sneaky. Most often they hide these behaviors and injure themselves on their arms or upper thighs. Both of these areas can be easily covered by shirtsleeves and pants, so you don't always notice this behavior until it has been going on for a while. When you ask your child how she got that cut, pay attention to whether the cut seems to be recurring.

As peculiar as it seems, remember that injuring one's self or self-mutilating behavior is a way for your child to let off some steam. The pain she feels from the wounds she inflicts on herself outwardly are often easier to deal with than the emotions she is experiencing inside.

Alert!

Parents typically freak out when they discover their child's self-injurious behaviors. Although this is not the time to underreact, try to keep yourself under control. Respond gently but firmly. Explain to your child that while it's hard for you to understand what she is doing, you are concerned and plan to share this information with her doctor or therapist.

The other behavior that may require inpatient treatment is when your child is psychotic. If he reports hearing voices or seeing things that do not exist, these are symptoms he cannot get rid of on his own. Often the voices will tell the child to hurt himself or hurt another person. If he cannot control his reactions to these voices, your doctor must be contacted immediately and inpatient treatment will need to be considered.

What If the Treating Professional Doesn't Agree?

Sometimes, you may actually wonder if your child needs more extensive treatment before the therapist or doctor does. This could be because many therapists don't like to give up. They continue to think there is just one more thing they'd like to try. Remember, inpatient treatment is a last resort, and therapists are often just as hesitant as you about making this decision.

Ask the treating professional why she is not ready to make this recommendation. If she has some other ideas, you may want to wait. But if you are feeling positive that this is the route you want to take, express this to her and move forward, with or without her help.

Treatment Settings

Therapy and medication management are considered outpatient treatment. If those methods have been exhausted or are not working, there are three treatment options for a child who needs more help: day treatment, hospitalization, and residential treatment.

Day Treatment

Day treatment is a step up from outpatient therapy. For example, if your child is seeing a psychologist for therapy, she is likely meeting with him on a weekly or bimonthly basis. Most therapists have a difficult time fitting in more than one session per client per week. If your child needs more intensive help than the few hours she gets each month, day treatment is an excellent option.

Day treatment usually occurs in a hospital or another facility that has a team component. This means that your child will be seen by more than one treating professional. A treatment team can include doctors, psychologists, and other professionals. Individual therapy is a must, and group therapy with other children experiencing the same problems is usually offered. Sometimes family therapy is included or required.

A child who enters day treatment can expect to be at the facility four to five hours each day for three to five days a week, and some facilities offer academic programs so that your child doesn't fall behind in his studies. He is allowed to return home each day, and the ability to be at home at night gives parents comfort and makes this an attractive treatment option.

Fact

You do not have to lose the professional who has been treating your child in his office! This is the person who will likely refer your child to day treatment and provide the facility with information about your child. Upon her discharge, she is typically sent back to her original therapist.

Sometimes you can hold on to your child's therapist if he has privileges at the treatment facility where your child is attending. If not, be prepared to start over with a new therapist, at least while your child is there. Once her condition is stabilized and she is on the road to improvement, she can return to an outpatient office.

While some parents prefer to have their children home at night, there is a downside. You are responsible for his safety when he is with you. If you are particularly worried about his impulse control (cutting, suicidal gestures), having him home at night may be too uncomfortable and frightening for you. Do not be afraid to address this with the facility you are considering choosing.

The other disadvantage to having your child home at night is that he is back in the environment that potentially caused or contributed to his depression. These are factors that you must consider before you choose this option.

Hospitalization

Inpatient hospitalization requires that your child stay at the facility day and night. She will be constantly monitored and will receive treatment from a team that can include a doctor, therapist, group therapist, and other professionals such as social workers and recreational or art therapists. The program is quite comprehensive and almost always has a component that requires the family members to participate in the child's treatment.

Psychiatric hospitalization typically lasts from a few days to two weeks. This is why the treatment team has to move quickly and effectively to provide your child with every opportunity to get better. If medication was a problem before your child was hospitalized, this is an excellent way for a doctor to try more aggressive medications because he will be able to observe your child carefully and continuously.

Residential Treatment

This is the most serious of treatment options outside the home because the child is there for an extended length of time. When other treatment methods have failed, residential treatment must be considered.

Residential treatment means your child will be living at a facility that operates much like a home. A length of stay is anywhere from three months to a year. Your child participates in intensive therapy, school, and physical activity. A facility like this tries to help a child live in a family-like atmosphere while learning new ways to interact with others and resolve his own emotional issues.

A benefit to residential treatment is that your child is immersed in an environment that makes him feel more at home and teaches him how to be a productive member of a family while addressing his own problems. Also, if your child was extremely disruptive and damaging to the rest of your family's functioning, this will provide everyone with a chance to get back to normal. Children who go to residential centers have drained and exhausted their parents to the extent that the other children were probably neglected. You should not feel guilty if you are relieved somewhat. Now you have some time to attend to the rest of your family.

Do not be fooled when you talk to your child living at a residential treatment center. He may be trying to convince you and the treatment team that he really doesn't need to be there. He may beg you to take him home, which will tug at any parent's conscience. Leave it up to the treatment team to make that decision since they are not emotionally invested like a parent.

Essential

Don't be surprised if your child's residential treatment prohibits your contact with your child for a specified length of time. Your child needs to get used to the facility and completely removed from his environment. It's hard to get used to being away from home, and forcing the child to focus on treatment is the best way to assure success.

Also, remember that the decision to place your child in an inpatient setting should include the awareness that what you were doing was not working and that your child seems incapable of controlling his impulses to hurt himself or others.

Picking a Facility

If your physician or therapist recommends day treatment, hospitalization, or residential treatment for your child, you do not have to agree right away. There are questions you need to ask, and issues you need to consider.

Why, How, and What?

The first question you should ask is: Why does my child need inpatient treatment? Explore with your treating professional if all other options have been exhausted. Remember, this is a big decision. There is nothing wrong with inpatient treatment if your child needs it, but it absolutely needs to be a last resort when nothing else is working.

Also ask how the inpatient treatment differs from what your child is doing now and how will it help him. When a parent hears her child needs inpatient treatment, she usually responds with surprise, sadness, and fear. Try to hear out your treating professional before you react. Remember, just because someone says you have to do something does not mean you have to obey.

Next you should ask about what will happen in your child's treatment. Find out what sort of program your child's therapist believes is best for your child. What are the goals for your child's treatment? Programs can often be designed to fit your child's particular needs and problems. Make sure your child will be in a program that is age appropriate. What kind of professionals will be seeing your child? What kinds of medicines might be tried?

Costs

The costs among treatment facilities can vary widely, but they are generally expensive. Get information about the cost per day at the facility. Are there different costs for different services? Is treatment covered by insurance, and how many days are covered? Is any payment expected up front? What if you can't pay? Can a payment plan be arranged? If your insurance won't cover treatment, and if your finances make it impossible for your child to attend this inpatient treatment, ask your doctor to recommend another. He usually has more than one option for you to pick from, and you shouldn't be embarrassed to ask.

 **Question?**

What if I can't afford the recommended treatment facility?
Balance the choice of a facility by picking what the most effective treatment for your child will be and what you can afford. Making this decision is difficult enough without you having the additional stress of being under tremendous financial pressure.

Family Involvement

Will you be able to visit with your child? Who else can visit? Is the family expected to participate somehow? Will you have the opportunity to visit with your child's treatment team, ask questions, and voice concerns? Remember that one of the reasons for inpatient treatment is to remove the child from her environment. Part of that environment is family. Most inpatient facilities will require some parental and family involvement to help the parents learn about their child and how to help. The child will learn new ways of coping within her environment and improve her relationships.

Other questions you might wish to ask before picking a facility include:

- Is the facility accredited, licensed?
- Is the facility designed for children or is there a children's unit?
- How long is the expected stay?
- How will your child be encouraged to participate? What if he refuses?
- Can your child's therapist be involved in the treatment?
- Will you be consulted when medication changes need to be made or the treatment plan needs to be altered?
- Will you be consulted when the facility thinks your child is ready to be discharged?
- Does the facility have a plan for your child after discharge?

Most treatment facilities have Web sites so that you can check them out in the privacy of your home. This is another great way to learn as much as you can before you make a decision. In addition, some facilities have kids and some parents who have already been where you are now. They might encourage you to speak with them to hear about their experiences and to give you some support.

What to Expect from Inpatient Treatment

Now that you have made the decision to place your child in a facility, you'll be entering foreign territory. Your child is also likely to be nervous and anxious about what to expect. Help your child to understand that you and his therapist have made the decision for his best interests and safety and that he will be undergoing a different kind of treatment. Reassure him that you will be in contact with him and the facility as their rules allow. Tell him that you are proud that he is getting ready to do something difficult.

Alert!

Children who enter inpatient treatment often think they have failed somehow at traditional treatment. Special care needs to be taken as to how you communicate your decision to place him in a facility. Tell him you love him and that this is not going to be easy for him, but that you have every confidence he will feel better soon.

It will be very difficult, if not impossible, to resist your child's pleas to not place him in treatment. "I'm so scared—you can't leave me here." "I'll be fine, you just go ahead and enjoy *your* life." "I hate you for doing this." You can imagine what other things your child would say! All such statements are meant to manipulate you, make you feel guilty, and to get you to spring your child from his "jail." Remember he is scared to death, and quite frankly, who could blame him? It's a strange, unfamiliar place, and kids don't like the feeling that they are imprisoned, which is what inpatient treatment can feel like initially.

You might want to wait as long as you can before telling him about the arrangements. It may seem unfair, but you are actually doing him a favor. There will be less time for him to work on you and find a way to get out of going. It decreases the chances for any acting out behaviors in response to your decision. Also, it will cut down on the time he has to start becoming anxious about what is getting ready to happen.

The Intake

The first thing that will happen in an inpatient facility will be an intake process. This will be the first point of contact for you and your child with an inpatient facility. Someone, usually a social worker, will try to put your child at ease. They are trained at dealing with your child's anger at being there, his suspiciousness, and his anxiety. The worker will likely take a social history from you. This includes questions about your child's development, medical and mental health history, and pertinent family history.

 **Essential**

One way to help your child get acclimated to his surroundings is to ask if he can have a favorite book, pillow, stuffed animal, or photo. Allowing him to have something meaningful may give him a bit of extra security that will serve as a reminder of home.

You might take the same folder you used when you first visited a treating professional to get a diagnosis for your child. A modified exam may be taken. Once the initial information is gathered, you and your child will receive a tour of the facility. You might be shown the room where your child will be staying. If he has a roommate, you may meet him at this time.

If you haven't already checked, ask at the intake what kinds of clothes you can pack for your child. Typically, you'll be asked to pack enough clothes for two or three changes. Your child's bag is likely to be searched upon entering the facility, so ask ahead what sorts of items are allowable.

Alert!

Do not let yourself be intimidated by the inpatient facility and its professionals. They understand that this is a new and bewildering experience for you and for your child. Ask as many questions as you need to in order to feel comfortable about your child's treatment.

Also during the intake process you and your child will be told the rules of the facility. You will likely hear about the means by which your child's confidentiality will be maintained. You will be asked who your child is allowed to contact on the outside once he is given the privilege of making phone calls. Also, you'll be asked who is *not* permitted to have contact with your child. This monitoring will not only maintain his privacy, but it will keep him away from any persons who might not be supportive of his treatment or who may draw his attention away from focusing on getting better.

Treatment Plan

Some facilities include you in the development of a treatment plan. Some won't, but the process is about the same. One of the members of your child's treatment team will meet with both of you or your child alone. The plan outlines what your child will be addressing while at the treatment facility. First, the specific problems that need to be addressed will be identified. Goals will be developed with steps to be followed in order to achieve them. The therapy process to be used with your child will be explained in depth, and if medication is required, you'll hear about it then.

An estimated length of time your child will be staying may be offered, but don't hold the facility to it. Many factors go into this decision, and sometimes things don't happen within the time projected. This doesn't mean that your child is not improving. It may take longer than normal to get his medications correct, or perhaps other issues integral to his recovery have emerged. It's best to remain as flexible as possible so that your child gets the most out of his treatment experience.

The Parental Role in Treatment

Your role in your child's inpatient treatment is simple and complex. As usual, it's more hard work! But you *can* do this, and your child's success in treatment will partially rely on you. Your child has to participate in order to succeed, but he will need your involvement as well.

Discussing Treatment with Your Child

First, be as honest as you can about why you have made the decision for him to have this kind of treatment. You have a better chance at convincing him this is a good choice if you present it with a team approach. He is the major member, but there are other members too. This includes his treatment team and you. You'll have to do your best to alleviate the stigma of mental illness and inpatient treatment. Kids don't like to be different, and inpatient treatment is certainly different!

 Essential

Do not argue with your child about treatment. You are the parent here, and ultimately this decision is yours. You want to be compassionate, but you will also need to be firm. Simply tell him you love him, and that your hope is to make him feel better as fast as possible so that he can return to his life.

If possible, keep your child's treatment arrangements low key. Be discrete about whom you tell and include your child's input on this. When he complains that it's going to feel like prison, understand that he's probably right. He is going to be watched, monitored, and intensively treated. He will have little freedom and this will be exasperating at first.

Facility Expectations

Second, find out the expectations the facility has for your involvement. You'll probably have a case manager assigned to your child. This person will be the one you call with your questions and concerns. You don't want to be too intrusive, but you also want to be available for family sessions and consults with the treatment team. Get a schedule of events to which you are supposed to attend. Unless you have a significant complaint, try not to criticize the treatment team. As a parent, you will naturally feel that some of what is happening to your child is too quick, too hard, and too much for your child. The treatment team understands that your child is your baby, but they are not going to do any special favors for him. He will be treated just like everyone else, and they really do know what they are doing!

Sharing the Responsibility

Third, be prepared to accept your share of the responsibility for your child's problems. Do not misinterpret this as being asked to take the blame. You read earlier that there are plenty of risk factors, causes, and predictors of depression. You are not perfect—you are a parent! Just as you have the ability to be a positive force in your child's life, you will make mistakes. Those mistakes may be influencing your child and how he sees himself. Your child needs to know that you are willing to examine your own behavior and make appropriate changes if necessary.

Inpatient Treatment Is Over—Now What?

When it is time for your child to return home, you and he will meet with the case manager or another member of the treatment team. You will be instructed as to what medications your child will be taking and what sort of treatment he will need on the outside. Generally, your child will be sent back to his previous therapist or doctor. Some facilities might have a partial discharge program where your child might attend group therapy. This is a great way to transition him out of inpatient treatment.

While it is certainly not designed to be self-damaging, a child can actually develop deeper feelings of inadequacy because he had to have this special treatment. In other words, he may be vulnerable to a recurrence of depression. This needs to be addressed as soon as possible in therapy.

Alert!

Understandably, your child is going to be sick of treatment. Once discharged, he will beg for a vacation from therapy, stating he just wants to return to his normal life. Don't let him talk you into it. Re-establishing a therapeutic relationship quickly after discharge will keep him on track and help avoid a recurrence of depression.

Removing Your Kid Gloves

It is important that your child return to his normal life as soon as possible. Let him visit friends, return to school, and do whatever he was enjoying doing prior to inpatient treatment. Resist the urge to walk on eggshells around him. It is reasonable for you to be worried about him, but treating him with kid gloves will only make matters worse.

While you are busy trying not to be too overprotective, also avoid asking him if he's all right. You'll want to ask about a million times a day, but it will make your child defensive. This is not the time for him to believe that you are worried about him or that you don't trust him to tell you when he is in trouble.

Keeping It Simple

Try to keep the tension and stress within your home to a minimum. Keep a stable routine because this can be especially reassuring for your child during this time. Don't make any major decisions, such as moving or changing schools, that will disrupt the family's stability.

Last, maintain a positive attitude. Express your happiness that your child completed treatment. Communicate to him that you understand how difficult it must have been for him and that you are proud of his hard work. And while you're at it, give him lots of hugs and love!

CHAPTER 15

Prevention

The prevention of depression is possible to an extent. There are ways to depression-proof your home and your child's life and there are ways to help prevent a recurrence of depression after your child has suffered from an episode. But don't misinterpret what is meant by depression-proof. It doesn't mean you can guarantee no depression. What you will learn here are techniques that will help your child develop emotional resiliency. It is that emotional resiliency that will help prevent depression.

Open Communication

Depressed children frequently have trouble expressing their feelings. When they do, they often say things in such a way that you miss the clues. If your child is talking with a lot less emotion than she normally does, it could be a sign she is feeling depressed. If she acts as though talking takes a lot of energy, and again, this is uncharacteristic of her, pay attention. So how do you get her to talk?

The sensation that your feelings are boiling up on your insides is uncomfortable and scary. Like a balloon filling with air, you have a breaking point. You feel as if a pin were to prick you, you'd explode and fly through the air! This is how a child feels if she is becoming depressed. That is why it's important to create an atmosphere where open communication is possible and encouraged.

Two Ears, One Mouth

Parents have a tendency to discount things children say. Parents are busier today than ever and the minutes spent with their children are few and far between. So when your very popular child comes homes and says, "No one likes me," your natural instinct is to respond with "Don't be silly, every one likes you. Don't feel sorry for yourself." But what if your child is really trying to tell you something? What if she is worried about something?

The funny thing is, when you ask your child what is wrong, she will probably go on and on about how no one likes her, as if she is trying to convince you, and herself, that this is really the problem. You are bound to become impatient and again, you will dismiss her words as trivial complaining.

Listen to what your child is saying. Maybe she really is feeling disliked. Or perhaps she is beginning to feel inadequate somehow among her peers. Remember, you have two ears and one mouth. It seems logical therefore that you should use those ears more than you use your mouth. Use those ears to listen to, or better yet absorb, what your child is saying.

Acceptance and Empathy

These are two words that are bantered about carelessly. In communication with your children, they need to feel that they are not being judged. The more you show acceptance and refrain from overreacting, the less likely they are to clam up and stop sharing with you.

You expect your children to tell you the truth, and they have the right to expect it from you. So for example, if Grandma is very ill and your child asks if she is going to die, don't assume that skirting the issue will be best for him. Give an honest, age-appropriate answer.

Your child needs to know that he can say what he needs to say. You have to learn the ability to separate your judgments and opinions from his words. That's where empathy comes in. You've heard the expression, "Walk a mile in another's shoes." This is what you must try to do.

You're probably saying that it's been a while since you've been a youngster so it's hard to know exactly what he's feeling. Well, you're going to have to try. Do you remember how you felt when a group of kids wouldn't invite you to play with them? Or when you knew something was up between your parents but your mom said, "Everything's fine, honey, don't you worry"?

When it comes to teens, they are the most difficult to get talking! Pushing usually ends up creating the exact result you don't want—he will dig in his heels and remain silent. Don't ask questions that he can quickly answer with a yes or no. Nudge him a little by asking open-ended questions. His answers may give you more information about what is bothering him.

So when your child says something, listen, don't judge, and remember how you felt when someone didn't do that for you.

Teaching Communication Skills

What if your child has trouble figuring out how to say something? In Chapter 12 it was mentioned that people are born not knowing how to name their emotions. If you have trouble labeling your own emotions, get some help and learn to do it. This is one of the most important skills you can teach your child and one of the best ways to prevent depression.

Ask and Show

Ask questions. "How are you feeling today?" "I know you didn't get invited to the party and that would make me disappointed. What about you?" Push a little, but not so much that you frustrate him. If possible, ask open-ended questions so that your child is forced to answer with more than just one-word answers.

Another way to help teach good communication skills is to model good communication. When you are feeling angry, instead of yelling or banging your fist on the counter, say out loud, "I am feeling angry right now because . . . ." While it sounds simple and that nothing will be learned this way, you are wrong. Children learn from what they see. You don't have to make a big deal out of expressing yourself, just casually describe how you feel. You'll be surprised the next time your child is feeling something when he imitates how you handled something!

Essential

Here's a great technique to teach your child to name his feelings. Play a game in which you act out an emotion and ask him to figure out what you're feeling. Then let him take a turn where you describe what he is enacting. It's a fun, easy way to learn and to spend some quality time with your child.

Coping by Communication

Helping your child develop good, solid communication skills is a super preventative for depression. And you are also helping him create skills for coping with adversity. When bad things happen, or when your child perceives something in a negative way, he needs a way to deal with it. Whether he has been neglected by the in crowd or made an uncharacteristic C on a math test, he needs skills to communicate how he is feeling or how he wishes to manage a particular problem.

If your child can talk about these events, he can also express his feelings. In turn, you are able to help him come up with options for coping. You don't have to be the perfect problem-solver, just a very good supporter and cheerleader!

Question?

How do communication skills prepare my child for adversity?
Kids must learn how to accurately communicate their thoughts and feelings. Without that ability, they cannot manage problems efficiently. Helping your child express how he feels, and then to develop options for action, is the perfect framework for managing adversity now and in the future.

A good exercise to try is to have your child list the way he feels about a situation. Then have him make a list of options for coping. After he does this, have him make another list of the pros and cons of his options. Discuss with him what the consequences of these actions might be and how they would affect him. This sort of plan will serve your child well in a number of settings.

Physical Activity

That physical activity is a good outlet for a depressed child has already been explored. But it is also a beneficial preventative to depression. Not only does physical activity activate the chemicals in the brain that makes one feel good, but it also helps individuals express their feelings. How? Exercise is a way to let off steam. When children are feeling agitated, bewildered, and anxious, exercise is an excellent outlet for reducing their discomfort.

Extra Benefits of Exercise

Exercise can also be good for helping a child develop discipline. Activities such as karate, ballet, or yoga demand a tremendous amount of focus. To focus on something positive can actually help a child work through her problems subconsciously and lets her take her mind off of her problems. These types of exercise require that the child place all of her attention on the activity and gives her time off from her worrying. The discipline she develops gives her another coping skill in her arsenal for preventing or fighting depression.

Essential

If your child shows interest in a certain activity, encourage it. You may not understand her interest, but she may actually need this activity. Kids often subconsciously know they need exercise to decrease their negative feelings. Do not assume that this is just a passing fancy. At least let her try and see if she gets anything positive from it.

Exercise as a Confidence Booster

The other advantage of participating in physical activity is that your child will hopefully experience some personal successes. Anything that gives her a sense of mastery and confidence is going to boost her self-esteem. Anything that bolsters her self-image will go a long way toward preventing depression.

A good way to interest an inactive child in physical activity is to get moving yourself. Exercising with your child sets an example for her, and it gives the two of you something to do together. You might even express to her how good physical activity makes you feel and how it helps you to cope with your emotions.

Creative Outlets

Playing with clay, painting, drawing, sewing—these are all excellent skills and fun activities to learn. What adults don't always realize is that these creative outlets can be expressions of what one is experiencing and feeling.

What Does It Mean?

Artists will tell you that it isn't until after they have finished a piece of art that they realize it was driven by specific emotions or a mood.

For children, creative projects are great activities to encourage emotional expression. Kids don't have to know that's what they are doing—they merely need to have fun. For children who don't know exactly how to verbalize what they are feeling, creative activities are instrumental in helping them relax, and whatever they are experiencing inside seems to come right out. And remember, creative expression doesn't have to be a structured activity. Maybe your child wants to paint his room, or he likes to cook, or he would rather write music for his guitar. Any activity that lets him play and explore who he is a great depression fighter. Adolescents also like these activities because they aren't being forced to talk!

Alert!

Just because your child draws something that seems dark and frightening, do not automatically assume she is depressed and needs help. Sometimes children like to depict negative things, and sometimes they are merely trying to be dramatic. Watch how she acts across the board before you form any opinions.

Keeping a Journal

Something as simple as keeping a scrapbook of successes and good times is a great antidote to a child's negative feelings about herself. Helping her to keep track of the positive things in her life keeps her less vulnerable to the thoughts that can lead to depression.

Education

Knowledge is power. The more educated you are about depression, its signs and its causes, the more aware you will be if it becomes a problem for your child. Your child needs to understand depression, too. It's not necessary to talk to your child about depression when she has never experienced it, but you do want to address any symptoms she may be exhibiting. Rather than lecturing her about depression itself, help her to understand the importance of communicating her feelings to you so that you can help her.

Modeling

Imitating preventative behaviors is a great way to teach your child the same skills without boring her to death with a lecture! Children and teenagers listen to about the first thirty seconds of what you are saying and then they begin to tune you out. Haven't you ever noticed the glazed-over look in her eyes when you are talking? She has merely stopped listening and has not one bit of interest in what you are saying!

Do you remember the old saying, "Do as I say, not as I do"? Teenagers are particularly adept at using that argument. He will be the first one to ask, "Why should I do it (whatever *it* is at the moment) if you don't do it?" Actually, he has a point. A child learns a lot by watching you. If you consistently do things to prevent depression or symptoms of it, your child will see that these skills benefit you and he will be more likely to take your advice. You don't even have to say anything—your actions will speak louder and teach your child more than your words.

Combat Skills

As communication skills help your child express feelings and thoughts that can possibly lead to depression, you can also pass on combat skills to prevent depression's grip. Unfortunately, sometimes the best way to teach your child how to cope with life's difficult moments is to let her live through them. You cannot protect her from every hurt she will experience and every mistake she will make. Hurt feelings, pain, and mistakes are inevitable. But the lessons learned can be invaluable.

When you support your child through the little things that cause her discomfort, you are preparing her for the bigger obstacles that life has in store for her. Combat skills are not designed to help her avoid those obstacles, but they will help her fight them and come out ahead.

Essential

> When your child enlists your aid in rescuing her from uncomfortable feelings or hard times, if she is not in present danger, encourage her to come up with her own ideas for combat. Do not make fun of what she perceives is the problem. Praise her efforts and let her know she has your support.

So what if your child makes a choice to do something that leads to more trouble? Your intervention needs to be in the form of listening, not lecturing. She needs a sympathetic ear, and someone to help her bounce back. Ask her what led her to make that specific choice. Did things turn out the way she had hoped and expected? What could she have done differently? Is there anything she can do now to improve the situation? Offer suggestions, but force her to sift through her options on her own. This will not only help her to accept responsibility for her actions, but it will also help her to see that most mistakes are not permanent. She will actively see that she *does* have the ability to change and make different choices.

Character is developed through adversity. As long as your child is not in danger of hurting herself or others, allowing her to make some of her own choices and mistakes is a gift you can give to her. As she learns better combat skills through every battle she fights, she will develop a stronger sense of self. These combat skills will also prepare her to fight off depression if it comes along.

Fostering Self-esteem

Self-esteem is an active, ongoing process. Your child's first sense of who she is comes from her family experiences. These relationships and interactions form the foundation for how she sees herself. Just like learning to label emotions, your child will need to learn techniques for developing a healthy, strong self-image.

Self-control

Self-control is not merely learning to keep quiet in class or to stay seated when required. The ability to control one's emotions and the actions that follow is one of the most important skills you can teach your child as a preventative against depression. When your child understands that she has some active part in controlling her emotions, she develops emotional resiliency and a healthy self-esteem.

 **Fact**

Believe it or not, one of the simplest ways to teach your child to get control over her emotions before reacting is to have her silently count to ten. This quick method gives her a few seconds to gather herself together and decide how she wants to behave.

When things happen, it's natural to think you have to react right away. Typically, when under stress or feeling pressured due to negative emotions, a child will blurt out or do something that is counterproductive. Teach her that she is not always required to respond to a person or situation immediately. If she is unsure what to say or do, she can take a time-out.

A time-out merely means she doesn't have to do anything until she has had time to consider her options. She can respond after she has considered how she feels and what would make her feel better as long as it doesn't hurt anyone else. If she doesn't know what to do, she can always say, "Let me get back to you." This gives her an out until she is able to respond appropriately. As she masters the skill of self-control, her self-esteem will naturally increase and her risk for depression decrease.

What Kids Can Do

Here are five things that your child can try to develop good, healthy self-esteem:

1. Make a list of all the things you like about yourself.
2. Make a list of all the new things you would like to try.
3. Think of the people you know who are very different from you and write down their names. Beside each name, describe how that person is different and what it might feel like to be that person.
4. What sort of goals would you like to achieve in the next month, three months, six months, and a year?
5. Do you have any role models? Who are they and why do they inspire you?

What Parents Can Do

While you are busy getting your child to work on his own self-esteem, here are five things you can do to boost him along:

1. Separate the behavior from the child. Help him to see that despite mistakes or blunders that he makes, he is still a terrific kid. You don't have to love the behavior, only the kid!
2. Accentuate your child's strengths. Parents find themselves often focusing on the negatives about their children. Try doing just the opposite.
3. Encourage respect for you, others, and for himself. One way to do this is to help him honor the differences between others. Help him to understand how he fits into his own world where not everyone will be like him.
4. Encourage your child to try new things. Gently pull him from his comfort zone and allow him to experience the rest of the world. He may succeed, he may fail, but he will have tried. And it is through trying that self-esteem is formed.

5. Write praise slips. These are little notes that you put in a lunchbox, under a pillow, or tape to a bathroom mirror that say, "Way to go!" or "I'm so proud of you for. . . ." These are sweet, tiny ways to let him know you are thinking of your child and all the wonderful things he does and how blessed you are to be his parent!

The bottom line is that while you can't always prevent depression from occurring, you can still try. You may never know if you have won that battle. You may also prevent depression from worsening or recurring. In any case, children need to have these skills to develop healthy patterns of coping. These coping skills not only will serve as excellent shields against depression, but also will build good self-esteem and offer a child ways to interact successfully for the rest of his life.

CHAPTER 16

All in the Family

You have read that depression is a difficult illness but one that is treatable and preventable. Dealing with the everyday stresses of life is difficult for any parent, but for a parent whose child is depressed, the stress increases exponentially. When a child is depressed, everyone in the family is affected. While the family does not cause the depression, the family's dynamics likely play a part in its development. Therefore, for treatment to be effective, it is best if the entire family is involved.

Depression's Effect on the Family

There are all sorts of effects on the family unit when a child is depressed. A parent feels the most responsibility for making sure everyone is all right. Parents want to heal everyone, and to make things better in whatever ways they can. They will spin their wheels looking for the magic cure even though they know there isn't one.

On the other hand, if the depressed child is aware of the family's stress, he will also blame himself for thinking he caused their troubles. Even though it is irrational for him to think this, he does it nonetheless. It is easy to see how the blame game and the guilt trip can occur on both sides. Talking about this with your child and the rest of the family will be important to help lessen the tension within.

Effect on Parents

Any parent will tell you that she does not want anything to be wrong with her child. It is difficult enough to deal with a physical illness, let alone something as scary as a mental illness! A parent is frequently consumed with guilt because she is sure that she either caused the depression or let it go on too long before seeking help. As you have learned, you are not the expert on depression, and unless you have dealt with it before, there is no reason to think you could have necessarily spotted your child's troubles early on. Part of the depression-diagnosis-treatment conundrum is that you have to observe your child for a while before making the decision that something is wrong. Doing this too hastily is no more productive than waiting too long.

 **Fact**

The way you react to the fact that your child has a problem is predictive of how he will handle it. If he senses that you are blaming yourself, or that you resent his illness, he is likely to blame himself and think that he is somehow bad for causing the family's strife. Stay positive and upbeat.

Often, parents will go through a process similar to grieving, although obviously not nearly as severe as when a death occurs. This is perfectly normal. A parent might first try to deny that a problem exists or that it will go away on its own. Then she may begin to feel guilty that she denied there was any trouble and didn't recognize a problem was present. She may feel angry and ask, "Why is this happening to my child?" Her anger might even be focused on the child as she feels resentful that this is something else she must handle along with the regular responsibilities and stresses of family life.

As a parent moves through this process, if she is successful, she will come to the point of acceptance. The realization that her child does indeed have depression may result in feelings of disappointment, more anger and guilt, and bewilderment. All of these reactions and feelings are perfectly normal, but they must be dealt with to minimize their effects on the child. Having a mental illness is not the worst calamity to befall a child if it is handled properly.

It is quite common for parents to disagree with one another about rules, discipline, and other matters related to the children. So it makes sense that they might disagree about how to handle a child's depression. One parent might blame the other for not handling things the way they were supposed to be handled, which really means, "Why aren't you doing it my way?" A couple who might already be under stress because of their own marital difficulties can break under the added pressure of having a child with depression.

Single Parents

Even though studies have found single parents with a depressed child are no more affected than a regular family, it seems impossible that this could be true. One parent is typically doing the work of two parents.

 Essential

When a child is involved, the ability of divorced parents to work together is critical. If your child has depression, he does not need the extra pressure of knowing his parents are disagreeing. Make sure you both are involved and are working in the child's best interests for recovery.

If the parents are divorced, there are often two kinds of environments at play. There may be two different sets of rules and discipline, and there may be other players within each system that will affect how the child's depression will be addressed. Trying to get two schedules together to attend appointments may be unreasonable.

The possibility that one parent will try to blame the other for the child's depression is a real possibility. A single parent may have less money and therefore fewer resources for helping her child. She will almost always have more time constraints. How can this *not* be more stressful?

Stepfamilies

Just the mention of a stepparent or stepfamily can strike fear in an adult. The separating of an old family and the merging of new families are always stressful, no matter how great the circumstances. Unfortunately and too often, this process is not a positive one and can leave many of its participants feeling left out, resentful, defensive, and neglected. Add to this mix of emotions a child with depression and there is the real chance for trouble!

A stepparent might refuse to be involved in his stepdaughter's treatment because it's not his child. He may resent the amount of time this child is taking away from the time he could be spending with his new bride. Likewise, the new wife might be defensive about her child and more protective than usual. She might be angry that her new husband refuses to participate in the treatment process and ultimately blame him if things don't go well for her daughter.

The scenarios of adults living with a depressed child are too many to mention. The important thing to remember is that depression *will* affect those closest to the child, and that is typically the immediate family. Failure to address how it is influencing each member of the family can prove to be more damaging than the depression alone.

Caring for the Caregiver

Parents never want to hear this, but you simply cannot be a good parent if you are not taking care of yourself. Parents will say, "But my children come first, not me!" This is true in many cases, but think of the family like a car and the parent as the motor. Without the motor, a car cannot move, operate, or be of much benefit to anyone. Of course your children are important. But if you want to be the very best, healthy parent to your child, you'd better make sure your "motor" is properly fueled and cared for!

Alert!

If you need another reason to take care of yourself, consider this: Children learn how to nurture themselves by modeling what they observe you doing. If they see you treating yourself as someone who is special and has needs, they are more likely to do the same for themselves.

Your needs matter—period, end of discussion. Your child's needs matter, too, and sometimes yours will have to wait until you take care of your child. But you simply cannot run yourself into the ground. If you do, you will become emotionally drained, physically exhausted, and you will have nothing to give to anyone.

Becoming a Good Personal Stress Manager

You try to help your child and your spouse manage their stress, right? Who's taking care of yours? Chances are the answer is nobody. There's no time. But this is the wrong answer. There are ways to organize your life so that you have time for yourself.

Look at some of the things you do for your child, such as laundry, cooking, cleaning the bathroom—the list goes on and on. Depending on your child's age, he can help with these tasks. Can your spouse take over some duties? Better yet, are there tasks, such as cooking dinner or raking the leaves, that you can do with your child? These opportunities allow you to combine two tasks—taking care of household chores and, even more importantly, spending some quality time with your child.

Are you exercising regularly? If this is hard to do, break up exercise into smaller chunks of time. Exercise with your child, again using it as an opportunity for him to observe healthy coping skills while spending time with you. How's your diet? Are you eating too much, too little, healthily? Are you drinking to reduce your stress? Are you getting enough sleep?

 *Essential*

It is perfectly reasonable to tell your child that you are taking a little me time. Ask your spouse or a friend for help if your child needs watching. Explain to everyone that you do not expect to be interrupted. Take a nap, go to a movie, or read a book, anything that quiets and relaxes you.

Look at your to-do list. Is it even close to being reasonable? Most parents will say their lists are realistic, but if you take a closer look, they are crazy! Does everything on your list really have to be done today? Ask yourself, "What's the worst that could happen if I don't do something?" Most of the time, if you are honest with yourself, you will see that you can skip a lot of things you thought you could've, should've, or would've done.

Isolation

Having a child with depression obviously stirs up many emotions within a parent. Yet parents are reluctant to talk with others about their feelings, believing that no one will understand what they are going through. They spend so much time trying to help their children that they think they simply have no time to interact with others. What ends up happening is that the parent becomes at risk for depression herself and isolates herself from other people, particularly if she feels it will bring on more stress to be with them.

Believe it or not, your friends do not have to have a child with depression to understand much of what you are going through. All parents feel overwhelmed by many emotions just by being parents. If you take the time to observe parents in conversation with one another, you will overhear them discussing the most recent antics of their children, or just how aggravated, scared, or worried they are about them.

Sharing how you are feeling accomplishes two things. First, letting out your emotions is good for your own mental health, and you need all the strength you can get to be able to help your child. Second, you may be a source of information for your friends. As they hear about what your child is experiencing, it might enable them to notice the symptoms of depression in their children, or at least to be on the lookout for the warning signs. Having a trusted group of friends will help you cope much more effectively with your child's problems and your own bundle of emotions.

Alert!

If you have a friend that is constantly comparing your child with hers, discussing your child's depression with her will only set you up for frustration as she tells you "how much better Johnny is" than your child. You already feel bad—you don't need this kind of support! Save the discussion of your child's depression for an empathic friend.

Nurture the Adult Relationship

Anyone who has children knows that the amount of time you have for a romantic relationship can dwindle to almost nothing. Between household chores, carpooling, your child's extracurricular activities, homework, and other family obligations, you might ask, "What romance?" You wouldn't be alone in that sentiment. Now add to the mix a child with depression and you begin to feel that not only do you have little time for romance, but also that you shouldn't be selfish to want anything for yourself.

Stop right there! This sort of thinking is unhealthy and unrealistic. It's part of human nature to crave the closeness of another adult. So whether you are single, dating someone, or married, this part of your life should not be neglected. But how do you fit it in when you are spending so much time parenting your depressed child?

Finding the Time

The first thing you must do is assess your schedule. Sure, it's probably chock full of have-to's and musts. On top of that, you have therapy and maybe doctor visits for your depressed child. By the time you finish your day, who cares about anything else but falling into your bed for a few precious hours of sleep before it starts all over again?

 **Fact**

Often, a depressed child will complain of feeling smothered by her parents because they want to make sure she is okay. Spend some of that time tending to your own adult relationship. It's also a great way to model healthy relationship behavior for your child. It also helps her escape from being under your microscope, focusing on her every breath!

It's been said before, but you need to understand that your needs are very important. If you are married, that relationship cannot be taken for granted. Research shows that when there is no focus on the relationship between a husband and wife, one or both partners can begin to feel neglected, angry, and lonely. Obviously, that's when trouble begins to brew in your relationship. The same is true for a single parent with a serious relationship.

A parent who is single and not in a relationship will often say she doesn't have time for dating because her main focus is on helping her depressed child. She may be right about her lack of time, but she certainly shouldn't ignore her romantic life just because she is burdened with many family obligations.

Talking

Communication with your partner is key if your relationship is going to endure. If you are feeling resentful because your wife is spending all of her time dealing with your depressed child, tell her. You are not being childish, just honest. Mothers in particular seem to become more engrossed and enmeshed with a child who is experiencing trouble. She doesn't mean to ignore her partner, but it does happen.

Recent studies have suggested that spending as little as ten to twenty minutes together every day is enough to keep your marriage on the right track. It gives both of you the opportunity to share news from your day, report on the children, and maybe indulge in a kiss or two!

What You Can Do

Parents worry about financial pressures, time, and other important matters. How can you make time with your partner without breaking the bank if your schedule is bursting at the seams?

- Schedule the ten to twenty minutes described earlier. It may sound contrived and artificial, but if it's on your schedule, you are more likely to actually do it!
- Schedule a weekly date with your partner. It doesn't have to be expensive or fancy. Take a walk together, go to your favorite pizza joint, or sit on your porch after the kids are in bed and enjoy a glass of wine. One caveat—no kids!
- If you can't find a babysitter or can't afford to have one, enlist your friends or family. Grandparents are always a pretty good bet for availability! Other parents are tight on resources, too, and good babysitters may be hard to find in your area. Offer to take care of your friend's kids for a few hours in exchange for her doing the same for you.
- Meet for lunch. If their work schedules permit, some parents use this time for a date. It might put some constraints on what you can do, but it's still a good way to have fun together.

Don't forget about flirting. Leave a note for your beloved listing all the ways you love her. Send flowers. Call her and tell her you are thinking about her. Make sure you make her feel loved.

Siblings

When a child is depressed, you may find yourself neglecting your other children. You aren't doing this on purpose, however, but because your child has a mental illness and takes a lot of your physical and emotional energy. But the siblings need support and attention, too. They have their own opinions and feelings about their depressed brother or sister. Unfortunately, a lot of what they are thinking and feeling is negative.

Sibling Reactions

There are several responses a sibling might have upon hearing that his brother or sister is depressed. While she loves her brother, she may not fully understand what is happening. You will have to educate her about depression at a level that is age appropriate. Explain to her that her brother is getting help, and that the whole family needs to support him. She may have questions and you should try to answer them as honestly as you can.

Alert!

Your natural tendency when your nondepressed child begins to ask questions is to minimize what is happening or to avoid answering. While too much information can be inappropriate, your child will sense that something is wrong. Don't make matters worse by being secretive. Let your child's depression be a problem that brings your family together.

A more natural reaction is for a sibling to feel left out. She is apt to be a bit envious of all the attention her depressed brother is receiving. Sometimes, a child cannot understand that the attention is not being given because he is more special than his sibling. She may begin to make comments such as, "You love him more than me," or "Why are you always doing stuff with him?" It will be your job to help her see that her brother has a problem and needs some extra time from you. Explain that she is just as important to you as he is, but that he has problems that must be addressed.

Sometimes a sibling will take her anger out on the depressed sibling. Again, while her anger is perfectly normal, she needs to learn ways to communicate it that don't push your depressed child deeper into that black hole.

Question?

Is it a normal sibling conflict or something more serious?
You should be familiar with your children's typical patterns of conflict. If your nondepressed child seems more physically or verbally aggressive than normal, she might be taking her feelings out on him. Encouraging the two of them to talk with one another about their feelings will improve their relationship.

Some siblings will try to take on more responsibilities to compensate for the depressed child's problems. They also crave attention, so doing more makes them more noticeable and possibly more appreciated. When a parent is emotionally and physically exhausted, she might allow this sibling to take on more duties. It is imperative that you allow her to be the child, not a grownup. Work to keep her life as normal as possible.

Avoidant Behaviors

Just like adults, kids have a tendency to avoid unpleasantness. When a sibling is depressed, the reaction of a nondepressed child can be tinged with embarrassment and a desire to keep the depressed sibling hidden. She may spend more time in her room to avoid dealing with her sibling. She may refuse to discuss her sibling's depression because she is angry, sad, and confused. You may find her not having friends come over in case the depressed sibling acts out somehow. While you may want to fuss at her and make her behave differently, remember that children express their feelings in all sorts of ways, some of which might not be attractive. Talk with her about what you are observing and help her develop other options for responding to her sibling's depression.

How to Help

In order to help your nondepressed child through her sibling's depression, there are some simple things you can do. First, as with your depressed child, the more each family member understands about depression, the easier its effects will be on the siblings. Help them understand that all of their feelings are normal and not bad. Spend some one-on-one time with your nondepressed child. Just a little quality time that she doesn't have to share with anyone else will tremendously reduce her feelings of being left out.

Last, think of how protective you want to be with your depressed child. Even with your nondepressed child, you may find yourself being stricter, more protective, and more anxious. You also know that depression can be hereditary, so you will be increasingly worried about your nondepressed child. It's only natural that you worry about this child getting depressed. You automatically have that feeling that you can keep her immune from depression, but you can't. You'll be better off accepting that and letting her be a kid.

Extended Family

Some people are fortunate to have a large, extended family. However, with extra family members comes the dilemma of who needs to know about your child's depression and how much information should be shared.

Who Needs to Know?

The best way to answer this question is by actually asking yourself why someone needs to know about your child's depression at all. While that might sound impolite, think about your child and how the news of his depression will be heard. If Grandma is especially nosy and has a tendency to enjoy gossip, she might unconsciously share this information with people you or your child would rather not have know.

Unfortunately, even though they are our relatives, some people enjoy others' misery, and they will tell anyone who is in earshot the latest news. Other family members may consider themselves to be experts on just about everything and will feel compelled to tell you how to handle your child's depression. Still others are uneducated about mental illness and may interact with your child very differently if they know about his depression.

Tell only the family members who are capable of respecting your child's confidentiality and who have regular contact with your child. They may be invaluable in helping you with your child.

Alert!

Your child's confidentiality should be held sacred. If your child does not wish to have his condition shared, respect his privacy. Explain that some people will have to know, while the decision to tell others is purely voluntary. Discuss with him before you tell anyone, and name the family members you will be talking to.

How Much Information Should Be Provided?

There's a fine line between sharing enough information and too much. Again, use your best judgment. If Grandma babysits for your child each day, she definitely needs to know about your child's medication, for example. But she doesn't necessarily need to know what he is talking to his therapist about in counseling. If your child wants to discuss some aspect of his treatment, while it might make you uncomfortable, let him talk. Children will usually be pretty discreet about what they share in terms of their depression.

Family Therapy

When a family member has an illness, they can quickly become known as what is called the *identified* patient. This means that whatever else is going on within the family, the sick member often acts out the family's problems. Unfairly, the depressed child gets pointed out and even blamed for the family's troubles. This is dangerous and family therapy is an excellent way to address the entire family's issues.

Who Has to Attend?

Family therapists prefer the entire immediate family to participate in at least the initial family sessions. After a few appointments, problems can be pinpointed, and if there are issues between certain family members, the therapy can take different directions. For example, if a formerly very close sibling bond is being threatened by your child's depression, the therapist might meet with the siblings a few times to help resolve those feelings. If parenting issues are a problem, the counselor might ask to see the parents.

 Essential

There is no hard and fast rule as to how long family therapy should last. How much family therapy is needed will depend on several factors: the severity of the child's depression, the ages and developmental stages of the children, and the issues within the family. Time and financial resources must be considered, too.

The most ideal situation is for the family sessions to be flexible and meet all of the needs of not only the depressed child but also the other family members.

What Will Happen in Family Therapy?

The first thing a family therapist will do is to get a good, thorough history about your child and the family. He will want to spend some time just getting to know the members and making everyone comfortable. With the family's input, he will help develop some goals for the therapy.

Each family member will be given the opportunity to talk and to be heard. Respect for one another's feelings and opinions will be encouraged.

Periodically, the therapist will ask the family to reassess their goals and change or modify them as necessary. If the therapy is successful, the tension within the family should decrease, empathy among its members will increase, and your child's depression will be reduced.

Family distress is almost always a by-product of a child's depression. The ensuing problems that emerge can either tear a family apart or bring them closer. The most effective treatment for your child will consider each family member's needs and will help improve how the family operates as a unit. While your child's depression is unsettling, it can have a positive impact on your family if you take charge and become proactive.

CHAPTER 17

Parenting the Depressed Child

Your parenting style ought to be the same despite having a child who is depressed, but often this is not the case. Parenting is not inherent in our personalities; it's a skill that is learned through trial and error. Hopefully you learn from the mistakes you make as a parent so that you do things differently in the future. This chapter is a primer on healthy parenting that can be useful for helping your depressed child as well as learning good parenting techniques that might prevent depression.

Avoiding the "Poor, Pitiful Me" Syndrome

How do children learn to get what they want? They become master manipulators! Early on, she discovers that with just a tiny smile, or the turning down of her lower lip, you melt. If she asks just right, or even asks enough times, you give in! See how simple it is? It's no wonder that as she ages she refines this skill such that she can maneuver with perfection and you never know what hit you!

While you are a softie when it comes to your child and her antics, you are even more vulnerable to manipulation when your child is ill. Think back to the last time your child was home sick from school. Chances are whatever she asked for you brought it to her. You knew she wasn't feeling that bad, but she looked so sad and miserable that you couldn't deny her.

When your child is depressed, you are going to experience the same emotions just like you would if she were physically ill. No parent wants her child to feel bad or to experience discomfort. You realize that illness is unavoidable, but that doesn't stop you from wanting to lessen your child's pain.

Essential

Sometimes there's a fine line between manipulative gestures and a child who has a true request. If your child is making uncharacteristic requests, he may be trying to tell you something important. It's up to you to decipher whether he is trying to communicate with you about his needs or if he is trying to cash in on your sympathy.

It's important not to allow your child to fall into the "poor, pitiful me" syndrome. This happens when a child realizes that she can invoke sympathy by pretending to be sad, uncomfortable, and needy. Of course, these are real symptoms of a child with depression, so you will need to consider how much of her behavior is real and whether she is actually using her illness to her advantage.

Signs of Manipulation

Consider how your child behaved when he wasn't depressed. With the depression, his behavior is bound to change. What you should look for is behavior that you find yourself giving in to despite your better judgment. This doesn't make you a bad parent, only a bit of a sucker! And your child knows it!

If your child is trying to get out of her chores, her homework, and other important tasks because she doesn't feel like it, she's using her depression. If she makes excuses for her behavior by using the depression card, she's manipulating. If she says, "If you'd only buy me a. . . .," she's trying to wrap you right around her finger.

 *Fact*

Separate your child from the depression. Your child is the same kid that he always was, but now there's a problem that needs to be addressed. Letting him off easy may send the message that he is weak and inadequate. Don't let his depression become a crutch that can hurt his self-confidence.

How to Respond

It's perfectly normal to want to grant your child's every wish, but it isn't realistic. When your child is depressed, you don't need to give in any more than you did before the depression hit.

There's no need to respond to your child by fussing or debating why she wants something. Instead, listen to her requests and ask yourself three questions. First, is she trying to get out of a responsibility or does she want you to buy her something simply because she feels bad? Second, will giving in to her actually help her or will it be a temporary fix? Third, are you encouraging her manipulative behavior?

Giving in is fine to a certain degree. Only you can determine where to draw the line for your child. If you do decide to give in, let your child know that it will not become a pattern and that she still has responsibilities even with her depression. Let her know that the new outfit she is begging for because it will make her feel better is not going to cure the problem, whether it's depression or something else. While she may enjoy the way she feels when she wears it, the depression will still be there. Giving in too much encourages the behavior to continue.

Let your child know that having depression calls for action, not helplessness. She can overcome her depression, but it isn't fair to use it to get attention. Just like any other illness, it will have to be addressed but it shouldn't become her identity.

Developing Trust

Having an open, honest relationship with your child creates a safe place for your child to share her thoughts, feelings, and opinions. When she feels respected, she will respect others. Trust is the cornerstone of good relationships, and without it your job as a parent is nearly impossible.

Alert!

Don't assume that because your child has secrets she doesn't trust you. It's healthy for a child and parent to have some boundaries and privacy. If you sense that her secret could be something that could harm her, encourage her to "spill." Otherwise, leave her alone and respect her privacy.

When a child is feeling the symptoms of depression, she can hide them pretty well if she thinks it might upset you to hear about them. No matter what might be wrong with your child, she needs to feel she can come home and lay it all on the line. Her level of trust in you is what will determine if she does indeed share with you her current situation.

Responding to Your Child

If you go home and tell your mother that you have done something you shouldn't have, how will she react? Ask your child that question and she will be able to answer with a pretty accurate prediction of how you'll respond. Her answer will tell you a lot about her perception of her relationship with you.

If she says, "Oh, she won't be happy about that. She would kill me," and she is not being dramatic, you may have some gaps in the trust department. If she senses that you will laugh at her, judge her, be angry, or overreact, she is apt to keep bad news to herself. Wouldn't you if you were in her position? Telling her that she can tell you anything and then reacting to her news in negative ways teaches her that you can't be trusted and that your responses will be, at best, unpredictable.

Remember to hold your tongue and watch your facial expressions. Don't give her the impression that you don't take her seriously. Withhold judgment until she has told you everything. If you are angry, take a few deep breaths and choose your words carefully. You may even ask for a few minutes alone so you can gather your thoughts. This will keep you from saying or doing something you might regret later. Your response now could determine whether she comes to you the next time she has a problem.

Practice What You Preach

If you expect your child to be honest with you, be honest with her. That doesn't mean you have to tell her things that are not age appropriate or for adults only. But if she asks you a question, you need to answer as honestly as possible. If you expect dependability, be reliable yourself. If you make a promise, keep it.

When you tell your child that if she comes home and tells you what she has done she won't get into trouble, mean it. A child needs to know what to expect and that you mean what you say. This is the best way to establish trust.

If you tell her that your love is unconditional, mean it. It will be more meaningful when she sees that your behavior and reactions match your words.

Effective Discipline

One of the most difficult tasks of parenting is deciding how you will discipline your child. Should you be permissive or rule with an iron fist? How do you mete out punishment? Is it wrong to spank? The questions can go on and on, with the answers varying greatly. Whatever method you choose to use, if it is going to be effective, it needs to be consistent and fair. Think of it as a means for teaching a child how to function within a unit and, later as an adult, in the world at large. Rules provide structure and expectations for how to behave. Rules exist for a reason and have a purpose.

Discipline teaches your child right from wrong—what to do and what not to do. This is why it bears repeating again. It is also important to separate the behavior from the child. Just like your child is not his depression, your child is not his behavior. Like the rest of us, he learns through the very act of behaving and, unfortunately, misbehaving! Children have to experience life, the good and the bad, if they are to grow and achieve their maximum potential.

Making Rules

How many rules are appropriate for your child? That depends on your child's age, developmental stage, and specific needs or problems. Some children need a lot of rules and others don't require as many. But all children need some rules.

Alert!

Don't develop and use discipline to mold your child into something you think he should be. Rules are not made to change a child's basic temperament and personality. Your goal for discipline should be to help create structure, limits, and skills for living for your child.

Rules should be clear and basic. The rules you create do not need to be negotiable at first. You have to start somewhere. Set a few rules first and see if they are applicable to your child. If not, change them or set some new rules. Explain the rules to your child and that you expect those rules to be followed.

In terms of your expectations for your child, set reasonable ones. What you may find reasonable may not be as practical as you think. A depressed child may not be able to meet as high of expectations as you would prefer, so you may have to lower them for a little while. As the depression decreases, you can raise your expectations gradually to keep up with your child's needs and abilities.

Rules are not supposed to be made to control your child's every move. Not every behavior or situation needs a rule to be followed. Sometimes the best way to teach discipline is to create rules that require your child to use her head. She needs to learn to think for herself and anticipate the consequences of her actions. Too many rules will prohibit her from having to do this.

 **Question?**

What if my child thinks a rule is unfair?
If you want to debate a rule with your child, go ahead. What usually results is that you end up changing the rule or forgoing it altogether. When in doubt, remember this: "No" is a complete sentence. Trying to convince your child that a rule is correct diminishes its importance.

Keep the rules consistent. As long as they are effective, keep them. When your child ages, changes, or circumstances warrant it, then you can change or alter the rules. Children need to know what it is they can and cannot do. This gives them structure, limits, and some sense of predictability.

Types of Punishment

There are many ways to punish a child, and one method will not fit every rule and every child's age. For a young child, ignoring a behavior can often have a quick effect. If a child does something and no one reinforces her behavior, she is apt to stop doing it. For some children, any attention is better than no attention at all, so even negative attention is attractive to this sort of child.

Time-outs are a popular method of punishment. Typically, this works best for children under the age of about six. For toddlers, a minute for every year of his age is appropriate. Time-out needs to be in a place where there is no attention or anything for him to do. It's not too punishing if you send your child to her room where she has access to all of her toys or a television. While your child is being punished, resist the urge to interact with him. This is not the time to argue with him about what he has done. What you are trying to do is get him to think about what he has done, not how to talk you out of the punishment!

The giving or withholding of tokens is another great way to work with younger children. For a behavior you wish to change, rewarding him with a token (such as a sticker on a calendar or a marble that gets placed in a jar) reminds him that he did well.

 **Fact**

Not every behavior deserves rewarding! Pick several things you'd like to see your child change and do. Reward these when he is successful. Don't let your child fall into the trap of thinking that he should be given a prize or privilege any time he does well or follows a rule.

Once he earns a set amount of tokens, he can trade them in for a toy or a privilege. What you have to remember is that the tokens and prizes need to fit the behavior. For example, remembering to brush his teeth each day is a smaller reward behavior, while finishing his homework each night and turning it in might warrant a bigger reward.

Loss of privileges and grounding work better with older children and teenagers. The key is in telling your child ahead of time what the rules are and what the consequences will be if the rule is broken. What you are teaching him is that he has a choice. He can either misbehave or do what he has been told. He will then know exactly what the consequences will be if he decides to misbehave, but he is being allowed to make a choice. This is an excellent way to teach him that he has control over his actions by choice. He will have to think for himself, make a choice, and find out whether the consequences were worth it.

Enforcing Rules and Consequences

The first rule of thumb when enforcing discipline is to refrain from acting when you are angry if you can help it. Responding under extreme emotion usually results in overreaction. Even the simplest rule infraction will seem like a major crime, and the focus will be on your behavior, not on your child's misdeed. Staying calm will also help you avoid saying things you shouldn't and that you will have to explain later.

You and your spouse need to present a united front. You may not agree on a rule or even the way it will be reinforced, but your child does not need to know that. As far as she is concerned, she needs to believe that the two of you have discussed discipline and that you back one another up. This will keep her from playing sides and escaping responsibility.

If at all possible, try not to punish a child in public. There is no reason to humiliate her or embarrass her. Punishment is not designed to make a child feel bad about herself. It is used to correct and reinforce behavior. Again, the child is not the behavior.

Last, it's always a great idea to say thank you when your child behaves favorably. Too often it's her bad behavior that gets attention. Rewarding good behavior lets her know how great she is and that you are proud of her.

🏠 Essential

Don't miss the opportunity to apologize for your behavior when necessary. You are not expected to be perfect, but when you make a mistake, take responsibility. Showing that you are willing to be accountable for your behavior is an important lesson that your child can learn by observing you behaving in an honorable way.

Knowing When to Back Off

This whole book has been about you being involved with your child's depression—it's diagnosis, treatment, and other issues related to it. You have been encouraged to be proactive and educated about your child. However, believe it or not, there are times when you need to back off.

Too Many Rules

Not every behavior is punishable. Kids are going to do silly things, hurtful things, and just plain bad things. It's hard to always know when you should correct a child and when you should just let it go. Ask yourself, "How much will this matter a year from now?" For example, if your son cheats on his spelling test because he says he panicked, this is punishable behavior. If your daughter was late for school and left her wet towels on the bathroom floor when she usually puts them in the hamper, you can let it go.

Too many rules create a very rigid, tense atmosphere. A child, depressed or not, wants to please her parents. When there are too many rules, she is bound to have more opportunities to get into trouble. When she perceives that her worth is based on her ability to follow all of the rules, she can easily fall into depression.

Pick Your Battles

Remember that you are supposed to be able to separate the behavior from your child. Back off when you are angry and being hurtful. When you are upset, as is normal you are prone to say things you don't mean. Again, you are more likely to hurt the child and take the focus off of the behavior.

Pick your battles. Decide what really matters and focus on that. And let the rest go. Preparing your child to be the very best she can be is what matters. What she will remember is that you loved her unconditionally, and that you didn't let the little things get in the way. She'll also be prepared to use her own head and make good choices.

Keep Perspective in the Midst of Chaos

A parent once said that being a parent was like being in the vortex of a tornado. The wind is twirling and you are trying to stop everything from being caught up in it. Sometimes, you can reach out and reduce some of the chaos, but for the most part you have little control.

This metaphor is correct. In today's world, parents are under even more pressure than ever before. You are bombarded with work, school, family, finances, housework, and activities. Just when you think you've got it all under control, something happens and your world explodes. When you have a child who is depressed, you want to make sure he is protected from anything that might make him worse, but you can't. Keeping your perspective will enable you to do what is best for your child.

Take the Pressure Off

When the pressure gets to be too much, give yourself and your child a break. Find a way to tune out the world for a few minutes. Taking time out will save both of you from making a decision or saying something you will regret.

Also, try to keep your child's schedule and yours, too, as predictable and dependable as possible. When a child is depressed, stability is a crucial factor in his recovery. Don't make any sudden, major changes in your routine. Keep situations that may be overwhelming or confusing for your child to a minimum.

You may think your depressed child shouldn't see you losing it for fear he will feel responsible and guilty. While you don't want to burden your child with your troubles, it's actually a good thing for him to see that you are not perfect, but that you do know how to cope.

Spend quality time with your child. It doesn't have to be long, just time that is focused only on your child. Kids talk at the strangest times, so make yourself available to listen. You don't want to miss an opportunity to hear what he has to say and how he is feeling. Little moments with your child can teach you a lot.

Don't Lose Your Funny Bone!

It's hard to maintain your sense of humor when your child is depressed and you feel that your life is falling apart. If you think you can survive all of this without your sense of humor, you are wrong! Finding the humor in any situation is a very effective way to reduce stress and help you not take yourself so seriously.

Your child's recovery from depression is going to be gradual, and possibly even slow. You may be spending so much time wishing he was better now that you miss the opportunities for laughter. As the saying goes, laughter is a great medicine. It just so happens that it's good for you and for your child!

Encourage Self-reliance

Self-reliance is one of the most important skills you will ever impart to your child. With self-esteem and the feeling that she is competent, she can go anywhere and do just about anything. Helping your depressed child understand that she has the ability to take care of herself is a powerful tool for her recovery.

Accentuate the Positives

Help your child find the positives about herself. It might be a talent for dancing, or perhaps she is a good friend. Whatever it is that she enjoys and does well, encourage it. Depression has a way of making her feel completely inadequate, so forcing her to find the positives may be difficult but not impossible. Try finding opportunities for her to embrace her positive attributes and talents. This is called scheduling positive events.

Question?

Isn't scheduling positive events a bit superficial?
It may sound like it, but it isn't. What you are doing is trying to find things that will make your child feel special and good about herself. You are merely placing her in the right spot at the right time to experience good things.

When something good happens to your child, celebrate it. You don't have to have a party, but at this time she needs special recognition. Take her out for ice cream or buy her a treat. Take her to dinner at her favorite restaurant. Remind her that she made that success happen, and that she can do it again and again.

Take Off Your Armor

There is no parent in the world that can protect his child from everything that is hurtful, bad, and dangerous. Being a parent is a huge responsibility, but your child is going to experience trouble. A depressed child makes you want to be even more protective.

When you overprotect your child, you undermine her self-reliance. Part of learning about who she is includes thinking for herself, making choices, and suffering the consequences. You aren't going to be able to live with her forever. Letting her live her life, complete with the bad parts, is the best way to build self-reliance.

Parenting may be the most underappreciated, difficult job in the world. When your child is depressed, you may feel extra pressure to do the parenting thing more perfectly than before. The most helpful thing you can do, however, is to resist making your child feel worse because of your own concerns about her depression. Get her help, be supportive of her treatment, and do whatever you can to make her feel better. But in the end, realize she is a child after all, and your parenting needs to offer her as normal a life as possible despite her depression.

Chapter 18

At-risk Parents and Depression

When a child is depressed, he has insecurities about his condition and his future. To make matters worse, if there are other problems within the family, these can have an effect on him as well. Parents who are at risk for certain mental illnesses and other problems unwittingly put added pressure on a child with depression, or they can cause a typically stable child to become depressed. These parental problems can make the parent unavailable to the child, and for a child with depression, this can lead to feelings of extraordinary loneliness.

Depression

When one or more parents are depressed in a family, the likelihood that a child will develop depression jumps to 40 to 70 percent. While this does not mean that the child is destined to become depressed if his parent also has the disorder, there is a greater likelihood that this mental illness can be passed on. As learned earlier, depression can be hereditary, and that puts a child with a depressed parent at risk.

Learned Depression

Children are capable of learning and catching our moods. As they experience life events with their parents and observe how they react, they naturally assume that whatever it is the parents are doing must be correct. Although depression can be inherited, children can also

learn to become depressed. Unfortunately, not everything you do in response to life's stresses and problems are healthy ways of coping. The more of these maladjusted skills kids learn, the more they are at risk for depression.

 **Fact**

> A Colorado University study found that when a mother's depression lifted after three months of treatment and medication, her child's risk of being depressed or developing other psychiatric disturbances dropped by 11 percent. This speaks to the need for a parent to get early intervention.

If a parent is not taking care of his own depression, a child will often take on the depressed parent's characteristics. For example, if a parent is becoming increasingly negative and hopeless, his child might begin to exhibit the same behaviors. Over time, these characteristics become more ingrained, and the child develops depression. It is harder to treat this kind of depression when these methods of coping have been learned at a very young age. This is another good reason for early intervention and treatment of depression.

Unclear Expectations

When a child has unclear expectations as to how he is supposed to behave or how he is supposed to interact in a family unit, he becomes insecure or uncertain. It's as if the rules change from minute to minute and no one knows how the family is supposed to operate, including the parents. Rules may be made then broken, forgotten, or changed. Trying to dodge the problems caused by such family chaos again puts an extra strain on a child and can cause depression.

Depression's Influence on the Ability to Parent

When a parent is depressed, there is often a decreased ability to take care of a child in the most appropriate manner. For example, if a mother is suffering from depression, she might be so busy focusing on her own problems that her child's needs get neglected or ignored. Most often, this is not something the mother chooses to do, but rather this is a sort of side effect of her own depression.

If you are depressed and are having trouble parenting your child, don't be so hard on yourself. Find several areas that concern you about your abilities at this time and focus only on those. As you begin to feel better, you can improve other areas. Some good parenting is better than none at all.

Unavailability

Depressed parents are often much more isolated and make themselves less available to everyone, including their children. They are less involved in their child's life and activities, and as a result, they are not involved in their child's inner psychological life. Children of this type of parent report feeling incredibly lonely at home.

 **Essential**

If you are suffering from depression, make it a point to spend some quality time with your child. As little as fifteen minutes a day is enough to make your child feel important and loved. It also increases the bonding between the two of you.

In these cases, it is not abnormal to see children doing tasks around the house that are normally reserved for adults, such as cooking dinner, doing laundry, and cleaning the house rather than spending their time just being kids. Although there is nothing wrong with children knowing how to do these tasks, parents with depression unknowingly put a child in the position of being the parent.

If this is something you are guilty of doing, encourage your child to participate in more "kid" activities rather than those of an adult. Some tasks can be left undone if it means you have more time with your child. Never has a child said they would prefer a clean house and home-cooked meal to spending time with his parent!

The Child Treating the Parent's Depression

Children have a natural tendency to want to please a parent, so when a parent is depressed, the child wants to make her well. A child will try to make good grades and excel at many activities in order to try to make her mother feel better, even though there is no direct correlation between her activities and her mother's depression.

 **Fact**

Parents often say they find it sweet that their child is trying to take care of them. If you find that your child is parenting you, find the healthy balance between a child who is being caring and one that is carrying too much adult responsibility. Thank your child for her involvement, but encourage her to use her energies elsewhere.

What the child is trying to do is to decrease her mother's unhappiness. She believes that if she is good enough, her mother's depression will be cured. Of course this is not the case. As she discovers that she really cannot make her mother happy, what often ends up happening is that the child will become depressed, too.

Drug and Alcohol Abuse

The abuse of drugs and alcohol raises a child's risk for depression in several ways. If a parent is abusing a substance, his personality is likely to become unpredictable and, at times, irrational. A child with a substance-abusing parent cannot count on him to behave consistently, or even to react to the same situation in a similar way. When a child feels his world is unpredictable, he is going to lack stability and security, important factors in the fight against depression.

Essential

If you have alcohol in the home and are not abusing it, do not lie about it. Be sure you educate your child about alcohol's effects and risks. A child who is exposed to alcohol in a healthy manner is less likely to use it in an unhealthy manner.

Unfortunately, parents with substance abuse problems are more likely to be verbally or emotionally abusive. This type of parent usually feels bad about himself, and under the influence of drugs or alcohol he will project those feelings onto his child. However, the child does not understand this and begins to think that she is bad and causing her parent to abuse substances. This type of child will avoid the parent who is abusing substances in order to stay out of his way and not create any trouble.

Medicating with Drugs and Alcohol

Another way that a parent with substance abuse can create depression for a child is best described in the saying, "Do as I say, not as I do." Much of the substance abuse today is found among adults who are trying to medicate other issues. For example, if a parent is depressed, stressed, or anxious, he may have a few drinks in order to calm himself down. He believes that this is an easy and quick fix to his problems, and before he knows it, his substance use becomes habitual. A child observes this behavior and begins to believe that this is an acceptable method for handling difficult times.

Competing with Alcohol and Drugs

Drugs and alcohol are powerful mistresses. Abusing these substances very often causes marital discord and even divorce. If this problem causes that much trouble among adults, imagine what a powerful competitor it is for a child! While a parent might say that he is not abusing substances in front of his child, the effects are nevertheless the

y other activity that becomes habitual, such as work
and alcohol use can make a parent unavailable both
d emotionally. It is difficult to be a good parent when one
with something that takes all this time and energy.

as children try to alleviate a parent's depression, children will
ry to fix their parents' alcohol and drug abuse. A child might
de alcohol or pour it down the drain rather than see his father use
it. What he doesn't realize is that his father can go and buy more, and
that this is a futile attempt. The more he tries to fix his parent's problem, the quicker he becomes at risk for depression.

Essential

Be honest with your child about your own struggles with depression
and substance use. You are not telling her so that she can watch out
for you; you are telling her so that she will reach out and ask for help
rather than trying substances to medicate her problems.

Divorce

When a couple is headed for divorce, the problems that this causes
create havoc within a family. Tempers are out of control, and emotions are running wild. There are all sorts of issues at play: who's
going to stay in the house, financial matters, who will have the children. The adults' world is falling apart, but the child can also be
severely impacted.

Children are very intuitive and can pick up on the stress and tension within the marriage. As they realize that their parents are divorcing, they are often left to take care of themselves. All of a sudden, they
are solely responsible for completing their homework, taking care of
their chores, and doing other things that routinely used to require
a parent's participation. Once again, they are at risk for becoming
mini-parents and depressed.

Question?

How much do we tell our child about our divorce without unnecessarily burdening her?

Tell enough to alleviate her anxiety about the divorce. Keep what you share at an age-appropriate level. She does not need to know everything. Keep a boundary between what are adult-only issues and what are family issues.

What about Me?

Children become quite concerned about what will happen to them. It is not uncommon for a child to ask, "Where am I going to live? What's going to happen to me?" In other words, children have a need to know what their future holds and how the divorce will change their lives.

In order to minimize the effects of divorce on your child, it is important for the two of you to sit your child down and discuss the fact that you are divorcing. It needs to be made clear that the child is not at fault in any way. While this may sound obvious to you, many children believe that they have somehow caused marital trouble and that the divorce is their fault.

It is also important to explain to the children living arrangements, as well as where they will be living. They need to be reassured that both parents love them, support them, and that you are both going to work very hard to see that their lives remain as normal as possible.

Staying Involved

Parents who are divorcing need to stay involved in the day-to-day lives of their children. If possible, share the parenting duties as equally as possible so that your divorce will have the least amount of stress on the child. An open line of communication needs to be available, and each parent needs to be cooperative with the other. A child

arents acting in a mature fashion will understand
d things do happen within the family, it does not
tely tear the family apart.

Alert!

Although you may be strongly tempted to do it, never tell your child
that it is your spouse's fault that you are divorcing. While you think you
are being honest with him, it places the child in the awkward position
of having to be mad at one parent while protecting the other.

Make sure that your child observes the two of you as a united
front. Even if you and your spouse disagree about the parenting of
your child, your child does not need to know. Distress and emotional
discomfort can be greatly alleviated if she believes that the two if you
are working together to make this process smooth. This also lets your
child know that she continues to be your first priority.

Mourning the Loss

From a child's perspective, a divorce often represents the loss of
a parent. If the father has left the home and is setting up house elsewhere, the child may grieve his absence. It is important for parents to
set aside their feelings about one another so that they can help their
child grieve healthfully and thoroughly.

Marital Discord

Just like a divorce can have devastating effects on a child, so can
marital conflict. If your home is constantly filled with tension and
disagreement, your child may be at a higher risk for depression. One
reason for this is that parents get so caught up in their arguments that
the children's reactions and feelings get neglected. Unfortunately,
sometimes the focus of the argument is on the child and how to

parent him. If a child is aware of this and thinks he is to blame for some reason, he will begin to feel guilty and angry and ultimately develop symptoms of depression.

Minimizing the Damage

To minimize the effect that your conflicts have on your child, do not pretend that you and your spouse never have fights. Not only is this unreasonable and silly, but it is also demeaning to your child. Children are not stupid, and they understand that conflict is occurring within their home. It's also perfectly acceptable to have arguments, and a child can learn how to handle his own conflict by observing how his parents behave.

Not all disagreements have to be voiced in front of your child, however. Normal, run-of-the-mill spats are appropriate to have when the children are present. In matters that are more serious or involve more adult material, help your child understand that you will be having that discussion time behind closed doors. Explain to him that there is nothing to worry about but that these conversations are for the grownups.

Parental History of Abuse

By now you have learned that a child develops his sense of trust in the world from the early relationships that he has with his mother and father. If these relationships were positive, nurturing, and close, then he is at less risk for depression. However, if that bond does not develop, a child has problems internalizing a sense of security and safety.

If you have a history of physical or sexual abuse, your early relationships were probably not very healthy. You learned to view the world as a scary and distrustful place.

Your sense of caution and unpredictability about other people has probably continued throughout the years. You may find yourself feeling damaged, unlovable, and unworthy. In these early developmental stages, these feelings probably made you vulnerable to depression.

Alert!

If you have a history of abuse, get help now! The damage caused by abuse is devastating and has far-reaching effects. Even though you may think the abuse didn't affect you, there is nothing further from the truth. You may be so used to feeling a certain way that you don't realize you are depressed.

Projecting Your Feelings onto Your Child

There is no specific way to handle this type of abusive history. However, you need to be aware that the feelings you developed may be projected onto your children. You may have trouble forming a relationship with them simply because you did not learn to do so as a child.

The problem is that children do not understand the fact that you have problems stemming from your past. It is not their job to fix that, but they want to try anyway. It is not possible for a child to make you feel loved all by himself.

As a child begins to realize that you are not happy and that he is unable to help you, he begins to see himself through the same eyes in which you see yourself. The best thing that you can do is to get professional help to understand how your current relationships have been affected by your past and how to avoid passing on these unhealthy patterns.

Toxic Parenting

From the moment you are born, you get messages about who you are and how you should function in the world. Again, the bonds formed early with a child's primary attachment figures have a tremendous influence on how she will form relationships with others. As she develops, she forms her identity from the messages she gets from her parents and other influential people in her life. If these messages are frequently negative, her self-image begins to form in a different way. She feels unlovable, unworthy, and unimportant.

There are several types of toxic parenting. This term suggests that when a parent disciplines or interacts with her child, or if the parenting is regularly negative and unpleasant, it does not serve to encourage growth but rather is toxic or damaging.

 Essential

> Like it or not, most people have been exposed to toxic parenting by their parents. And as a result, you will likely expose your children to it. This doesn't make you a bad parent, just a normal one who makes mistakes. The point here is to reduce the negative effects of your parenting and increase the positive ones!

Rigid Bonds

You may have heard that a family can't be too close. This is simply not true. There is a distinct and important difference between a close family and an abnormally rigid family. When the bonds of the family are so tight that they do not allow for relationships outside the family, or when the bonds foster too much dependency, this is known as enmeshment. Rather than encouraging a child to jump out into the world and experience it, this type of family communicates to the child that the world is not a welcome, safe place. Sometimes these boundaries are so rigid and impermeable that relationships with extended family members can't even develop.

Absence of Emotional Expression

One type of toxic parenting is a family's inability to express emotion. This is a family where parents have not learned to express their own emotions or it was unacceptable to do so as children. It is so uncomfortable for them to do this as an adult that it is not surprising that they cannot encourage their children to express feelings. As a result, the child is forced to keep her feelings to herself. Ultimately, she cannot find a way to alleviate the discomfort she is feeling, and depression occurs.

Revolving Limits

Another type of toxic parenting is poor consistency in setting limits. You've heard of the need for discipline to be stable, consistent, and fair. When the rules are constantly changing, unpredictability sets in.

Alert!

Some parents allow themselves to be bullied by their children so that the rules do not have to be followed. Don't fall for this! Even though they whine and complain, children report that they really do prefer to have rules and structure so that they know exactly what is expected of them.

When there is no order within the family, a child loses the ability to behave appropriately. The best she can do is to respond to whatever the rule is at the time.

Taking Criticism Too Far

While it is important to point out to their children the behaviors that are unacceptable, toxic parenting occurs when there is too much criticism. Often, parents get caught up in picking out all of their child's faults rather than pointing out his strengths and talents. Because parents want to make sure that their children behave and fit in with their peers, the potential for becoming overly critical is a very real possibility.

The more negative messages a child receives about herself, the more at risk she becomes for depression. This is why it's important to separate the behavior from the child when you are trying to discipline her.

Question?

Being Too Lenient

Just as being overly negative with a child can create depression, overindulging your child is also a form of toxic parenting. Most parents want to get their children everything that they wish for and to not deny them anything. However, when a child is overindulged, she begins to believe that this is how the world should treat her as well. As she begins to discover that she cannot always have her way, this can be upsetting and confusing to her. The best way to overcome this is by teaching her that while she is deserving of all the good things in life, there are limits, and she will have to work for some of the things that she wants.

Over-the-line Teasing

Although family members are prone to tease one another, when the teasing becomes mean and overly critical, it is toxic. Many parents grew up in a family where teasing was as natural as breathing. They will say, "My brothers teased me all the time and I've turned out fine." This does not mean it was necessarily a good thing. Good-natured ribbing amongst family members is a healthy way to bond and form close relationships. However, when the teasing becomes too personal and cruel, a child begins to feel unsafe, even in her own family. A child that receives this sort of teasing is likely to become a bully herself.

Essential

Parents often say they want their child to have a thick skin so that other's teasing won't bother him. Having a thick skin means a child doesn't take himself so seriously and that he can laugh at himself. But bullying should not be tolerated at all.

Again, the negative messages that he receives about himself put him at risk for depression. Teasing should be gentle comments about a child's behavior, habits, or characteristics. It should never be aimed at demeaning a child or making him feel self-conscious.

Overprotectiveness

There is nothing wrong with wanting to protect your child from all of the evils in the world. You know, however, it is not possible to do this. Parents often try to excuse their overprotectiveness by insisting that they are merely watching out for their children.

Overprotectiveness becomes toxic when a child is sheltered so much that when she is out in the world, she has no idea of how to behave or interact. This is the child who typically becomes rebellious, and she may even begin to lie about her whereabouts so that she can do some of the things she wants.

Being so overprotective that a child cannot make some mistakes or experience life sets a child up for depression as she becomes more and more angry or resentful toward you.

Avoidance

In contrast to the overprotective parent, toxic parenting can also take the form of avoiding a child. When a child has problems such as depression, it is not unusual for even the best parent to wish to avoid the unpleasantness. In addition, most parents cannot stand to see their beloved children in pain. Often, the parent is so uncomfortable about what is happening that he simply does not know what to do. This type of extreme avoidance is more of a defense against a parent's own insecurities and concerns. However, a child does not always understand this, therefore, she feels left out and ignored. These feelings ultimately result in a child who thinks that she is being a bother or that no one wants her around. Obviously, depression is not far behind.

Rules, Rules, and More Rules

Rules are important and there's no getting around that fact. Too many rules, however, create a jail-like atmosphere in your home. Part of the child's healthy development lies in his ability to make some choices and to make mistakes. Many of life's lessons are learned this way. When there are too many rules, a child will either rebel or he does not learn how to handle himself in situations that are troublesome. There is so much structure that he does not have to use his head and merely operates as a robot.

Toxic parenting is something that most parents are guilty of at one time or another. The reason is because no one is perfect, and you operate as a result of how you grew up. However, too much toxic parenting can result in a child who feels unacceptable, inadequate, and unprepared to face the world. The resulting depressive symptoms can be devastating.

As an adult, you bring to your family the baggage that you had from your childhood. In addition, you cannot always correct or fix every problem that you may have. What's important to understand is that your history and your problems can have an effect on your children as well as the possibility that he might develop depression. Working to minimize the impact of these issues is the most effective way to guard against that.

CHAPTER 19

School

Because most cases of depression last longer than a couple of months, a child's depression can affect an entire school year. This means that his grades, his ability to learn, his relationship with his peers, and his extracurricular activities are going to be influenced by the depression. Deciding how the school portion of your child's life will be handled will have to be addressed if your child's treatment is to be successful.

Should the School Know?

Actually, the time that a child spends in school is longer than the time he spends with you. Therefore, if he is experiencing depression, it only seems reasonable that the school needs to be in the loop. Just how much information you want to share is another issue. Although teachers and other school professionals have had classes about childhood development and other problems, their education about mood disorders and how these problems can affect academic performance has been general at best.

Who's Who

Consider your child's school professionals as a team. Of course, there are the teachers who are the most frequent point of contact for your child. In early childhood education, this is the one individual who spends the

majority of her day with your child. Later, there may be more than one teacher involved.

Guidance counselors are also members of the school's team. Some schools do not have a guidance counselor on duty full time, so she might not be very available to your child if he needs help. As a rule, these individuals have usually had only a couple of classes in psychology. Little of that class time was spent learning about childhood mood disorders. Still, they are often a good source of information for a parent. Guidance counselors can also help teachers and other school professionals understand what your child is experiencing. They are a good liaison between the staff and the family.

Essential

Find out who on the school's team will be interacting with your child most of the time—a teacher, the homeroom teacher, the coach. These are the people who will most likely be able to provide you with information about how your child's depression is affecting him at school.

Some schools provide school psychologists, but in most school systems they are typically few and far between. Often one school psychologist might serve a few schools or many in a school district. Obviously, this means her time is quite limited and it may take a while before she is able to see your child.

The school psychologist is often relegated to mostly performing school testing and helping place your child in the most appropriate academic setting for his needs. However, if you observe your child having trouble learning or you suspect your child is having significant difficulties, a school psychologist is the perfect professional to turn to for evaluation, diagnosis, and a treatment plan. She can also help you learn how to help your child at home.

What to Tell

So what information do you provide the school about your child's depression? The best way to determine this is to ask your child's treating professional. Often, this individual will know how severe your child's depression is and how it manifests itself at school. For example, if a child with depression is frequently and easily agitated or frustrated, this is information a teacher might need to have to understand why your child is behaving out of character. On the other hand, if medication needs to be given during the day, obviously a teacher needs to know this, particularly considering today's school regulations about medications on their property.

The treating professionals will also be able to help you decide how you will present the information. Saying too much might scare the teachers or cause your child to be treated negatively. Saying too little can be disadvantageous, too. Get some help with this so that the information you share is appropriate.

Question?

Won't a teacher become offended if I try to teach her about my child's depression?
A good teacher won't. Most teachers will want to know how to distinguish your child's normal behavior from what is out of character. Without that information, your child may be completely misunderstood and treated very differently.

Although it may sound disrespectful, consider that teachers are not prepared to deal with your child's depression. With that said, think ahead about how you want to present information about your child. The last thing your child needs is for a teacher to view him negatively or to treat him so differently that it makes him uncomfortable.

Before informing any school professional about your child's depression, consider having a meeting with his major teacher and perhaps the principal. This allows you to sit down in a quiet setting and explain what is happening with your child. Typically, one of the individuals will know who needs to have this information and who does not.

Ask if accommodations need to be made to help your child cope during the day. For example, your child may need more breaks than what is typically allowed. If he is easily frustrated, how does the teacher plan to handle his discipline? Will he be able to take his medication at school?

Reasonable Accommodations

Schools are overcrowded these days and it is easy to neglect a child's individual needs. For a child with depression who happens to be very quiet and withdrawn, he can easily fall through the cracks in a large classroom. For a child who is more aggressive and angry, a teacher's response may be to send him to the principal's office or discipline him harshly. Therefore, it is understandable that making accommodations for your depressed child is not on the top of a teacher's list of priorities.

Are Accommodations Welcome?

Just because your teacher may not take a proactive approach with your child does not mean that you shouldn't try to get accommodations for him if necessary. As mentioned earlier, childhood depression can affect an entire school year and can make a huge difference in how he sees himself, his academic performance, and how he views school in general.

If you are concerned that your child's depression is going to affect his grades, discuss with the teachers ways in which this can be avoided. For example, if a child is having problems completing his work and having things done in a timely manner, is there a way for the teacher to incorporate a plan whereupon he gets credit for what he *does* complete? Are there extra credit assignments that would be appropriate so that he can keep his grades up? Is there a certain project that might interest your child, thereby engaging him in trying to bring up his grades and to motivate him? Does he need a tutor or a mentor such as a classmate?

Essential

Accommodations are often made for children with learning disabilities. This is done to improve learning, promote a successful school experience, and boost the child's self-esteem. Many schools will make similar accommodations to help a child with depression, too. Though the school may be limited in how it can meet your requested accommodations, it never hurts to ask.

Your teen may be a member of a sport's team or another group that has as a requirement for membership a certain grade point average. If your teen is depressed, his grades might not be where they are normally and could be placing his participation in this activity at risk. On the other hand, perhaps being a member of a particular team or group is the one thing your child continues to enjoy and benefit from, so the thought of being kicked out can make a child's depression worse. This is a touchy topic for schools because they don't want to let some students slide while others are not given the same preferential treatment. Talk with your teen's coach or the teacher who sponsors his club. Express that your teen needs this activity because it is about the only positive thing he is experiencing at the moment. Also, stress that as soon as his depression lifts, you expect your teen to return to his higher level of functioning.

Be Specific

When a depressed child's behavior is interfering with his ability to learn, you need to explain this very carefully to the teacher. While you do not expect your child to receive special treatment for misbehavior, a child with depression is going to act out more often than he did prior to developing depression. It will be up to you to help the teacher understand what she should be on the lookout for and be ready to address it. This can be especially tricky, as they prefer that their students behave no matter what. Help the teacher understand that being overly harsh and stern with your child will be counterproductive at this time. However, stress to the teacher that you do expect your child to be disciplined when appropriate.

What if the teacher thinks that your request for accommodations is going to result in babying your child rather than helping him? What if she refuses? You have two options. If you are certain that your request is not unreasonable or that it will not cause a lot of disruption in the class, try talking to the teacher again. When you tried the first time, perhaps she was feeling pressured by the demands of all of her students. Maybe she didn't hear you accurately.

Second, if you try again and she still refuses, take a step back. Decide how important the request is to your child's success. You will likely be dealing with this teacher again so the relationship between the two of you needs to remain positive. If there are other more important concessions you will be asking for, then scrap this one. If you feel the accommodation is absolutely necessary and that it should not be overlooked, ask the principal. But be sure to inform the teacher that you will be speaking to the principal about it so that she doesn't feel you are going over her head. Explain that you might be wrong, but you'd like another opinion. If in doubt, discuss this with your child's treating professional first.

Putting School Resources to Good Use

Some schools have excellent resources available to your child, while others are stretched to their limits already. In either case, you have the right to expect help for your child, but it will be up to you to take action. In other words, you are probably the most important component to getting help for your child within the school system.

Approach with Caution

When preparing to meet with your child's school, it is difficult not to be anxious about your child and more confrontational than usual. You probably don't need to be told that this approach will not be helpful. School systems are crowded and teachers and other school personnel are very busy. Encountering a parent who is too forceful, rude, or combative will not be something that is met with enthusiasm. Again, your best approach is one of measured enthusiasm, concern, and gentle strength.

 Essential

Some states have government resources and programs that are specifically designed to help children with special needs. Ask your guidance counselor to see if your child qualifies. If you do research on your own and find something, take it to the school and see if they would be willing to help you get your child approved.

This means that you do not cave in when or if a school official seems unconcerned or ignores you, but you should also understand the predicament that they are in.

If you have some information about your child's depression, such as an article or a letter describing your child's specific symptoms, sometimes this is a good way to break the ice with teachers and other school officials. This gives them some information that they can use to learn about depression and possibly help other children. It is also a way to put your child on their radar without you being a nuisance.

Find Out What's Available

If your school has programs in place for children who have specific problems, inquire about these and see if your child could benefit. If no programs are in place, you might ask the guidance counselor to meet with your child, or to set up a group for children who have similar problems. Again, because these people are so busy, they do not always come up with programs for prevention purposes. It is only when they are confronted by a parent that they take action. This does not mean that they are disinterested, but sometimes they just need a nudge.

 **Fact**

Some guidance counselors will involve the parent in group activities for children. For example, she might enlist your help in being a co–group leader to address specific issues, such as social or coping skills. Ask if your participation could be beneficial or if you can help with research-ing to find helpful information.

Another way to put your school's resources to good use is to have one school official with whom you have regular contact. This could be the guidance counselor, the teacher, or another trusted school employee. Rather than trying to keep communications going with several people, you can have one individual with whom you are shar-ing information. This keeps misinterpretation of information to a min-imum, and it keeps you from being known as that "pesky" parent.

The Parent's Role at School

While you do not want to be the parent from whom the teachers run at the first sight of you, or the one who is going to be a troublemaker, you also need to make it clear that you plan to be a presence in your child's academic life. This means that they can expect you to ask questions, share information, and voice your concerns with them.

Communicate by Phone

Communicating with your child's school can be done in several ways. As stated earlier, having just one person to communicate with is appropriate and easy. If this is the route you choose, find out when this teacher is most often available and contact her then. Do not make repeated phone calls during the day every time you think of something you want to say. Keep a list of questions and concerns and have them ready for when you're able to talk with her.

Notes

Another way to communicate with your child's school is by sending a short note. Some teachers prefer this method because they can address your questions and needs when it is convenient for them. Keep the note short, to the point, and make it specific enough so that the teacher is somewhat forced to address it.

E-mail

E-mail is a convenient way to communicate with your child's teacher. Many teachers make available their e-mail addresses at the beginning of the year as a means for you to contact them. Take advantage of this, but don't abuse it. However, it is a great way to share information about your child's depression as well as articles or books that you think they might find helpful.

Alert!

If a teacher or school professional tells you that he has everything under control and does not need your help, ask yourself if this was said because you are being a bother or for some other reason. It may also be a sign that this teacher doesn't plan to address your child's needs any differently from the other students!

Volunteer

If your child's class needs a room mother, or a parent to head a charity project, volunteer to help. This is an excellent way to get to know your child's teachers as well as to observe your child in their presence. And though it might sound sneaky, it's a great way to catch a minute of the teacher's time!

Don't be afraid to ask your teacher or other school official how you can be the most helpful to the school regarding your child's depression. Often, they will welcome your support and involvement and may have creative ways to use you that no one has thought about.

Manage Depression's Effect on School Performance

Depression can affect your child's functioning at school in several ways. Tardiness and absenteeism increase as a result of depression. Often, children will be late to school because they are reluctant to go. This is the child who finds ways to create distractions at home in the morning—everything from not being able to find her shoes to not liking what she has to wear to having a temper tantrum—so that she can be late. A child may be chronically absent from school due to depression because she simply does not feel like going to school. If she is depressed, remember that she is already running low on motivation, so she probably really doesn't feel like going anywhere.

Teens with depression are frequently truant. You might believe that your child is not doing this. After all, you dropped him off and you watched him go inside, right? Unfortunately, the school personnel can't monitor your child every minute. Many a depressed child will report that he has spent most of the day walking the streets or going to the mall—anything to escape the pressure of school. If you discover that your teen is doing this, explain that it is against the law for him to be truant and that you will not tolerate it. Depression is not an excuse for skipping school. If he ignores you and continues, it might be beneficial for him to suffer the consequences so that he can understand the seriousness of his actions.

Essential

Make sure your child's teacher understands how his depression manifests itself in terms of symptoms. Your child becomes known partly by his behavior. You don't want your child to be identified solely by his depressive behavior as it will usually be in a negative context.

Children with depression typically have some cognitive difficulties such as an increase in poor organizational skills and a low attention span. This is the child who is seen as not being able to concentrate, or he might not be able to finish an assignment. He might be described by the teachers as a daydreamer. He may lose his books or other important materials for a class. He simply may not be able to organize himself in a way to keep distractions to a minimum. In these cases, he may not be able to tolerate the structure of a classroom, and this will need to be addressed with the teacher.

Social Relationships

Depression can also have an effect on a child's social relationships at school. When a child is depressed, he is more likely to be socially withdrawn or very aggressive. In either case, peer relationships are affected. Obviously, a lack of friends and the feeling that he is not liked will only make his depression worse.

Kids can find the smallest thing about others and tease them mercilessly. When a child is depressed, he often stands out, making him the perfect target for being made fun of or becoming the butt of jokes. Watch out for this since it will only serve to make your child's depression worse.

Another issue that influences social difficulties at school is that of poor judgment. When a child is depressed, his judgment can also be impaired. He may say or do things that typically he would never do. This can lead to embarrassment or humiliation, particularly if the teacher calls him on it in front of everyone. This further increases the child's social isolation, leading him to feel more frustrated and lonely. Remind your child that he needs to think before acting or speaking. If he does something that gets him into trouble, stress to him the importance of being able to simply say, "I'm sorry," and to take responsibility for his behavior.

 ***Fact***

If your child's social skills are suffering as a result of his depression, get this addressed in treatment. Typically, these skills can be learned, and a child can begin to understand that how he interacts with others can be changed for the better. An increase in positive attention with his peers will decrease his feelings of depression.

How to Help Your Child at Home

There are many things you can do outside of the school day to help your child cope with his depression. Discuss with him what he believes his problems are as they relate to his depression and encourage his participation with you in finding ways to minimize his symptoms.

If these have become increasing problems as a result of your child's depression, consider making a list of tasks that must be completed before your child goes to school each day. You might try getting him up fifteen minutes earlier to avoid the pressure of having to rush.

If your child is still reluctant to go to school, consider using being on time and going to school as a reward. For example, if he is ready to go to school on time for five days in a row, he may earn a specific privilege or treat.

If your child is having difficulty with concentration or staying focused at school, ask the teacher how she can help minimize distractions for him. Can he take some extra breaks? Does he need to be seated in the front row of the class?

Essential

Although a morning routine is important, it might be a good idea to keep it as simple and stress free as possible. With increasing chaos comes the exacerbation of his anxiety, and before you know it, your household will be out of control. Keep your expectations clear and keep tasks to a minimum for morning success.

At home, help him set up a quiet space where he can study. Some children do better with white noise while they study. Parents are often reluctant to let their children study while listening to music, but research shows that this helps many children, particularly those whose attention is drawn away by other problems, such as depression. This enables them to tune out other stimuli that would otherwise be disruptive. If the noise bothers you, get him a set of earphones.

For younger children, set a timer for study times and break times. For example, if your child can tolerate staying focused for only fifteen minutes at a time, set the timer for fifteen minutes. At the end of this time, he gets a five-minute break. Obviously, this will result in him taking longer to complete his homework, but he is more likely to finish it because he is not frustrated. This also sets him up for a successful school experience.

In terms of social difficulties, encourage your child to have friends over. This will give you the ability to observe your child in a social situation so that you can help him develop more appropriate skills. At school, you might ask the teacher to check on your child during lunch or recess to make sure that he is engaged with his peers.

 **Fact**

Some children are so full of agitation and energy once they get home from school that they simply are not able to sit down to do more school-work. You can help by letting him play outside or engage in another activity that will let him burn off this energy before he has to do his homework.

When the School Isn't on Board

Unfortunately, there are certain institutions that will not address your child's depression, nor will they make any special accommodations to help him. When this is the case, you have a real dilemma.

Do you withdraw your child from the school he is attending and place him in one that is more attuned to his needs? Do you continue to push the present school system until you find anyone who will listen?

Only you can make these decisions, but if the school is absolutely not going to be helpful, you will have to find ways to help your child on your own. This may require finding him a tutor or mentor who can help him develop ways to navigate through school life.

Homeschooling

Some parents find that when the school cannot or will not participate in helping a child that is depressed it's easier to homeschool him. This concept has been growing in popularity and more parents than ever are homeschooling their children for a variety of reasons.

There are obvious advantages to homeschooling your depressed child. First, you can help him minimize his distractions and find ways to help him tolerate the process of learning. You can also allow him to take more breaks if necessary, and he can do his schoolwork at times that are easier for him.

Enlisting the Treating Professional's Help

Perhaps his therapist who is treating his depression can help him learn skills to overcome or to compensate for the cognitive changes he is experiencing. As well, he may need help learning new social strategies to compensate for his difficulties. The most important thing to do is to make sure these issues get addressed whether at school or at home.

Alert!

Get lots of information and advice before taking on your child as a student. Your role will be that of a teacher, not a parent. Can you tolerate the time it will demand, and can you be an effective teacher? If you aren't able to discipline and motivate your child as his teacher, you might consider another alternative.

Often, if your treating professional is willing, a letter or a phone call from her can get the school's attention. Just because the teacher hasn't listened to you, do not overlook the authority the treating professional appears to have that the school might be more open to hearing from.

Understand that even though your child may spend the majority of his time at school, the school is not going to be the major player in the treatment of your child's depression. The school is merely another piece of the treatment team, and they need to be kept informed as much as possible. Encouraging the school to be involved in your child's treatment of depression can have an effect on the length of time your child is depressed, and can prevent him from having an unsuccessful school experience.

CHAPTER 20

What Does the Future Hold?

Although your child's depression may be under control or even gone, you still feel worried and uncertain. How do you proceed now that the proverbial white elephant has left your home? The immediate future after your child's depression should be a time of refocusing and regrouping. Family priorities can shift and life can get back to normal. The problem is that you may have spent so much time in that tunnel of despair with your child that you have difficulty remembering what was normal for you and your child!

Is the Depression Gone?

It's finally here, or at least you think so! This is the moment you've been waiting for since your child began to show the first signs of depression. The depression seems to have lifted, and the constraints that it placed on you and your child are gone. Or is it really?

What Does Recovery Mean?

To most people, the word "recovery" means that an illness is over, that a person is cured. For depression, recovery is a more ambiguous state in which your child seems better but may still have some lingering symptoms. For the most part, what you are looking for is a significant decrease in his symptoms and a gradual returning to his prior self. His energy and interest in

things will return. He may be sleeping and eating better. His concentration and focus may be back. In other words, he is turning into his old self again and seems ready to move ahead into the future.

 **Fact**

Children get disappointed and frustrated when their symptoms don't totally go away. Don't let your child be discouraged if he still has lingering symptoms of his depression. Remind him that this is not an illness where the symptoms magically disappear all at once. Recovery is a gradual process and this is normal.

It's important to know whether your child has the coping skills and other things in place to move forward. Recovering might mean that he has to stay on his medication for a bit longer, and he may even need to see a therapist occasionally to stay on track.

 **Question?**

When is it okay to let my child stop counseling?
Just because your child's symptoms appear to be decreasing or gone does not mean it is time to stop treatment. Typically, a child will decrease the amount of time he goes to treatment, but it doesn't stop altogether. Discuss with your treating professional what is best for your child.

The fact that your child is feeling better and enjoying his life more is a terrific change that is taking place. Even though his recovery is not totally symptom free yet, this should still be considered a time for rejoicing.

How Do You See Your Child's Progress?

Another way to determine if the depression is gone is to ask yourself, "Does he seem better?" Is your child ready for more responsibilities at home? Is it time to renegotiate your rules and expectations for him? Listen to that all-important gut of yours. If you are getting responses that make you feel excited about his moving forward, then recovery is in full swing.

Overparenting

It's been said in previous chapters that there is a tendency for parents with a depressed child to be overprotective and overly engaged in their children's lives. This is perfectly normal. But now you are in a new phase—recovery—and this means that it's time for you to pull back. Your child is finally getting well. Revel in this, and congratulate yourself that you and your child have survived a very difficult time.

Keep Doing Your Homework

Because depression can recur, it's important to remain knowledgeable about depression and the way that it manifests itself at different ages. While you don't want to keep your child under a microscope, you do need to be on the lookout should symptoms reappear.

If your child experiences negative emotions reminiscent of his depression, he is likely to worry that his depression is returning. Stress to him that bad feelings are a natural part of our daily functioning. It will be important for him to learn how to discern between what are normal ups and downs and the more serious symptoms of depression.

Watch for signs of environmental stress. Is something different at school that might be putting pressure on your child? Has he started a new school year with a new teacher? Is he getting along with his friends? Any type of event that is causing significant changes for your child can be a trigger for a return of depressive symptoms.

Keep a Positive Attitude

When you are projecting a positive outlook, your child will likely model this as well. Promote positive emotions by reminding him that thinking affirmatively and creatively will keep depressive symptoms at bay. Foster a sense of self-reliance. Remind him of the skills he learned while depressed to manage his emotions and behavior. These skills are still excellent ways for dealing with whatever challenges he might be facing. Help him to remember that it is this new set of self-management tools that can possibly prevent depression from returning.

Whose Life Is It Anyway?

It bears repeating that the dreams and expectations you have for your child are not always the same as those that he has for himself. If this is the case, consider whether you are trying to force him to be someone that he is not or whether you are being unreasonable.

Essential

You should have certain expectations for your child in terms of his behavior, his treatment of others, and his fulfillment of his responsibilities. The expectations you should keep in check, however, are more about wanting to mold your child into a person that you think he should be rather than honoring who he really is.

Also, there is nothing wrong with your child having different hopes for himself than you do. The fact that he does have these expectations is a sign that he is looking ahead and is feeling better. Keep your personal feelings in check, and try your best to promote his expectations for himself.

One of the hardest tasks in a child's recovery is allowing him to become more independent. There are things that you have done for him in the past that he can now do on his own. You must resist the urge to do these things for him so that he does not become excessively dependent on you.

Maintain a Close Relationship

Obviously, the closeness that you developed during the difficult period of your child's depression is one that you want to keep going. While your child may not need your attention in the same way, he nevertheless continues to need it. Your child needs to have quality time with you, even though he might say he doesn't. Particularly with teenagers, even though they think they do not need you at all, this is not the case.

Children

For a younger child, find activities that you enjoy doing together. Better yet, if there is something your child truly enjoys, participate in that whether you enjoy it or not. Find things that the entire family can do together that will continue to encourage the bonding process.

 **Fact**

Studies show that families who do things together have closer relationships. Take turns with your child in planning a family night. Let him decide what to have for dinner or what fun activity you will do together. This will help remind your child that he is an integral and enjoyable part of your family!

Continue to ask your child how he is feeling but not necessarily as it relates to his depression. Keep him engaged by asking his opinions on all sorts of things such as what's going on in the world or school happenings. Foster an atmosphere of acceptance and nonjudgment so that he will feel free to share his feelings with you.

Adolescence

Teenagers are famous for not wanting to be around their parents. This does not mean that they do not value your input or your presence—you just probably won't hear about it! You may not get a lot of positive reinforcement from your participation with them, but understand that they are aware that you are available to them.

Essential

As a parent, you want to avoid being too intrusive and yet you wish to stay knowledgeable about what is happening. Are you asking a question because you need to know something or you are actually being a bit nosy? Respect your child's privacy and save the questions for important matters.

Whatever you do, keep talking and trying to engage your child. Ironically, a teenager will usually report that no one listens to him. He may roll his eyes or act as though you are irritating him, but ignore this and ask him how he feels about certain things. Encourage his open expression of his opinions and thoughts. Spend time with him, but don't smother him.

Teens are famous for finding strange times to share their feelings and worries with you. Your teen may wait until late at night or right before bed to approach you. She might crawl into your bed and snuggle beside you while she talks in the dark. This actually provides her with a sense of being invisible that in turn makes it easier to talk. She may prefer to call you on the phone with the distance between you providing that same sort of a barrier of invisibility. She may talk more freely by writing you a letter or e-mail.

Don't overlook these conversations just because they aren't always happening face to face. Remember that these very important conversations you'll have with your teenager need to happen in a way that makes your child feel secure and not judged. Most of the time it will happen off the cuff. This means that they will happen when you least expect it. When your teenager does decide to talk, be prepared to stop what you're doing and listen.

Prepare for Developmental Changes

You known that the symptoms of depression are different for certain stages in the child's life. After depression, you need to be prepared for their developmental growth to have an effect on their feelings and be aware of the factors that can possibly make depressive symptoms recur.

Children

As children age, they are going to be introduced to new experiences. This can be something as simple as a new grade in school, the arrival of a new student in his classroom, or maybe a new sibling! Now that his depression has lifted, he is ready to take on new tasks and responsibilities at home. Do not be afraid to make changes in that regard, but be sure they are commensurate with his level of ability.

Alert!

Your child may use his depression as an excuse for not doing what you've asked. He will masterfully remind you how he was feeling when you asked him to do something when he was depressed. You may feel a twinge of guilt that perhaps you shouldn't make him do something. Not so, and don't buy into his manipulations!

Encourage your child to make new friends and try new things. Help him find people and activities that fit his personality and interests. It is time for him to re-enter his social life, but he may need a little push from you.

It also may be time to renegotiate the rules in your home for your child as he changes, such as bedtime or the amount of TV he can watch. Introduce new freedoms and privileges that he can try out. This will give him, and you, the opportunity to see how much he is able to handle at a certain age.

Adolescence

Teenagers are strange creatures! On the one hand, you'll meet "Mr. Independent" who will scream for you to leave him alone and get off of his back. Next, you'll encounter "Mr. Whiny Baby" who wants you to take care of him like a five-year-old! The problem is that you never know which personality you will get. Your teenager's personalities can take on even more forms than just these two, so living with him will be like riding on a constant rollercoaster.

Adolescence is wrought with the battle between a teenager wanting his freedom and a parent not knowing how much freedom to give. This dilemma is heightened when your child has suffered depression. You don't wish to put him in any situation in which he might re-experience symptoms. But you can't shelter him forever, and deep down you know this.

Part of what a teenager will have to learn is that with freedom comes responsibility. Part of what you must accept is that you will have to give him some freedom in order for him to learn responsibility. What you both need to recognize is that it is a give and take process between the two of you and that your teen will make plenty of mistakes along the way. This is how he will learn and grow.

Meet His Friends

Although he will protest, it is perfectly reasonable for you to expect your child to bring his friends over for you to meet before he goes out with them. Knowing who he is with gives you insight into what your teenager is experiencing and thinking. If you're uncomfortable with his set of friends, it's also okay to restrict his time with these people. Explain to him that while he has a choice to make friends with whomever he wishes, you also have the choice to manage that as you see fit.

Communication with Other Parents

Another way to stay engaged with your adolescent in terms of what he is doing is to call other parents. When your child tells you he is spending the night with John, call John's parents. Will they be home that evening or is your child really going to be there? If there is a party planned, ask if adults will be present, and call to make sure.

 **Question?**

Shouldn't I be able to trust my child?
Of course you should, but your child is under a lot of pressure to fit in. He will naturally want to do things you don't want him to do, and he may even lie about his whereabouts. Keeping a close watch on your teenager is part of being a healthy, responsible parent.

Pay Attention

Listen to the music that your child listens to. You may not enjoy it, but it will help create a bond between you and your surly teenager and you might also get a glimpse as to whether this music is affecting him negatively or positively.

What is your child reading? Who is his favorite author and what is his favorite subject? Is there anything in the news that he finds fascinating or is concerned about? Is there a particular kind of art he would like to try and pursue? Help him maintain enthusiasm for what he enjoys by being interested yourself.

Pay attention to what kind of events he is engaged in after school. For example, if he is on the basketball team, then you know that he will have practices in the afternoons. On the other hand, if he says he is hanging out with his friends, find out where he is going and what he is doing. These are times when a teenager can easily get into trouble, and you need to be on top of your game.

Dream with your child. Play "what if" and "what would you do?" games like:

- What would you do if you won a million dollars?
- What would you do if you ruled the world?
- If you could be anyone in the world, who would you be?
- Who are your heroes?
- Where would you go if you could plan the perfect vacation?
- If you could have a super power, what would it be?

Questions such as these are a great way to get a conversation started. You'll learn new things about one another while having fun.

New Rules

Obviously, the rules between childhood and adolescence are going to change, and you must be prepared to make the necessary alterations. Your teenager may not need for you to tell him when to go to bed and went to get up. It may be time for a curfew change now that he is not depressed and enjoying his social life again.

Driving

Driving is probably the scariest word for a parent. However, it is a rite of passage for your teenager and should be celebrated. If he is not ready for this responsibility, practice driving with him until he is better prepared. Enroll him in a drivers' education program. Limit the amount of kids who can ride in the car with him to minimize distractions.

 **Fact**

Many states have laws in place that limit how many passengers your teen is allowed to have in his car. Some states allow only one nonfamily member. These laws are typically strictly enforced. Find out if your state has any restrictions and be sure your teen is aware of them as well as any consequences should he not comply.

First Job

This is also a time when your child may be getting her first job. Often, teenagers are worried that their previous history of depression will become known and somehow affect their jobs. Help her to understand that no one needs to know about her history unless she wants them to know.

She may be overly anxious about the first job. What will she wear? How is she supposed to act? What if she messes up? All of this anxiety can put her under extra pressure that in turn can put her at risk for developing depressive symptoms again.

 **Question?**

Should I let my child quit her job if her symptoms are returning?
If she's using her depression as an excuse to leave her job, no. Work is not a cause of a recurrence of symptoms, but it can add extra stress. If she cannot handle the pressure, it's better to let her quit rather than feel bad about herself.

Help her to understand that this can happen, but it can be avoided by employing the healthy self-management skills she has learned.

Generating a Plan B

When all else fails, help your child to develop a Plan B. Research shows that individuals who are able to generate alternatives are much more emotionally resilient and are less vulnerable to depression.

It would be beneficial for your child to recognize and accept that plans are going to fail, hopes will be dashed, and setbacks are going to happen. Having a Plan B means that when changes are happening too fast, or whatever plan of attack he had in place is not working, there is always another option.

Your Child's Identity after Depression

Now that your child's depressive symptoms are gone or are present to a much more limited degree, it is time to help him plan for life after depression. His depression is *not* who he is, and it is time for him to evaluate himself in a new light.

Who Is He Now?

One of the most important things you can do is to help your child develop an independent attitude. This means that he feels competent to face new challenges in the world and has a healthy "I can do it" attitude. This does not mean that he is so independent that he never needs your help, but he needs to feel that he has the skills within him lying in wait for these new challenges.

 Essential

Successes always need to be celebrated, and this is true whether your child is depressed or not. Your child needs to understand that the good things he does continue to have importance and that he is a capable individual. This gives him the confidence to continue moving forward.

Important to his new identity is the ability to take personal responsibility for his actions. The excuse, "I have had depression so you'll need to give me a break" is not going to work. Your child needs to understand that whether he has a problem or not, he has choices about how to behave, and when he does the wrong thing, it's up to him to take the blame.

Mistakes Do Not Equal Failure

Continue to separate your child's mistakes from your child's identity. It's important to help him do this as well. Reiterate that your approval is never contingent on his successes or failures. Again, what you see as a success or as a monumental moment may not mean anything to your child. Take your lead from him in order to understand what truly matters in his life.

Major Life Events and Stressors

You cannot control what the future holds for your children, although you certainly want to be able to do that. A child who has had depression is prone to having a recurrence, and this is especially true when life creates extra stress.

Major Events

Chapter 2 introduced the Coddington Life Stress Scale. This was a list of major life events and stressors that have varying degrees of relevance in a child's life. After your child's depression has lifted there's a tendency to not want to look back, to only look forward with optimism. There is nothing wrong with this. However, you need to realize that major life events in your child's life are going to have an impact on him, either positively or negatively. The way the child handles and interprets these may determine whether depressive symptoms will return. In times of major changes or extreme pressure, watch for signs that the depression is coming back and nip it in the bud.

Manage Stressors

In times of extraordinary stress, remind your child that she learned coping skills during her depression that will be helpful now. For example, here are some things she can do to minimize the effect of a major life stressor:

- Take a time-out to refocus and relax
- Write in a journal about her feelings and options for behaving
- Find something pleasurable to do
- Talk to you or a trusted friend about what is happening
- Express her feelings in a positive, nondamaging manner
- Ask for help

Conclusion

You now have a solid understanding of what depression is and how it looks. You know that there are treatments out there and that help is available. You grasp the significance of your role in helping your child get better. You know how to put together a plan of action that is most beneficial to your particular child.

Life is going to give you lessons that you will learn from making mistakes, having setbacks, and celebrating successes. Many who have suffered from depression actually say they are better off for having experienced it. Think they are crazy? Probably not. In the movie *Oh God*, comedian George Burns's character was asked why bad things have to happen. His response? "You can't have an up without a down. You can't have a right without a left. You can't have a happy without a sad. How else would you know when the good stuff happens?" This is probably what those depressed people mean. Now they know what good really feels like!

Hopefully, what you will really remember is this: Your child is *not* his depression. With your love, support, and participation, he can get better. Depression doesn't have to be a permanent way of life. He can learn important life lessons from it while realizing that he has the power to control his life and move toward a brighter future.

Resources on Childhood and Adolescent Depression

BOOKS

American Psychiatric Association. *Diagnostic and Statistical Manual of Mental Disorders*. 4th Edition. (American Psychiatric Association, 2000)

Beck, Aaron T. *Cognitive Therapy of Depression* (Guilford Press, 1979)

Berlinger, M.D., Ph.D., Norman T. *Rescuing Your Teenager from Depression* (HarperCollins, 2005)

Brooks, Robert, and Sam Goldstein. *Raising Resilient Children: Fostering Strength, Hope, and Optimism in Your Child* (Contemporary Books, 2001)

Copeland, Mary Ellen, and Stuart Copans. *Recovering from Depression: A Workbook for Teens*. Revised Edition. (Paul H. Brookes Publishing Co., 2002)

Cytryn, M.D., Leon, and Donald McKnew, M.D. *Growing Up Sad: Childhood Depression and Its Treatment* (W.W. Norton and Co., 1998)

Ellis, Albert. *Reason and Emotion in Psychotherapy* (Lyle Stuart, 1962)

Faber, A., and E. Mazlish. *How to Talk So Kids Will Listen and Listen So Kids Will Talk* (Avon Books, 1999)

Fassler, David G., and Lynne S. Dumas. *"Help Me, I'm Sad": Recognizing, Treating, and Preventing Childhood and Adolescent Depression*. (Penguin Books, 1997)

Goldberg, Arnold, M.D., Jill S., and Mary A. Fristad, M.D. *Raising a Moody Child: How to Cope with Depression and Bipolar Disorder* (Guilford Press, 2003)

McCoy, Ph.D., Kathleen. *Understanding Your Teenager's Depression* (Penguin Group, 1994)

Nicholson, Joanne, Alexis D. Henry, Jonathan C. Clayfield, and Susan M. Phillips. *Parenting Well When You're Depressed: A Complete Resource for Maintaining a Healthy Family* (New Harbinger Publications, 2001)

Reivich, K., and A. Shatte. *The Resilience Factor: 7 Essential Skills for Overcoming Life's Inevitable Obstacles* (Random House, 2002)

Riley, Douglas A. *The Depressed Child: A Parent's Guide for Rescuing Kids* (Taylor Trade Publishing, 2000)

Seligman, M.E.P. *The Optimistic Child* (HarperCollins, 1996)

Shaffer, David, and Bruce Wastick. *Many Faces of Depression in Children and Adolescents.* (Psychiatric Press, 2002)

Simon, L. *Detour* (Simon and Schuster, 2002)

Stillman, William. *The Everything® Parent's Guide to Children with Bipolar Disorder* (Adams Media, 2005)

WEB SITES

www.childpsychologist.com

The Child Psychologist—a site about children's problems *www.4therapy.com*

Locator service for therapists and information about childhood disorders *www.healthyplace.com*

A great place for information about all kinds of health information *www.nmha.org*

Mental Health America *www.pbis.org*

Positive Behavioral Interventions and Supports *www.wingsofmadness.com*

Depression information

Depression Questionnaires

Symptom Checklist

Please read each statement carefully. If the statement is true about how you felt over the last week, circle the number of that statement. If the statement is not true about you over the last week, then just read it and go on to the next statement.

1. I felt sad, or down, or unhappy, or like crying.
2. I was angry.
3. I felt guilty.
4. I felt like no one loved me.
5. I didn't like myself.
6. I felt like life was harder on me than on other people.
7. I had aches and pains.
8. I worried about my health.
9. I was tired.
10. I had trouble concentrating.
11. I couldn't sit still.
12. I felt like I was moving in slow motion.
13. I wanted to be by myself.
14. Nothing seemed fun.
15. I had trouble sleeping.
16. I slept longer than usual.
17. I didn't feel like eating.
18. I ate more than usual.
19. I tried to hurt myself.
20. I thought about hurting myself.

The Choate Depression Inventory for Children (CDIC)

Answer true or false.

1. I feel sad lots of the time.
2. I have trouble sleeping.
3. I feel tired lots of the time.
4. I don't have many friends.
5. I cry a lot.
6. I don't like playing with other kids.
7. I don't feel as hungry as I used to.
8. Other kids don't like me.
9. I feel lonely.
10. I have lots of stomach-aches and headaches.
11. I don't like school.
12. I have bad dreams.
13. Sometimes I think about hurting myself.
14. I worry a lot.
15. I don't like myself.
16. Other kids have more fun than I do.
17. I don't do as well in school as I used to.
18. Sometimes I have trouble concentrating.
19. I feel angry lots of the time.
20. I get into lots of fights.

If your child answers "True" to three or more items, she should be evaluated by a qualified mental health professional; she may be clinically depressed. And if she answers "True" to Item 13, which reveals self-destructive or suicidal thoughts, she should be evaluated immediately to ensure her physical safety.

Other Inventories Used by Professionals

The following are for use by a qualified professional.

Children's Depression Rating Scale-Revised (CDRS-R)
Multiscore Depression Inventory for Adolescents and Adults (MDI)
Multidimensional Anxiety Scale for Children
Reynolds Adolescent Depression Scale, 2nd Edition (RADS-2)
Beck Depression Inventory-II (BDI-II)
Beck Youth Inventories-Second Edition for Children and Adolescents (BYI-II)

Index

THE EVERYTHING® PARENT'S GUIDES SERIES (CONTINUED).

The Everything® Parent's Guide to the Strong-Willed Child
ISBN 10: 1-59337-381-3; ISBN 13: 978-1-59337-381-8

The Everything® Parent's Guide to Raising Siblings
ISBN 10: 1-59337-537-9; ISBN 13: 978-1-59337-537-9

The Everything® Parent's Guide to Sensory Integration Disorder
ISBN 10: 1-59337-714-2; ISBN 13: 978-1-59337-714-4

The Everything® Parent's Guide to Children and Divorce
ISBN 10: 1-59337-418-6; ISBN 13: 978-1-59337-418-1

The Everything® Parent's Guide to Raising Boys
ISBN 10: 1-59337-587-5; ISBN 13: 978-1-59337-587-4

The Everything® Parent's Guide to Childhood Illnesses
ISBN 10: 1-59869-239-9; ISBN 13: 978-1-59869-239-6

The Everything® Parent's Guide to Raising Girls
ISBN 10: 1-59869-247-X; ISBN 13: 978-1-59869-247-1

The Everything® Parent's Guide to Children with Juvenile Diabetes
ISBN 10: 1-59869-246-1; ISBN 13: 978-1-59869-246-4

The Everything® Parent's Guide to Children with Depression
ISBN 10: 1-59869-264-X; ISBN 13: 978-1-59869-264-8